Generation Rising

A New Politics of Southeast Asian American Activism

Loan Thi Dao, Ph.D.

Eastwind Books of Berkeley

Generation Rising: A New Politics
of Southeast Asian American Activism

Author: Loan Thi Dao, Ph.D.

Copyright © 2020 by Loan Thi Dao, Ph.D.

Published by:
EASTWIND BOOKS OF BERKELEY
2066 University Avenue
Berkeley, CA 94704

www.AsiaBookCenter.com
email: eastwindbooks@gmail.com

Eastwind Books of Berkeley is a registered trademark of
Eastwind Books of Berkeley

Published 2020. First Edition
Printed in the United States of America

For more information or to book an author event, contact www.
AsiaBookCenter.com

Cover Design: Kelly Yan Wong

ISBN: 9781734744033 (Paperback)

ISBN: 9781734744040 (E-book)

10 9 8 7 6 5 4 3 2 1

GENERATION RISING
Table of Contents

To my dad and mom, the first community leaders in my life.
You showed me how to love and serve the people.
Thank you for your sacrifices to let me be free.

Acronyms

American Council for Nationalities Services (ACNS)
American Friends Service Committee (AFSC)
Asian American Movement (AAM)
Asian American Pacific Islander (AAPI)
Asian American Youth Promoting Advocacy and Leadership (AYPAL)
Asian Pacific American Labor Alliance (APALA)
Asian Pacific Environmental Network (APEN)
Asian Prisoners Support Network (APSN)
Black, Indigenous, and People of Color (BIPOC)
Cambodian Community Development, Inc. (CCDI)
Cambodian Mutual Assistance Associations (CMAAs)
Catholic Social Service (CSS)
Committee Against Anti-Asian Violence (CAAAV)
Community Safety Act (CSA)
Community Defense Project (CDP)
Desis Rising Up and Moving (DRUM)
Direct Action for Rights and Equality (DARE)
Freedom Training (FT)
Grassroots Asians Rising (GAR)
Immigration and Customs Enforcement (ICE)
Minnesota Immigrant Rights and Action Committee (MIRAC)
Mutual Assistance Associations (MAA)
National Network for Immigrant and Refugee Rights (NNIRR)
non-profit industrial complex (NPIC)
Office of Refugee Resettlement (ORR)
Olneyville Neighborhood Association (ONA)
Project Safe Neighborhoods (PSN)
Providence Youth-Student Movement (PrYSM)
Returnee Integration Support Center (RISC)
Socio-Economic Development Center (SEDC)
Southeast Asian American (SEAA)
Southeast Asian Freedom Network (SEAFN)
Southeast Asian Queer leadership (SEAQuel)
Southeast Asian Resource Action Center (SEARAC)
Vietnamese American Youth of Louisiana, New Orleans (VAYLA-NO)
Youth Leadership Project (YLP)

List of Figures

CHAPTER ONE
Introduction: Refugee Resistance

Each generation must out of relative obscurity discover its mission, fulfill it, or betray it.[1]

In the late 1990s, I directed a community organization that ran after-school programs for low-income Vietnamese American youth, grades 5 through 12, in Oakland, California. I noticed an insidious pattern of youths and their relatives entangled in the criminal justice system and then "disappearing." A lawyer on our board of directors represented one of these cases, and they informed me that Vietnamese and other refugees from Cambodia and Laos who did not have United States citizenship were being detained after they served their time. Based on the Illegal Immigration Reform and Immigrant Responsibility Act (IIRIRA) of 1996, these youth were targeted for mandatory deportation, but they were being detained indefinitely since the United States did not have repatriation agreements with those countries.[2]

On March 22, 2002, the United States State Department signed a Memorandum of Understanding (M.O.U.) with Cambodia's Ministry of Interior to allow for repatriations—a euphemistic term for deportations—and entered into similar negotiations with Viet Nam and Laos.[3] This agreement rendered over 10,000 Southeast Asians in the United States vulnerable to removal from the country that had offered them refuge in the aftermath of the American War in Southeast Asia, commonly referred to in the United States as the Viet Nam War.[4] The majority of people immediately impacted by the M.O.U. were refugees who had come to the United States as childhood arrivals, teenagers, or young children, and had been survivors of the American War in Laos, Cambodia and Viet Nam between 1954 and 1973. For many Southeast Asian Americans who grew up in the United States, the fundamental claims to this country and refugee families' sacrifices in migration were at stake.

Then, in the summer of 2002, I represented an all-volunteer organization as one of twelve Southeast Asian American-based organizations nationwide at the offices of the Youth Leadership Project in the Bronx, New York.[5] The three-day retreat included: 1) Southeast Asian American (SEAA) activist youth groups that had begun in the late 1990s into the early 2000s; 2) Mutual Assistance Associations (MAAs) that were originally created for refugee resettlement in the 1970s and 1980s; and 3) grassroots leftist groups from the Asian American Movement (AAM) that emerged in the 1960s. One purpose of the gathering was to strategize about how to educate our constituent communities and respond to the deportation of Southeast Asian refugees. We were familiar with the typical format of professional meetings and excited to share information and engage in political discussions.

On the first day, we started late after awaiting a new group called Providence Youth Student Movement, or PrYSM, to drive in from Providence, Rhode Island. We had spent the morning in intellectual discussions intended to give context to the strategic planning for the rest of the retreat. Around lunchtime, as we all gathered in a circle on the floor of the main room, five carloads of people arrived led by two men, PrYSM founders Sarath Suong and Kohei Ishihara. In walked twenty-five young, male, formerly incarcerated and former gang members—they completely shifted the room dynamics. The majority of activists present were college-educated and trained organizers. It dawned on me that despite all our "radical" thinking, the retreat's esoteric language, format, and content was going to marginalize and silence the very people we claimed to be developing as leaders. When they sat down with us, I realized that in all the years I had been working in Oakland, this was what social justice really looked like: everyday people who had been directly impacted by systemic oppression developing their collective power to create social change. By the end of the retreat, with leadership from PrYSM, our organizations formed the Southeast Asian Freedom Network (SEAFN), a national coalition of Southeast Asian American youth-based groups that laid the groundwork for the first Southeast Asian American youth movement for social justice that began in 2002.

In this book, I demonstrate that regardless of the state's liberal-minded attempts to resettle refugees, its contradictory policies of neglect and surveillance failed many of them, along with other communities of color. The critical intervention of PrYSM for refugee children and the children of refugees sharply contrasts those official governmental agencies responsible for refugee resettlement. While government agencies and local institutions served as social service providers or regulators of social control, PrYSM provided the socio-cultural needs of young people in ways that simultaneously gave them a sense of self, belonging, pride, and empowerment. In doing so, they centered the priorities of SEAA youth to build new generations of leaders for a social movement that emphasized on their lived experiences as well as their strengths and collective power.

Figure 1.1. PrYSM Gang Truce BBQ, 2002 (Courtesy of PrYSM Archives).

Subverting Dominant Narratives of Southeast Asian Americans

Between the mid-1970s and 1980s, a dominant narrative emerged in the research on Southeast Asian refugees in the United States based on Cold War discourse.[6] The arrival of the first two cohorts of refugees after the American War in Southeast Asia incited a body of publications documenting their escape from perilous, traumatic experiences and ending with their arrival in the United States. Anthologies of testimonials pieced together migration narratives offering an archive rich with testimonials, but those collections were often spliced into a master narrative that situated refugee flight within a Cold War discourse of fleeing Communism. Consequently, refugee resettlement was analyzed only to the extent that their economic progress could be measured as a signifier of successful assimilation to justify the unpopular decision by the government to resettle the largest refugee population since WWII.[7]

From the 1990s to the early 2000s, social scientists shifted their focus from refugee resettlement to the assimilation process for 1.5- and second-generation adolescent youth. Yet widespread conflation of the cultural and social infrastructure of these ethnic groups created a binary in social science analysis between the refugee youth and other East Asians, where 1.5-generation adolescent youth, or youth who arrived in the United States a adolescents, struggled to assimilate compared to their second-generation, or American-born, counterparts. Scholars have attributed these differences in socioeconomic mobility among Asian Americans to the cultural environment of resettlement and lack of adherence to the positive cultural values based in Confucianism, which is a problematic fallacy that invokes the model minority myth.[8] This narrative continues to dominate social science research on SEAA youth, and directly influences policy and philanthropic approaches to the communities and organizations that target cultural preservation and individual behavioral change rather than systemic failures to meet the needs of these youth.

In the wake of the World Trade Center tower bombings on September 11, 2001, Immigration and Customs Enforcement (ICE) engaged in increased immigration sweeps but did not provide families, advocates, or even lawyers with basic information, such as the whereabouts of individual detainees, and the hearing dates or dates of deportation flights. Through the high concentration of information-gathering and information-sharing among families and loved ones in the physical space of PrYSM and other youth groups, moreover, community members gained invaluable knowledge of detention and deportation that would be the foundational research for a national campaign. Through the process of information sharing between families, these youth organizations simultaneously built the trust and leadership of community members who had too often been neglected by Mutual Aid Associations (MAAs) that provided social services to Southeast Asian refugees.

The Evolution of Asian American Activism

These re-framings of Southeast Asian American communities and scholarship did more than challenge the inequities of power hierarchies. The stories revealed intersectional identities of race, class, and sexual orientation that occupied a new terrain in social movements. In doing so, PrYSM and other progressive Southeast Asian American youth groups have charted a unique path to develop new voices and leaders. They mark a new period in Asian Pacific American activism and in Southeast Asian American studies since the American War in Southeast Asia between 1954 and 1975, and subsequent refugee resettlement between 1975 and the mid-1990s.

The post-9/11, anti-immigrant climate also galvanized the first critical mass of Asian American activists for the Millennial generation on a national scale, and arguably a transformative shift in the dominant narrative of the Asian American Movement (AAM), which embeds its foundation within the period of the anti-Viet Nam War Movement, and for which it allied with Vietnamese calls for self-determination.[9] The Millennials and post-Millennials[10] involved in PrYSM has been central in the renaissance of progressive activism that is emblematic of the 1960s. They represented the unique perspectives of refugee children, both as childhood arrivals and the U.S.-born children of refugees fleeing Communism from Laos, Cambodia, and Viet Nam.

To be clear, this book does not aim to create a comparative analysis between the Asian American Movement of the 1960s through the 1970s to the contemporary movement. I also recognize the multiplicity of campaigns, movements, advocacy, and activism that has evolved and shaped Asian Pacific America since the early years of AAM. Through this book, I emphasize the unique relationship between the early years of AAM and today's SEAA activists through the historical lineage that both found life: the American War in SEAA and its aftermath, and how this history has been articulated as a historiography of radicalism that centered the war *without* the refugees that arrived on these shores with divergent politics than the dominant narrative of the war espoused by the Asian American Left as articulated in the canon of this literature. That lineage extends to this moment in the centering of a radical refugee positionality that holds both a critical politics of this early generation of activists and the reality of war, imprisonment, torture and starvation that inform the anti-communism of many in SEAA communities. This book does not try to ignore the decades of activism in between; rather, I point to the unique relationship between the early radicalism and this generation of leaders and the ways in which they carry on the lineage of the elders—including their ancestors—with whom they find inspiration in the movement. While carrying this lineage, I argue they also carry the burden that has been bestowed on them as a "gift" to be honored in their embodiment of both co-ethnic refugee and Asian American Movement elders.

When Mutual Assistance Associations (MAA) formed to support refugee resettlement in the late 1970s and 1980s,[11] their priorities of refugee survival were often at the expense of many childhood arrivals living in what Tang (2015) refers to as the "hyperghetto," the cycles of government neglect and over-surveillance.[12] Some MAA leaders forsook those in the community who did not aspire to embody the model minority stereotype— they were ostensibly either poor reflections of the entire community or "too Americanized" because they had lost their roots and adopted negative behaviors associated with American youth. Sometimes the neglect of newer refugees were remnants of class differences carried over from Southeast Asia. Regardless, this rejection of later cohorts ultimately ostracized many working-class youth whose families often arrived in later cohorts with fewer governmental safety nets.

Since 2000, MAAs have faced a crisis of relevance as the U.S. Office of Refugee Resettlement (ORR) and other funding sources have turned toward new refugee populations from South America, Africa, and other countries in Asia to support refugee resettlement and integration, thus diminishing the allocation of funds for MAAs involved with Southeast Asian refugee resettlement. These bureaucratic choices symbolize the arbitrary markers of timelines and compassion fatigue to determine when the Southeast Asian refugee should be integrated and no longer considered a refugee.[13] Consequently, MAAs had to search for new funding sources and justifications for their continued existence. As SEAFN began organizing against deportation, it offered an opportunity to sustain the viability and relevance of the MAAs through increased attention from private funders and media.

Generation Rising documents PrYSM's participation in national and local organizing coalitions such as SEAFN between 2002 and 2017. This project is in dialogue with other movements of young Black, Indigenous, and People of Color (BIPOC)—spanning #BlackLivesMatter, Undocumented and Unafraid, and more—about the state of social movements in the United States with regard to generational shifts in leadership and the predicaments of social justice movements in relation to the non-profit industrial complex, the "entrenched set of relationships [between organizations, state, and private funders] that maintains relationships of power and fails to address issues of structural inequality."[14]

The term "non-profit industrial complex" emerged in the early 2000s with the proliferation of nonprofit organizations in the 1990s.[15] They were the private, institutionalized response to diminishing state service providers since the 1980s and professionalization of the social movements of the 1960s. The non-profit industrial complex consists of grant makers, including government agencies, large family and corporate foundations, independent small foundations, and individual donors, and non-profit organizations that function as subcontractors who implement smaller grants from these large donors, or groups that receive grants directly from these donors. These identities may overlap for any individual organization; for example, an organization may give out grants from money they received from a large foundation, and they may be direct recipients of other grants. These donors, foundations, and non-profits have constituted the majority of political, social service, and youth organizations in the United States since the mid-twentieth century.[16] This web of networks and individual power brokers control the resources of funding sources and the actors who serve as gatekeepers between funders and communities. The term non-profit industrial complex carries a negative connotation because of the increasing influence and control of funders in the daily operations, political activities, and long-term vision of the grantees. It has also been used to reference the co-optation of the more radical vision of past movements, such as AAM, to become career pathways and organizations that follow corporate models of management rather than the grassroots mission and working-class-centered leadership of the movements in which many of these organizations became rooted.[17] The power relations within the complex remain a contested site for the small grassroots organizations within SEAFN, including PrYSM, throughout *Generation Rising*.

PrYSM embodies the collective identity of contemporary SEAA youth activists through their organic expressions of political power; a development of a new cadre of movement leadership; and their contradictory relationship to older, more established organizations and funders. In *Generation Rising*, I illustrate how PrYSM engages with those three categories of organizations in its journey to find its identity and determine its positionality within the movement. This web of organizations in this book represents a microcosm of the non-profit industrial complex. Older Asian American groups have occupied two different positions within the non-profit industrial complex. MAAs, which were sustained through subcontracts of federal grants for refugee resettlement, became a product of a wave of philanthropy in the 1990s that promoted the hierarchal, patron–client model for non-profits, whereby service providers, or patrons, offer specific kinds of assistance in short-term, transactional exchanges to alleviate a narrow problem for the client. Conversely, the client offers allegiance and validation of the patron's power and even identity. The client and patron model fluctuates continually throughout their relationship as an implicit negotiation of power, influence, and exchange of resources.[18] This model provides the groundwork to the relationships among the categories of groups discussed in this book.

Funders are organizations that provide financial and technical resources to non-profit organizations and often request deliverables to justify their financial investment. These may include enumerating outcomes of programs or activities, attendance, and outreach numbers, budgets of spending, success or impact measurements of campaigns, as well as meeting or adjusting to meet grantmakers' evolving funding priorities. Since these entities have the reputation of being staffed by college-educated, predominantly white, upper-middle-class professionals, grassroots, working-class non-profits have often characterized them as inaccessible or unapproachable.

Another category of organizations are the non-profits with deep roots in AAM as defined by earlier Asian American Movement scholars. These are groups that tend to have founders who were active in progressive organizations during the 1960s and 1970s as student or youth activists. Although the founders themselves may come from working-class backgrounds and have radical visions for social change, the organizations' evolution to professionalize their volunteer work into larger institutions as non-profits that provide services to broad swaths of people had the incidental consequence of narrowing the political mission of their services and staff. Consequently, they have created either corporate-like structures of management and operations, or attempted to maintain informal, volunteer-based management styles that were no longer realistic for the size of the organizations. Some of these organizations have also become subcontractors of grants, blurring their roles as both patrons and clients.

Recent transitions over the past fifteen years have led to increasing numbers of college-educated, middle-class Vietnamese Americans hired into established organizations and former staff moving into grantmaking organizations. As non-profit organizations formed by co-ethnic Southeast Asian refugees to assist with refugee resettlement since the 1970s, MAAs remain largely social service-oriented groups staffed by first- and 1.5-generation immigrants and refugees who tend to be bilingual and live within their co-ethnic communities. Although not many of these groups originally had grantwriting skills or social capital in the private grantmaking world, some have adapted by hiring staff who had received their college education in the United States or have subcontracted professional grantwriters who receive a percentage of each funded grant. The majority of SEAA MAAs nationally have been in a precarious state due to decreased government funding and lack of support from private funders.[19] PrYSM belongs to the category of new SEAA-based youth organizations that represent a merger between the social service and activist-oriented groups who are still developing their own characteristics and negotiating their relationships with these other three categories of influencers.

Generation Rising explores the impact of the pressures inherent in the non-profit structure manifested in PrYSM as they underwent changes in organizational culture, campaign priorities, and staff turnover after the group achieved 501(c)3 (non-profit) status.[20] In general, MAAs had been reticent to participate in any political activities and later viewed groups like PrYSM as radical outliers of the community. On the other hand, members of the earlier generations of activist groups had more diverse roles in the non-profit industrial complex. They occupied multiple positions within that web of relationships, spanning program officers for funders to social service providers within the non-profits. Through PrYSM, activist groups that transitioned into non-profit organizations found themselves restricted by the existing power relations with funders and funder-driven agendas at the expense of social justice ideals. Kwon (2013) refers to this set of relationships as the "funder-fix," whereby "nonprofit youth organizations, charged with developing and improving the life chances of 'at-risk' youth of color, are imbricated to neoliberal policies and reconfigurations of civil society that aim to manage and regulate the production of moral economic actors who are receptive to opportunities for self-empowerment and community governance."[21] In other words, the funder-fix serves as a social control to structural change that would revolutionize existing power differentials. It leaves the work of social justice actors constrained to the parameters of reform that relieves, not upends, the institutional hierarchies in which the web of funders and organizations are complicit.[22]

Political Indebtedness: From Refugee to Revolutionary

SEAA Millennials and post-Millennials like those in PrYSM have become entrenched in a discourse of political indebtedness. Mimi Thi Nguyen refers to the "gift of freedom" as a neoliberal relationship characterized by the debt of war and, by extension, freedom as "a revenant, a ruin, a reminder of what has been lost—but debt is also a politics of what is given in its place."[23] Nguyen refers to the contradictory role the United States played in both creating the circumstances of the refugee situation during war and its claim that it is the "savior" of those same refugees. That claim inevitably reconstructs the plight of refugees and their resettlement in the United States as one of indebtedness for refugees. The debt of war, like its memory, takes root in intergenerational transference sometimes too intricate to untangle. I interpret the notion of debt as a power relationship between the person with the power to give as a unidirectional act on its surface, while implicitly expecting reciprocity through loyalty, political alliance, or behavior that benefits the giver in reputation, legacy, or material outcomes. The generational burden of the immigrant experience, whereby the sacrifices of co-ethnic elders, manifested in the MAAs, embodies the role of refugee parents who sacrificed their own lives for the betterment of the family. In essence, the debt of war assumes the symbolic and discursive articulation of the patron–client dynamic that frames the relationships between SEAA youth groups, established Asian American groups, and funders.

In the context of social movement, 1.5-, 1.8- (who migrated as pre-adolescents), and second-generation Southeast Asian refugee children inherited that "gift of freedom" as a burden of political indebtedness to their Asian American mentors, who developed refugees' critical analysis of their social situation and taught them skills for organizing.[24] SEAA organizers needed to navigate between competing ideologies of progressive Asian American activist groups and their co-ethnic elders in the MAAs. Older Asian American activists perpetuated the legacy of an anti-imperialist past and refugee narratives of anti-Communism in its narrative framing against deportation. MAAs used Communism in current Southeast Asian countries as the justification to not send their community members back to those authoritarian regimes. In turn, the SEAA youth constantly negotiated these dualistic loyalties toward activist elders and co-ethnic communities in trying to express their personal and political identities. The youth activists in *Generation Rising* found themselves resisting the burden to perform the role of the indebted refugee victim in order to be legible to some Asian American leaders and funders that would sustain the normative paternal relationship between funders and grantees.

Young SEAA progressives have chosen to shift the public narratives of their collective identity to construct their own political movement. The intra- and inter-ethnic tensions that manifested in PrYSM's story illuminate the generational, class, and ethnic clashes and collaborations that face this generation of activists. Their resistance symbolizes the interwoven legacy of past social movements with a concrete rejection of the established organizations' embeddedness in the non-profit industrial complex. This new iteration of the movement locates itself at crossroads of what Schlund-Vials describes in her analysis of Cambodian refugee youth culture as "a legible set of refugee coordinates that identifies distinct points of U.S. foreign policy, modern Cambodian history, and contemporary Cambodian American survivor memory."[25] Her astute theorization of Cambodian American experiences informs my map of that transitional moment in Asian American Movement history as it relates to Cambodian American youth and their collective identity formation. Southeast Asian American youth groups across the country like PrYSM see themselves as an extension of a collective refugee experience in the discourse of U.S. foreign policy and refugee resettlement.

I assert that this generation's refugee resistance marks a third space informed by pre-existing expectations about politically loaded identities mapped onto their bodies by the debts of the war and the debts of the patron–client relationships in the non-profit industrial complex. From the youth's perspectives, the refugee imaginary projected by their co-ethnic elders necessarily means that they transform from a refugee to a model minority in order to fulfill the state narrative of repaying their debt to the savior United States. Simultaneously, I argue that the relationship of many older Asian American groups to Southeast Asian American youth has mirrored the paternal relationship between the youth and the United States. The youth feel obligated to perform the ideological discourse of radical activism from previous generations to garner approval of many of their movement elders, as well as benefit from resources from it. Their refugee resistance is thus not simply resistance to state policies that criminalize, incarcerate, and detain youth; it also occupies a resistance to a non-profit industrial complex that makes its own claims outside the narratives of both the model minority and the radical activist imposed onto the youth by both co-ethnic and pan-ethnic elders, mentors, and potential funding gatekeepers. Their resistance signifies a watershed moment of a generation rising because it marks a new opportunity for a syncretic subject-making that engages with the multiplicity of identities within their generation. The third space of refugee resistance simultaneously adopts and adapts the narratives of their elders and continually interjects their narratives with the intersectional priorities of contemporary generations' multiple identities as working-class, queer, and female SEAA youth. The new narrative frames represent a critique of the ways in which the previous generation's narratives have contradicted one another. Yet, even as they redefine themselves and their political selves, they struggle within the confines of the patron–client model that frames the landscape of the movement through the non-profit industrial complex.

As Sarath and Kohei tried to secure PrYSM's sustainability and organize for immigration reform, they relied on advice, networks, and other resources from allies and mentors from older progressives to become a non-profit organization, fund its campaigns, and engage in policy-making coalitions. However, the necessities of a funder-driven organization fundamentally change an organization's internal culture. PrYSM felt established groups and funders tried to confine and control their mobilizing activities, campaign messaging, and political positions on immigration reform. The organizations appreciated the youth's activism to the extent that it garnered funding and media attention. The ally organizations invited directly affected community members to share personal stories through testimonies. But for the first ten years—between 2002 and 2012—they never invited the youth groups to sit at the decision-making table or take control of shared resources. They encouraged and mentored the youth groups to the extent that youth participated within boundaries that maintained the status quo of the movement. While the youth perceived their allies as well-intentioned, the perception of well-educated, middle-class professionals masking their privilege and power behind reified images of a grateful refugee in order to leverage resources left many SEAA youth groups feeling disempowered and at times exploited. Consequently, the movement that has emerged has an uneven and contradictory relationship to the Asian American progressive movement since it never addressed or rectified the power dynamics of the "gift of freedom" between the movement and the refugee communities in the context of community organizing and empowerment.

Movement Transformations: From Solidarity to Indebtedness

The anti-war sentiment of the Asian American Left during the Viet Nam War era contextualized the war as part of a racist endeavor against Asians that travelled from the streets of America to those of the Asia Pacific region. Between the late 1960s and mid-1970s, AAM had reached a pinnacle of multi-faceted activism. This included historian and activist Yuji Ichioka's coining of the term "Asian American"; the development of Serve the People programs—modeled after similar programs begun by the Black Panther Party—that provided basic needs to underserved communities, such as free food and educational programs for children and their families; and the student movement on college campuses for curricular transformation with the inclusion of ethnic studies by Third World Liberation Fronts.[26] That transformative period of Asian American history served as the backdrop against which the first cohort of Southeast Asian refugees arrived on American shores, setting the stage for the paradoxical ideologies of the movement against the very "imagined community,"[27] or reified notion of pan-Asian solidarity, that AAM had supported during the war.

Solidarity with the Vietnamese people was generally shared by the radical Left in the anti-war movement; a particular point of inter-racial solidarity connected the analysis of American intervention as an imperialist endeavor to control the Asia-Pacific and as a racist war toward a formerly colonized country.[28] The anti-war activists articulated their support for the Vietnamese people (as opposed to Southeast Asian) to the extent these Asiatic kin shared the goal to counter American imperialism and saw themselves as victims of capitalism.[29] The anti-war movement contributed to a conflicting set of emotional and political relations between AAM and future refugee cohorts who would be inserted into the demographic groups that AAM sought to organize.

By the 1990s, the evolution of Asian American grassroots activism into federally recognized, non-profit status, 501(c)3 social service organizations built an infrastructure that paid for organizers to become career staff. The transition to a non-profit patron–client model required more overhead, more robust funding sources, and the professionalization of staff to maintain the bureaucratic requirements of government awards, such as grant writing and reporting. The non-profit patron–client model rendered groups vulnerable to funders, including those in local, state, and federal governments. The professionalization of Serve the People programs and anti-imperialist campaigns into service and reform activities that were legible to funders increasingly restricted much of the movement's traditional rank-and-file activists into middle-class, educated, professionals and encouraged a paternal, patron–client relationship.[30] While the emphasis on electoral politics and policy-making within the non-profit framework drew college-educated, middle-class members to career leadership roles, by default, this bias excluded most first-generation, working-class immigrants, like newly arrived Southeast Asian refugees who lacked the educational training for non-profit positions or an understanding strategies and tactics to maneuver of the American political system.[31] In the end, refugees embodied the client in need of assistance, in need of saving, and in need of a voice, and only those who were legible to policy-makers could advocate in the name of these "worthy victims."

From the 1980s into the 1990s, the strategies of reform and the emphasis on essentialized identity politics of Asian American representation (in other words, the emphasis on Asian American inclusion as the singular priority) blinded some activists to the daily struggles affecting Southeast Asian refugees, who were being resettled into urban housing projects and welfare system. The evolution of the Asian American Movement and the rise of Southeast Asian American political power developed in two disparate paths, grassroots, working-class activism and professionalized non-profit.[32] By 2000, Southeast Asian American youth still found themselves negotiating discrepancies between the political agenda and messaging of their ethnic communities and their mentors.

With the American war and subsequent failed socialist projects in their homelands as points of reference, PrYSM carved out a mission based on anti-imperialist positions, juxtaposed against the realities of the refugee experience under post-1975 Communist "re-education" initiatives in their countries of origin. Through our strategic framing of the detention and deportation issue, PrYSM tried to defy what Espiritu refers to as American rescue fantasies:

Constituted as existing on the other side of freedom, Vietnamese could only be incorporated into the modern subjecthood as the good refugee— that is, only when they reject the purported antidemocratic, anti-capitalist (and thus anti-free) communist Viet Nam and embrace the "free world."[33]

PrYSM, and other SEAA youth groups, faced an impossible conundrum. They struggled with the expectation of performing the role of good refugees, as an inherited debt owed by their parents to the United States, the receiving nation, as they fled war. By challenging the dominant historical narrative of the anti-war stance of the anti-imperialist sentiments of radical Asian American activists that found solidarity with its own romanticized version of Vietnamese people, PrYSM simultaneously had to confront demands for justice in ways that ran counter to the spirit of Asian American critique of American imperialism in Southeast Asia.[34] These contending narratives extend the analogous relationship of indebtedness between the older refugee generation and the United States as well as the Millennial generation of SEAA activists with the movement.[35] The Millennials featured in this book inherited the burden of war from the 1960s, from both their parents as represented in the MAAs and from Asian American activists as their political mentors. Their ability to make claims on their own terms—especially to a socio-political identity that frees itself of those debts—would take yet another generation of activists, as witnessed in the last chapters of this book.[36]

Crossing Borders: Intersectionality as Refugee Resistance

The years of major refugee resettlement, spanning 1975 to 1992, revealed the threshold of compassion fatigue by the U.S. government and society.[37] Southeast Asian refugees resisted federal attempts at fast-track assimilation—they refused to anchor themselves in locations where there were no available ethnic and cultural support structures. Rather, they engaged in secondary and tertiary migrations that created ethnic enclaves. These enclaves created the necessary institutions that have provided political, social, and economic opportunities not available in mainstream society, and are the bedrock of community leadership. The politics of refugee resettlement situated many of the enclaves alongside other marginalized BIPOC. The concentric circles of ethnic-based resources and racialized oppression molded youth's collective identity, as well as mobilizing activities and coalitional formations.

Movement Forward

The Asian American Movement today primarily consists of an overlap of the Millennial generation who grew up in the late 1990s and early 2000s, and post-Millennial, who grew up in the 2000s. Post-Millennial SEAA youth in this book are the current youth members who are on the cusp of taking leadership roles in the movement. The challenge for SEAA organizers from these two generations is twofold. First, these leaders must devise a strategy of how to create sustainable collective resources within the community and with allied support that allows them to act freely apart from the inherently competitive nature and politics of the funding world. That strategy has the advantage of building community solidarity internally and externally, concretizing the foundational pillars for movement-building independent of a funding model that relies upon notions of debt and patronage, and removes the pressure to professionalize youth organizing such that it depoliticizes their political campaigns.

Second, as PrYSM demonstrates, the movement's viability in working with co-ethnic communities and achieving solidarity externally with progressive groups required a balance of two highly contested ideologies. As part of the SEAFN coalition, these youth leaders created a localized map that allowed them to employ early movement organizing tools while creating a unique perspective that encompassed the memories of war and torture under Communist regimes in Southeast Asia. Rather than succumb to the dominant pro-U.S./anti-Communist rhetoric, SEAFN critiqued U.S. foreign policy, arguing that it should have been held accountable for refugee resettlement. Additionally, it also evoked a critique against deporting refugee childhood arrivals. The development of those critiques derived from a combination of knowledge PrYSM founders had gleaned in college courses in ethnic studies, critical studies of the Viet Nam War, and study groups in local progressive organizations.

Refugee youth organizers tend to view immigrants not as blank slates upon immigration, but as active agents of change who carry political and cultural values that are transmitted across generations. Those values are neither adopted wholesale by Southeast Asian youth from their parents nor from the hybrid urban landscapes in which they grow up. The youth's strategic choices allow them to make sense of disjointed spaces between Asian American radicals and their co-ethnic communities. Their ability to merge these two somewhat disparate worldviews have become a source of strength in which they find a new political direction for movement building. In carving out the "liberated zones" of social movement, these new leaders embrace what Kelley views as "the time to think like poets, to envision and make visible a new society, a peaceful, cooperative, loving world without poverty and oppression, limited only by our imaginations."[38] During the last fifteen years, PrYSM has continually attempted to prioritize love, generosity, inclusivity, and creative expression to build community and its collective identity. The re-branding of social activism characterized by love instead of anger represents a shift in the strategy and tactics from previous generations. By sculpting what social movement scholars call the "repertoire of contention"[39]—the strategies, frames, and tactics activists can draw from to achieve their immediate objectives and goals for social change—these youth form an oppositional consciousness embedded with syncretic values and politics that has the potential to shift an entire generation's worldview.

Auto-Ethnography and the Myth of the Unbiased Researcher

Virtually nothing has been written about Southeast Asian American youth political engagement, or about the mobilization against Southeast Asian American detention and deportation beyond the legal studies field, which is the impetus for the activism for many PrYSM and SEAA working class youth.[40] From the rich data with "thick" descriptions in my field notes and interviews, I created identification numbers and aliases for all subjects. Some subjects have requested to not be identified, and I have respected this request. Other subjects and their respective organizations have requested that their names be used. Throughout the book, I do not designate which names are pseudonyms in order to further protect my subjects. At the beginning of each chapter, I provide short vignettes of my first-person experiences to introduce the chapter and situate myself within the narrative.

Generation Rising is an auto-ethnographic study that started with my participation as a student activist against SEAA detention and deportation. Ethnography involves the study of relational processes within a culture from the perspective and for the benefit of encouraging mutual understanding between those inside and outside of a culture. According to Ellis, Adams, and Bochner, an auto-ethnographer must "consider ways others may experience similar epiphanies; they must use personal experience to illustrate facets of cultural experience, and, in so doing, make characteristics of a culture familiar for insiders and outsiders."[41] In this book I offer my own self-reflective insertion as an actively engaged scholar committed to developing knowledge about the "hidden transcripts" of lived experience.[42]

I include an analysis of my personal involvement in my field research as a Southeast Asian refugee, community member, and former youth organizer concerned with Southeast Asian deportation without centering myself as a main character in the narrative. Personal field notes and journal entries from participant observations helped me reflect on my participation in the groups, gatherings, and events. These include numerous times I participated in SEAFN and PrYSM activities.[43] While the traditional ethnographic approach historically viewed a subject from the space and time of a racialized other and as inherently less civilized or developed, the postcolonial turn includes the researcher as a part of the research process. Auto-ethnographic research, especially one that incorporates a racial, LGBTQ+, and feminist critique, can potentially equalize the scholar–community power dynamic as well as generate a study that deepens our understanding of a topic by validating the perspectives of the subjects as critiques of dominant scholarship.[44] As a co-ethnic activist-scholar and generational peer of the early activists of this movement, I embody this methodological shift in ethnography because my overall identity removed much of the power dynamics between myself as the researcher and the communities of inquiry. In short, I situate myself as a part of the movement such that I have long-term accountability to the communities about which I write.[45]

In the summer of 2017, Sarath asked me to join the board of directors of PrYSM after another board member stepped down. I did this on a temporary basis until they were able to recruit new board members. My choice to join the board was difficult because I was in the very last stage of preparing this book for review. Ultimately, my decision was influenced by my main purpose for writing this book: to support and document Asian American social movement history from the perspective of a small but influential grassroots organization located in a modest metropolitan area with limited resources. As a community-engaged scholar, I felt a responsibility to reciprocate to those with whom I conducted research, as a principle of conducting community-based research, by meeting the needs of the organization as it requested assistance rather than defining the terms of my reciprocity. Chapter Two includes an analysis of the reflection and strategic planning process that occurred while I participated on the board. I made sure to be careful not to participate in or influence this process as a board member and recused myself from this process. I also received permission to include the outcomes of the process and topical descriptions of the workshops in this book.

Throughout *Generation Rising*, I reflect on my own "insider/outsider" positionality within the SEAFN dynamics as a 1975 Vietnamese refugee woman who grew up in a well-respected but low-income (and later middle-income) refugee family. While I have this shared background of coming to this country with literally no material possessions but the clothes on our back, my positionality shifted as an adult and over the course of this study. During the timeframe of this project, I started as a graduate student and a peer of many of the activists, and then evolved into a position of a scholar at a public higher education institution, and thus had significantly more income, power, and privilege than the post-Millennial youth leaders. While the research is focused on a case study—PrYSM and the group's role in coalition such as SEAFN—this book does not purport to represent the "activism" of an entire, multifaceted, multiethnic racialized group. Additionally, evident throughout the narrative are my own experiences as a founding member of SEAFN and a SEAA community member with shared generational experiences. I recognize that my own activism and the role I played in the early years as a member of SEAFN represents a biased political position. In exposing these biases, I assume the political position that aligns with what I understand to be the original mission of ethnic studies: to challenge the dominant narratives of historically oppressed people through counter-hegemonic narratives that re-center those who have been marginalized with academic research.

Finally, I situate myself at the porous border between "insider" and "outsider," in the recognition of my activist role as an historian documenting a movement in which I have been an invested member. This public recognition of my positionality marks the difference between an auto-ethnographic project and a more traditional ethnographic methodology. Sociologist Linda Vo recalled her decision to refrain from passing judgement or engaging in political debate that might distract from her own interviews and access to the Vietnamese American community as well as bias her observations and analysis of her ethnographic study.[46] I also attempt to offer a critical analysis and withhold bias or judgement, but I choose to do so by making transparent to the participants and my readers of the inherent subjectivity scholars embed in their studies.

I situate this project as an auto-ethnography rather than an ethnography because of my public and active participation in the campaign against deportation that originally became the impetus to use my research skills to the benefit of the movement of which I was an active participant. My contribution to the movement evolved from one of a co-coordinator of events, fundraisers, and strategic planning to a scholar-activist whose role was to document and critically analyze the movement. My original role gave me entrée as a trusted member of the community, both as a Southeast Asian refugee and as an activist with shared political position, which allowed me to more readily build rapport and trust with my subjects. While engaging in "thick description" in my ethnographic activities, I had to engage in ongoing reflexivity to acknowledge implicit biases that might lead me to overlook important critiques or observations during my field work. Similar to Milann Kang's description of the challenges she faced with determining the boundaries of her role as a trusted accomplice to the Asian American women nail salon workers who viewed her as "one of their own," I also had to manage and continually negotiate the boundaries of my study with my sense of obligation to the anti-deportation movement that gave me access in the first place.[47]

The subjectivity at the forefront of my research privileges me to delve more deeply into what Kelley calls the questions of the "how" rather than "why." Early social movement scholars of the Civil Rights Movement fixated on the question of why people would join as the first stage of social movement theory, which seemed like a contradiction of social theories that suggested the conditions of socio-economic class privilege correlated with political participation. However, Kelley suggests that the perspective internal to social justice movements assumes the necessity of activism as its instigating factor, and that the more interesting question for those within a movement is to better understand the internal dynamics and the campaigns themselves as lessons for future leaders.[48] The emerging generations of activists have expressed these same sentiments to me, and so these questions underlie the framing of the book: How do social movements operate, particularly in the context of the non-profit industrial complex? How do grassroots organizations deal with their internal struggles? How can intergenerational challenges be overcome within ethnic-based movements?

I followed grounded theory methods to develop themes from the data rather than rigidly pursue pre-set themes. Grounded theory approach allows for the data to guide the researcher to decide on the trajectories to pursue based on existing data, and then to develop themes based on what emerges organically from the data.[49] This approach allowed me to integrate scientific data collection methods and analysis while maintaining the integrity of community-based research, where the communities of inquiry involved the co-creation of knowledge by defining what is important to them.[50] By allowing the data to breathe, I am more honestly giving life and precedence to the communities of inquiry that are leading my research project. I created both axial and theoretical coding systems that helped me to develop main points for narrative development and academic analysis. Axial coding synthesizes large amounts of qualitative data to create broad frames under which more precise codes can be created. These frames often fall into the categories of: conditions, or circumstances, in which the study emerges; actions, which are the responses to the conditions or circumstances; and the consequences of those actions.[51] The process of combining these primary source materials in the context of secondary academic sources allowed me to engage in what grounded theorists identify as "reconstructing theory,"[52] which develops new theoretical understandings or models in relation to existing literature that derives from the data, rather than having theories grafted onto research subjects.

In addition to my participation in movement activities, I conducted formal semi-structured interviews with twelve staff from policy and legal organizations and with forty youth participants connected to SEAFN.[53] Of these forty, I conducted in-depth interviews with sixteen of the approximately thirty members of PrYSM multiple times between 2002 and 2006. Interviews lasted between thirty minutes to two hours per session, and twenty interviews were with new members and follow-ups with PrYSM leaders and ten leaders from ally organizations who worked in coalition with PrYSM, in addition to conducting participant and non-participant observations with PrYSM from 2002 to 2006 and 2011 to 2016. The depth of this book—an engaged case study where I focus on this one main organization in the anti-deportation work over an extensive time period—offers me sound insight through which some contributions related to Asian American activism might be understood in the development of social movement theory.[54]

Auto-ethnographic research involves transparency, and reflexivity of one's involvement in the research topic. For this reason, I detail my methodology and begin every chapter with a vignette of my first-hand observations. Fieldwork was documented through journals, notes, and collecting archival materials of events, protests, and campaigns. I engaged in non-participant and participant observations with PrYSM and its ally groups between 2002 and 2006, including programming, workshops, social events, immigrant rights marches, court hearings, and meetings at the Returnee Assistance Project (RAP) in Phnom Penh, Cambodia from 2002 to 2004, and conducted semi-structured and unstructured interviews with ten Cambodian American deportees. Upon my return, I continued email, phone, and social media communications with individuals and with the organization, now known as Returnee Integration Support Center (RISC). Between 2002 and 2006, I attended immigration hearings for client-members of SEAFN organizations, testified as an expert witness in immigration court, and sat in on immigration court hearings once or twice a month. In addition to formal interviews, I maintained ongoing informal conversations, as well as email, text, and social media exchanges with my research subjects over the years, which directly inform my analysis. I was witness to SEAFN's resurgence at the Racial Justice Gathering in New Orleans, LA, in August 2013, and the Advancing Justice conference in Los Angeles in March 2016. Finally, I also used personal reflections and field notes of my involvement in SEAFN (including bimonthly to monthly conference calls and biannual gatherings) and PrYSM events, meeting notes, public presentations, protest/campaign materials, newsletters, and media productions.

Chapter Descriptions

At the beginning of each chapter, I introduce a vignette of my auto-ethnographic experiences by presenting a first-person scenario that relates to the topic of the chapter. In Chapter Two, I introduce PrYSM's emergence in the historical, political, and geographical setting of Providence, Rhode Island through the oral histories of current and former PrYSM members. PrYSM's origin story offers insight to the dynamics and political contexts indicative of Southeast Asian refugee communities across the country that either do not constitute a majority-minority population or emerge from a long-history of Asian Pacific American activism. I argue that the collective identity formation unique to PrYSM's intersectional social location situated them within the ethnic community without competition, while also pulling resources from various allies in different movements throughout the country. It allowed for an innovative structure and programs that were grounded in values and identity formation while retaining a critical social justice agenda. The post-9/11 crucible in which PrYSM began proved critical to their preparedness to address the anti-immigrant climate in the aftermath of the 2016 elections I discuss later in this book.

Chapter Three follows PrYSM's internal operations and growth as a leading Southeast Asian American youth group in the country. This chapter unpacks the process of the development of their political consciousness and leadership skills through their main programs for queer youth, young women, and campaign organizing. The culture of the organization and the make-up of the founding members modeled a space for intersectional identities along the lines of pan-ethnicity and mixed-race, gender, queer, and class identities. The chapter examines their process of developing an oppositional consciousness to mainstream society's stereotypical representations of these marginalized youth. Over the years, moreover, the challenges of intersectionality also manifested in the differential growth between queer youth and young women's programs, and in the inclusion of cis-female leadership as the face of the organization. The growth of young women's participation in the organization challenged the invisible norms of male privilege and opened the door to opportunities for increased public representation and leadership.

Chapter Four examines the campaigns and coalitional activism that PrYSM participated in locally and nationally. In this chapter, I highlight the complicated nuances of operationalizing intersectional collective identity and relationships in social movement coalitions. I focus on issues of marginalization of youth activists as serious political actors to their tokenization in testimonials without the power to actually negotiate policies that affect them. PrYSM leaders recall their role in the formation of SEAFN, the first national coalition of SEAA activist youth groups that formed in response to the deportations of Cambodian Americans, as they attracted external major funders and media attention through their national mobilization against detention and deportation. This chapter magnifies the local social terrain of relationships and power imbalances to the national stage. PrYSM helps us reframe the deportation narrative to privilege the voices of those directly affected by deportation through the intersections of class, ethnicity, and queer identity. With the retreat from funders toward more winnable causes that they could celebrate and use to demonstrate success to donors, and the internal challenges within SEAFN member organizations, the first iteration of SEAFN dissolved quickly, with individual organizations disbanding or restructuring. PrYSM survived this period by refocusing on local organizing and recentering their base-building activities.

The new generation of leaders began talks with multi-racial allies about the issues of police surveillance and formed a coalition of local organizations that created a bill to stop surveillance, hyper-policing, and immigration enforcement by local police, called the Community Safety Act. Through their coalitional campaigns, they began to build inter-racial alliances and organizing skills, while the revamped coalition, SEAFN 2.0, focused on their immigration histories and identities as Southeast Asian refugees growing up in the United States. These coalitional campaigns allowed the emergent post-Millennial activists—particularly female leaders—to articulate the third space of refugee resistance that they embraced from the original PrYSM members, and internally, these transitions centered on the role of women within the organization. Over the course of these campaigns, we see how these youth activists evolve in their roles as tangential partners to enacting their own agenda on their own terms. Coalitions thus vacillate from being advantageous for small groups or groups in isolated geographical locations to being sites that reproduce power imbalances amongst allies.

Chapter Five examines the attempts to build a transnational movement to demand a "right to return" for those who have been deported to Cambodia. This is a turning point for the movement in its efforts to transition from local and domestic policy to a framework driven by international law. In an attempt to have power over their own narratives, PrYSM leaders joined other SEAFN activists to travel to Southeast Asian American enclaves and to Cambodia to interview community members, deportees, and other stakeholders. They released the interviews on social media as part of the launch of their Right2Return transnational campaign. In analyzing their engagement with the human rights framework, I consider its effectiveness in building a mass base as well as the problematics of a juridical dependency to define these rights in the campaign against deportation. The call for human rights as the basis for demanding one's rights is fraught with legal contradictions. It also forces two major shifts in PrYSM. First, as a small organization that could easily be dismissed as a localized campaign, PrYSM's involvement in this transnational effort centered them on an international stage. It also challenged them to internally consider their strategic messaging, which at that point had become quite localized, and thus politicized their youth members to consider their world and politics beyond that which they had become accustomed. Finally, their testimonies to the U.N. and meetings with the Cambodian government offered opportunities for a new generation of leaders to rise as the voices and faces of this emergent campaign in Asian American social movement history.

Chapter Six discusses the ways in which the presidential election of Donald J. Trump impacted local politics and alliances, as well as the process by which post-Millennial youth leaders chose to respond to the differences and tensions that manifested during this period, with an emphasis on heightened hate violence and the racial politics of policing and safety. One major shift during this time was their positionality and choices in relation to funders. The non-profit industrial complex (NPIC), particularly funders, have shaped and impact the culture and activities of PrYSM. The organization's transitions in membership, leadership, and campaign priorities over the years were directly linked to the availability of funding resources and funders' agendas on a national level. They evolved from a grassroots volunteer group of college-age youth who organized high schoolers and gang members, to an organization with a budget of approximately $500,000 with professionalized titles, roles, and responsibilities to funders. As youth funders shifted their attention and back again to youth organizing and deportation enforcement, PrYSM's campaigns also flowed from national to local organizing campaigns. In this chapter I focus on three major funders that directly and indirectly impacted PrYSM's campaigns and coalitions: the Four Freedoms Fund, the Kellogg Foundation, and the Coulter Foundation. As the group's reputation became solidified and leadership became more adept in the philanthropy world, they made a conscious choice about identifying funders who aligned with their political vision and diversified their funding portfolio so that they would not be unduly influenced or dependent on one source.

PrYSM's journey in the present historical juncture is a microcosm into the tensions and successes of the passing of activism across generations for both the Asian American Pacific Islander communities and other ethnic and racial groups. PrYSM must react to the increased discourse of racial hate after September 11, 2001 and after the 2016 presidential election in ways that align with their core values. The chapter reiterates how the path forward for AAM may shift with the intervention of the emerging landscape of power brokers with the intervention of SEAA youth at the helm. The campaigns and programmatic activities outlined in this book gave the youth a concrete grounding in how to lead campaigns and accumulate their own resources; as a result, they viewed themselves as agents of their own life choices and paths. Their communal and individual futures were something they could shape, as opposed to being pre-destined by the structural barriers surrounding them. As they developed their power, however, the realities of constraints within social movements were put in relief. Simultaneously, the debates within the immigrant rights movement about immigration policy have direct impact on the local work against criminalization of PrYSM youth, and the extent to which they are perpetually framed as the "undeserving immigrants." Their achievements to gain recognition and at the very least nominal public support from national Asian American policy groups represents a huge advancement in their ability to influence public discourse, but they continue to face significant obstacles in the anti-immigrant climate under the Trump administration that require innovative strategies and tactics of resistance. In *Generation Rising*, I provide the framework to analyze the spaces in which their collective identities create new paradigms for social change that meet the demands of the historical moment. This is a testament to the possibilities for the Millennial and post-Millennial generation forge a new paradigm for social change.

CHAPTER TWO
Core Values: Peace, Love, Power

But a new Asian America was being honed as the Asian American Movement was birthed, and new goals, perspectives, values, priorities, and even lifestyles began to change for many... Out of the chaos and criticism, a new breed of cultural artists and thinkers emerged [55]

As a graduate student ethnographic researcher, I made my first visit to Providence, Rhode Island, in 2003 to meet members of Providence Youth Student Movement (PrYSM) and conduct observations of their activities. PrYSM co-founder, Sarath Suong, picked me up to take me to the house he shared with his partner, Ross, and one other PrYSM member. As we headed to their house, I noticed the gradual changes from modernist, late-twentieth-century architecture to small, one-story, locally owned markets and Victorian homes, some renovated and others barely standing.

Sarath and Ross rented the top floor in a Victorian house on a street with homes that were mostly densely packed, renter-occupied three-story homes in which each floor was a separate unit. Their roommate, CK, another member of PrYSM, was also gay and Khmer American. After climbing three narrow, circular staircases, I entered a bare, dark living room. Down the hallway past the kitchen, they showed me my bedroom, which was along the right wall between the other two bedrooms. My room was their storage space and had a semi-inflated airbed on the floor. The window looked straight into the next-door neighbor's, about three feet away. There was no air conditioning in the middle of the humid summer, and they shared only one fan. They carefully placed it in the kitchen so that it could reach all the rooms. And on my first night there, Sarath and Ross hurriedly concocted a special Khmer beef soup from scratch for the PrYSM "family."

As if on cue, as soon as Ross turned off the stove, people streamed into the apartment without knocking. For the rest of the evening, they came and left at will. Some sat down immediately at the round dining table, ate the home-cooked Khmer meal, and rushed off, while others sat at the table joking late into the night, talking about updates in their lives, and integrating PrYSM discussions into the conversation. Almost all of the 15 or so people who stopped by that evening lived within a five-block radius of the house, and despite the heat, they congregated for hours in Sarath's apartment. Most were Southeast Asian Americans (SEAA) under 27 years old, and all had some connection to PrYSM. Sarath later told me the visitors often had to figure out meals on their own at home, rather than share meals with their families, as is usually a family tradition in Southeast

Asian households. Consequently, Sarath and Ross' social role in the group had become one of reconstituting family. By the end of the night, the entire organizing leadership of PrYSM had come through to eat, check-in, and share their lives with one another.

Over the next three years, I visited PrYSM and other youth organizations in the Southeast Asian Freedom Network (SEAFN) to conduct observations, interviews, and participate in gatherings to strategize on the national organizing work for immigration reform. Among these American-born children of refugees and childhood refugee arrivals, I documented issues of ethnic identity formation, and generational and class-based marginalization by older community leaders. While PrYSM shared these challenges with other SEAFN groups, their autonomy in the first few years—especially as a grassroots group without non-profit status—sparked the creative ways they articulated their collective identity without the confines of a professionalized staff and formal membership base. They expressed themselves in messaging and organizing strategies and tactics that made sense to working-class Southeast Asian refugee communities.

This chapter addresses the misperceptions of immigrant and refugee children's integration by centering the perspectives of 1.5 and second-generation youth within the context of their hyper-criminalized neighborhoods and social support networks. In many ways, PrYSM embodies experiences and the organizing potential of the majority of SEAA youth throughout the country who do not live in large, urban cities with extensive infrastructure of progressive organizations. After introducing the emergence of PrYSM and the context of resettlement in Providence, I explain how their four organizational core values—"family, love, ghetto roots, and movement building"—inform their structure, cultural practices, and identity formation as forms of political development. The honesty with which PrYSM members during this nascent period embodied those values was a transformative challenge to the sterilized ways in which many organizers embedded in the non-profit industrial complex had been trained to represent themselves.

Southeast Asian Resettlement in Rhode Island

The resettlement of Southeast Asian refugees represents an extension of the aftermath of U.S. military incursions into Viet Nam, Laos, and Cambodia in the name of saving the victims of Communism.[56] Tang explains, "If we begin by viewing the Cambodian refugee as merely a subject of humanitarianism, we might conclude that her presence in the hyperghetto marks a major programmatic failure, as if something went terribly awry in the resettlement process . . . "[57] He argues that refugees became collateral damage to the structural state violence against long-term Black and Puerto Rican residents in the Bronx, one of New York City's "hyperghetto, inner-city neighborhoods that warehouse the poorest of the urban poor, particularly the black subproletariat—those who, since the late 1960s urban insurrections, have been stripped of virtually every opportunity for livable-wage work."[58]

Relatedly, Southeast Asian refugees in Rhode Island fluctuated between the hyperghetto and relative economic stability based on life events and opportunities through social networks. Rhode Island began accepting large numbers of refugees as part of the 1975 dispersal policy to distribute the first cohort of refugees across the fifty states. The main influx of Southeast Asians did not arrive *en masse* in the state until the second cohort in the early to mid-1980s and through tertiary migrations, particularly from Lowell, Massachusetts and other parts of the Northeast in the 1990s to early 2000s. In 1980, Asians accounted for 6.3% (9,894) of the total state population (156,804), and by 1983, an estimated 2,800 Cambodians, 2,000 Hmong, 500 Lao, and 100 Vietnamese, in addition to the existing 118 Vietnamese, had moved to Rhode Island, increasing the state's Asian population by almost 50%.[59]

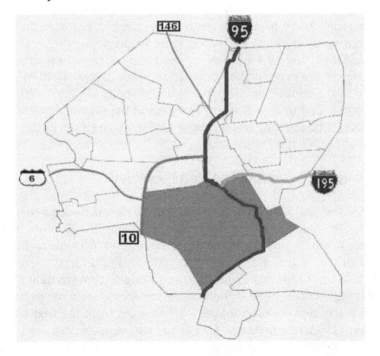

Figure 2.1. Map of Rhode Island/Providence South Side.

The majority of refugees resettled in the West End of Providence, on the city's formerly industrialized south side. The West End is known as the city's most diverse neighborhood today, but as industrialization moved abroad in the 1970s–1980s, the middle class moved out to the suburbs, turning the area into what was then called an inner-city neighborhood. Between 1990 and 2000, the population was 30% Hispanic, 30% African American, 14% White, and by 2000, 13% Asian Americans made up of mostly Southeast Asian refugees. One in three people lived below the Federal Poverty Line, and 44% of adults had not completed high school.[60]

Between 2000 and 2010, the population of SEAAs in the state remained constant at an estimated 11,971, with Khmer being the largest ethnic group, followed by Laotians (Hmong, ethnic Lao, and other ethnic minorities from Laos). The socio-economic situation in the state, especially for Khmer and Laotians, very much resembled the national statistics for Southeast Asians in the United States, with poverty rates higher than the national average (18.2% and 12.2%, respectively), household sizes almost double the United States overall average (3.87% and 3.82%, respectively), and workers concentrated in agricultural occupations and a largely low-income, and economically and politically vulnerable labor force.[61] Surveys conducted in Providence found that only 4.6% of Khmer Americans and 10.4% of Lao Americans had a bachelor's degree compared to 18.5% of the general population and 23.2% of the entire state Asian population.[62] Moreover, 21.1% of Khmer and 19.4% of Hmong lived in poverty, more than twice the percentage of the general state population living in poverty (8.4%), while almost half the population of all four groups "spoke English less than very well," as opposed to only 8.4% of the general population.[63] PrYSM youth lived this reality, and they saw the organization as a medium through which they could change their situation.

Early Nonprofit Assistance and MAA Formation

PrYSM's critical analysis of the structural barriers in the local community became the foundation for movement-building for Southeast Asian American youth throughout the city, and the progressive movements began to view this new group as a promising ally in multi-racial social justice activism. In the 1970s and 1980s, the pro-immigrant government of Rhode Island recognized the need for immediate services for new refugee arrivals. It hired thirty new K–12 bilingual teacher aides from the first cohort of refugees in 1975, who had some formal English language education, to meet the needs of incoming refugee students. The state also hired translators at police departments, social service agencies, health centers, and three major hospitals, and created the Southeast Asian Support Center for mental health at St. Joseph's Hospital.[64]

Two major non-governmental organizations that served as subcontractors to the Department of State led resettlement efforts in Providence: The International Institute, an arm of the American Council for Nationalities Services (ACNS) and Catholic Social Service (CSS), of the U.S. Catholic Conference. In lieu of local churches or individual sponsors, these agencies served as the umbrella sponsors for refugees entering Rhode Island as their point of arrival until 1982, when ACNS cited Rhode Island as a "high impact" state that should no longer accept refugees unless they had immediate relatives residing there.[65] From that point on, refugee resettlement largely consisted of secondary or tertiary migration, mostly for family reunification or clan reunification (Hmong). The Rhode Island Office of Refugee Resettlement records indicate that in 1984, one in four residents in Providence was Southeast Asian.[66]

Soon after the first cohort resettlement, each of the four Southeast Asian communities—Hmong, Khmer, Lao, and Vietnamese—created their own MAAs. In 1987, these merged to form an inter-ethnic, coalitional organization, the Socio-Economic Development Center (SEDC), which became a nonprofit 501(c)3 in 1998. SEDC is a multi-service organization that has assisted in job placement, English language skills, case management, crisis intervention, translation services, and family reunification immigration services. As SEDC began to partner and integrate into the governmental infrastructure, its roles also evolved. In the 1990s, its staffers became community representatives, liaisons, and trainers for state projects, like tobacco and substance abuse prevention, elderly services, early childhood educational programs, and youth development. The organization eventually changed its name to Center for Southeast Asians.[67] The MAAs became the primary voice of their communities to governmental agencies, politicians, and funders throughout the 1990s. They were the gatekeepers between the community, external resources, and power brokers.[68]

In addition, Buddhist temples, funded through private donors in the community, functioned as sites for community information sharing, spiritual practice, and social and cultural expression. Providence had the reputation as the center of Theravada Buddhism for Khmer Americans by the 1980s, and monks from the local temple were deployed to ethnic enclaves throughout the country.[69] In all, the progressively-minded state of Rhode Island seemed to do everything *right* in its efforts to resettle and integrate refugees. By the late 1990s into the early 2000s, however, most MAAs did not see the issues of incarceration or deportation as a priority in their work and did not have human or financial capacity to assist families. Families either exhausted all of their legal possibilities, and often, MAA staffers did not know how to address issues of incarceration and deportation. Many individuals with criminal records have long been marginalized or even ostracized by legal and social service institutions. Consistent with this pattern, MAAs came to represent the class divisions within their ethnic communities.

The Economic Vitality in Rhode Island

While Rhode Island had a long history of immigration and a strong middle class based mainly on textile manufacturing, dominant narratives of immigrant histories in Rhode Island are based around the migration of Irish, Italian, Canadian, Portuguese, Polish, German, Scandinavian, Russian Jewish, and Armenian populations. Rhode Island, the second most densely populated state in the country during the first half of the century suddenly faced a dramatic exodus as manufacturing significantly declined between 1950 and 1970, particularly as its textile companies moved out of state and abroad.[70] By the 1980s, the major industries that remained were in (custom) jewelry, machine, and metal manufacturing, with the majority of job openings for entry-level, low-wage labor that required little formal education and minimal English language skills. Hence, although unemployment was the highest in New England and wages the third-lowest in the country, Southeast Asian refugees who had little to no English-language or industrial skills found employment as entry-level, mostly seasonal assembly workers in and around Providence.[71] Statewide, public housing was scarce due to an abundance of low-income housing in the private sector. Consequently, local media reports demonstrated the success of refugee assimilation without burdening the welfare state.

Surveillance of SEAA Youth Through Policing and Funding Mechanisms

Since the Clinton administration's passage of various immigration, welfare, and crime reforms in 1996, state and local governments had been encouraged to promote tough on crime initiatives in the name of creating safer streets.[72] The result was youth being tried as adults in the late 1990s, and increased penalties, convictions, and longer sentences largely targeted at black and brown youth.[73] SEAA youth were growing up in a period of public policy in which "structural rather than individual solutions [that] called for increasing institutional opportunities for low-income youth"[74] were no longer the premise for creating policy that targeted low-income youth of color. Instead, programs introduced in the post-September 11, 2001 context only heightened the surveillance and criminalization of

BIPOC and immigrant youth of color under the Bush administration; even liberal stakeholders and non-profit organizations benefitted from the programs' attendant funding. SEAA bore the dual burden of heightened economic stress due to decreasing social safety nets by the government and hyper-criminalization of youth of color. By the early late 1990s, there were increasing numbers of SEAA entering the criminal justice system and being turned over to immigration detention to linger indefinitely, only to be deported to a country they often did not remember.[75]

The trend to criminalize youth of color, including SEAA, amounted to what Victor Rios terms the "youth control complex" of "the web of institutions, schools, businesses, residents, media, community centers, and criminal justice system, that collectively punish, stigmatize, monitor, and criminalize young people in an attempt to control them."[76] The youth control complex might take the form of material physical punishment, or it might be symbolic in the form of surveillance, profiling, or harassment, particularly of youth of color.[77] The state apparatus evolved into a pervasive intrusion into youth's lives in the early 2000s as surveillance and social control increased with the introduction of gang databases and funding for additional surveillance to schools and non-profit organizations. Many local school systems and organizations accepted this money, though not necessarily without prior understanding of the surveillance expectations attached to it.

On May 14, 2001, George W. Bush's administration introduced Project Safe Neighborhoods (PSN), which would hire 113 U.S. attorneys dedicated to prosecuting gun-related offenses. The administration also dedicated $75 million to: hiring and training 600 new state and local prosecutors nationwide; funding schools and community programs to surveil youth and collaborate with local police; and providing equipment for technological surveillance for local police departments. The program was introduced as Bush's key anti-crime initiative and PSN was framed on five key components: 1) partnerships; 2) strategic planning and research integration; 3) training; 4) outreach; and 5) accountability. These components maximized the investment of federal resources through a focus on the contexts driving gun crime in particular jurisdictions. Research would assist in allocating resources and local and state partners to fully understand local conditions as well as resources to the interventions.[78] By the end of its first year, the Department of Justice included both Boston and Lowell in a report that touted cities with high prosecutorial rates—these two Massachusetts cities showed a 13.1% decrease in violent crimes, essentially proving the success and needed expansion of PSN.[79] The support for Bush's initiative gained that much more traction in the wake of the 9/11 World Trade Center tower bombings.

Rhode Island and the city of Providence began to receive funding from PSN in July 2003, implementing a Gang Intervention Unit, Gun Task Force, and Street Workers Program. The Gang Intervention Unit would enhance the detection and intervention of gang activity by expanding local gang databases and sharing those databases across local and state police departments in Rhode Island, Massachusetts, Connecticut, Maine, and New Hampshire. The Federal Bureau of Investigation (FBI) provided an operating budget, surveillance equipment, cash for informants, and funding for investigations.[80] Providence modeled its computerized system, ProvStat, after those in Boston, Detroit, New Orleans, and New York City, and reported a decrease in murders by 13%, robberies by 44%, assaults by 31%, and shots fired by 45% by 2005.[81] The Gun Task Force buttressed the gang intervention unit by sharing information with federal agencies. Gun-related offenses were automatically reported through the system to the Rhode Island U.S. Attorney's office for possible felony prosecution. ICE databases were cross-referenced and notified the task force of any previous immigration violations, rendering the individual deportable. The Street Workers Program hired seven full-time and one part-time certified nonviolent trainers to intervene in violent situations and engage in conflict resolution.[82] These combined programs, while seeming to decrease crime on paper, in fact served to increase criminalization of youth of color by targeting and entering them into this newly formed system as gang members.

In what was publicized as a form of community policing to liberal advocates, Providence School District, Rhode Island Training School, and community-based organizations received funding from PSN to collaborate with the Attorney General's office and local police departments. The local police conducted school visits and attended community meetings and youth programs to explain gang recruitment and the role of citizens in preventing and reporting gang participation or activities.[83] Liberal and conservative stakeholders alike applauded the combination of surveillance, gun control for criminals, and prevention services, and the question of increased surveillance on bodies marked as poor, immigrant, and racialized never expanded into public debate.

PrYSM's emergence in the community coincided with the national and local efforts to lessen crime and gang activity, and PrYSM youth as well as community members were swept up in the youth control complex that entered innocent youth into gang databases. SEAA caught in the dragnet of the gang database found refuge in PrYSM when MAAs and other social service organizations had rejected them as outcasts, did not have the capacity to serve their specific needs, or participated in their criminalization through the PSN community-funding gang intervention initiative.

Together, surveillance and attempts to reform young people's behavior with PSN-funded after-school programs and educational institutions began to damage trust with local youth. Some youth who had gone to PrYSM instead no longer viewed these places as safe for their marked bodies. PrYSM had built the needed trust among community members and youth to create the space for truces between gangs. In turn, opportunities for collaboration developed on the community's own terms. In the process, PrYSM articulated a discourse on the issues of surveillance, detention, and deportation from the unique intersectional perspective of their LGBTQ+ youth members.

PrYSM's Emergence

In the next section, I closely examine the beginning stages of PrYSM. First, though, I must explain the urgency and importance of what they do. Despite other parts of the U.S. having larger SEA youth populations, Rhode Island maintains a significant connection for SEA youth organizing work.

Throughout the 1990s, marginalized SEAA youth developed their own oppositional spaces based on their intersectional identities, such as through gangs or programs provided by non-profit organizations that addressed their unique experiences as refugee children in urban America. With external support networks provided by movement groups, "at-risk" youth programs began to recruit SEAAs in low-income communities. As the youth grew to assume leadership positions or start their own groups, they prioritized issues relevant to their intersectional identities and ways of understanding and analyzing their varied human experiences.[84] PrYSM and the majority of SEAA youth leaders occupy the interstitial spaces of identity, class, gender and sexual orientation. Those activists organized around Crenshaw's premise that non-intersectional organizing creates a narrowed understanding of shared problems in which "one discourse fails to acknowledge the significance of the other, [and] the power relations that each attempts to challenge are strengthened."[85] The creation of a third space such as PrYSM articulates a "collision of perspectives" whereby competing scripted narratives of identity intermix to the point that "a representational contract is broken; the queer and the colored [and the poor] come into perception and the social order receives a jolt."[86] As I discuss in detail in future chapters, PrYSM's intersectional culture allowed for LGBTQ+ leadership to emerge without question, and this included their willingness to make space for Kohei, a gay, middle-class Japanese American, to serve as executive director in their formative years. Yet, in PrYSM's adoption of this philosophy of intersectionality, they remained unable to secure strong involvement of young women in the group.

PrYSM took advantage of the confluence of resources from progressive, LGBTQ+, and immigrant rights movements to tilt the power balance in co-ethnic communities. By becoming a voice for SEAA youth in other movements, their collective intersectional identities also influenced the perspective and priorities for a younger generation emerging in the ranks. In later chapters, PrYSM leaders discuss organizing the youth within their membership by integrating the history of refugeeism with the contemporary reality of poor youth of color in America. They realized early in their political development a complex phenomenon that the Combahee River Collective had also pointed out: "When it comes to social inequality, people's lives and the organization of power in a given society are better understood as being shaped not by a single set of social divisions, be it race or gender or class, but by many axes that work together and influence each other."[87] PrYSM's curriculum to raise the political consciousness of its youth highlighted this philosophy so they could better understand the confluences of their identities and the intricate ways in which their perceived or imposed identities interacted with the state. By the time a new generation had grown up in PrYSM, they expressed themselves and their political organizing through this intersectional lens.

The expressions of marginalized narratives in their campaigns allowed PrYSM youth to view themselves as part of the history of BIPOC in the United States, not solely as the umbilical extensions of a war lost in a homeland they did not know. They crafted a platform to connect past movements concerned with race, gender, and sexuality with the call for refugee rights and self-determination. The hybridization of those multiple identities led to the flourishing of an oppositional community that simultaneously occupied and rejected each of its fragmented identities.[88] The youth featured in *Generation Rising* continually worked to uproot the power differentials that Crenshaw claims are a result of the fragmentation of political identities.[89] To this end, we must prioritize lived intersectionality as we study the multiple sites of SEAA political identity formation in social movements since 2001.

In 2000, Sarath Suong and Kohei Ishihara, two Asian American students at Brown University, recruited local Black, Caribbean, and SEAA students at other colleges in Providence to start a local youth group, Providence Youth-Student Movement, or PrYSM. Due to the diversity of their membership, PrYSM's vision for the organization was to build a space for local Lesbian, Gay, Bisexual, Transgender, Questioning, and others (LGBTQ+), and those who identify as Southeast Asian American youth in a social justice movement to represent the intersections of their sexuality, poverty, immigration, and race and ethnicity. Since there were virtually no similar groups in the city, PrYSM soon became a multi-racial space for other queer[90] youth of color in working-class sections of Providence who did not have such spaces in their schools, colleges, or neighborhoods.

Although PrYSM began its work with a vague idea of the political impact it wanted to make toward social justice, it still had no clear path of how to materialize that vision. The founders encouraged the local youth of color—mostly Cambodian, Laotian, Hmong, Vietnamese, Black, and Dominican—to set the organization's agenda by identifying the main challenges they faced in the vacuum of services available to them as hyper-criminalized youth of color. In response, they set forth priorities concerning the racial profiling of SEAA and other youth of color through the creation of a gang database; the need for queer youth support networks; and a leadership and mentoring pipeline for SEAA youth in Rhode Island.

In the aftermath of the destruction of the World Trade Center buildings on September 11, 2001, the narratives and images of violent Muslim immigrants as terrorists catalyzed a social climate of fear that fomented new, sweeping immigration enforcement policies by federal and local law enforcement.[91] In response, PrYSM fought the hyper-criminalization of youth of color as imminent societal threats in the post-9/11 climate.[92] The blurring of rights and legal privileges between "refugee," "noncitizen," and "naturalized citizen" left many youth of color, regardless of their religion or geographical origins, vulnerable to hostile immigration enforcement policies that swept poor immigrants of color into anti-terrorism initiatives that ostensibly targeted South Asian, Arab, and Muslim communities. The lack of due process rights in immigration proceedings, a surge in deportations, and a lack of transparency by Immigration Customs Enforcement (ICE), left families feeling virtually defenseless and communities fearful of accessing government services and agencies. The stakes became exponentially higher for working-class immigrants whose alleged crimes point to larger issues of structural poverty, such as theft or welfare fraud, while the political will and government-sponsored safety nets to assist those communities dissipated with withering financial and social assistance under the Bush administration.[93] No longer was a person who committed a crime of poverty solely meant to answer to the criminal justice system; they had to independently navigate the immigration system and enforcement practices intended to combat non-citizen terrorists.[94]

The mission and vision of groups like PrYSM forced the question of how disenfranchised segments of the population might obtain political power beyond electoral politics. They developed tactics of direct action, participatory action research, and independent cultural and media production. They produced counter-hegemonic narratives with those tools as part of the national mobilization strategy within the newly formed youth organizing coalition, Southeast Asian Freedom Network (SEAFN), to target

ICE for its due process violations and re-humanize targeted members of the community through a critical analysis of U.S. intervention abroad and neo-liberal policies at home. PrYSM's story represents how a generational shift of leadership must navigate the competing forces of elder expectations and resource-rich allies. Since PrYSM's geographical location extends beyond the epicenters of Asian American activism, such as Los Angeles, the San Francisco Bay Area, Seattle, Boston, and New York, we can view this generation's struggles through underrepresented narratives about AAPI activism.

Sarath's Political Development

Sarath is the only founding member of PrYSM who has been involved with the organization in some capacity since its inception. His personal values and beliefs both influence and reflect much of the organization's culture and vision. Sarath was born to Khmer parents in 1978 in Khao I Dong refugee camp in Thailand. In 1983, Sarath, along with his parents and his four siblings, were sponsored to the United States and reunited with relatives in Lowell, Massachusetts. Like many Cambodian refugees, they soon moved to a more affordable, though increasingly violent, area in the nearby city of Revere. The family of seven lived on the top floor of a New England triple-decker, a three-story house converted into three separate rental or condo units. Their apartment was about 700 square feet, with two bedrooms, one bath, a kitchen in the center, and a living room converted into a master bedroom. Sarath's father worked as a clerk in a gas station until he was shot in the hand during an armed robbery. He has not been able to work since that incident, and the family has had to depend entirely on Sarath's mother's income from various low-wage jobs.

Sarath is the youngest of the five siblings, all of whom were involved in gang activity while he was growing up. He learned valuable lessons from their mistakes, and they did everything they could to protect him from street life. However, Sarath believed that the institutional support given to him through the educational system made a huge difference between his academic success and that of his siblings:

> I was placed in a special program at Revere High. They had this strategy of picking a handful of kids, who they saw something in—I don't know what—and they focused all their energy on us.... It's because of them that I even applied to Brown, and that I got into one of the best schools in the country. All of us did— Harvard, medical school—everyone in the program got into great schools and did some great things. My older siblings weren't chosen, and I see the difference. They just got lost with all the other kids. It wasn't really fair.

Still, he almost did not escape from engaging in gang activity. Sarath fortunately had strong mentors at school who protected him from gang recruitment in middle and high school, but he still felt he lacked a co-ethnic mentor who genuinely understood his family trauma. The first role model he identified with early in high school was a gay Filipino American advocate who introduced Sarath to youth organizations in the Greater Boston metropolitan area. Sarath recalled:

I was so close to ending up on the streets like my brothers. And I guess I sort of had a dual case growing up in America. And I know, for me, I grew up in this inner-city urban community. And we hear about all these Southeast Asian gangs, these killings and shootings and stuff, and for me it was reality—it was happening right outside my door. My brothers and sisters were all involved, and I guess a lot of that comes from my parents and the parents of teens ability to talk, and the ability to communicate to the kids. I was lucky . . . I had mentors that taught me about organizing, not just staying outta trouble, but thinking with a social justice philosophy. That's what I wanted to create with PrYSM.

Sarath was able to express social problems, solutions, and critiques through the supportive mentors and staff in his after-school programs, and it shaped his vision for PrYSM in later years. That self-growth translated into Sarath's academic achievement and his grades and classroom engagement improved. His teachers encouraged him to apply to Brown University in his senior year—he describes how he had to "fight my way into Brown as a Southeast Asian" youth from a working-class background.

At Brown, located in Providence, Rhode Island, Sarath felt isolated and had little in common with the general privileged class status of the campus and many of the students. The distance from home allowed him the space to come to terms with his sexuality, and he found support from other LGBTQ students on campus. He and classmate Kohei Ishihara, a biracial, Japanese and white, upper-middle-class student from California, were two of the few openly queer Asian American students on campus in the early 2000s. They became close friends as they challenged each other personally on their political outlook in regard to social justice.

Sarath also found strong mentorship in an Asian American professor, Robert Lee, who validated Sarath's desire to reconcile his community commitment, political activism, and newly articulated sexual identity. While both high school and college mentors guided Sarath toward political engagement, his parents and his own ethnic community pressured him to stay away from politics based on their own experiences with political revolution. Sarath recalled, "I remember coming to Brown, and someone asked me what I wanted to do, and I said, 'I'm going to go into political science.' And my parents would say, 'Oh, no, why do you want to go into political science? You know, people in politics get killed, usually politicians get physically abused, disciplined in the middle of the night.'" He felt clear dissonance in his sense of obligation and indebtedness to both his mentors and his parents, who were pulling him in opposite directions. Sarath's parents' comments are a common sentiment among SEAA refugees who have fled their homelands due to turmoil in which one's political participation could easily lead to incarceration, physical harm, or death to the person and their family. Upon resettlement to the United States, the reluctance to organize and integrate Asian Americans and immigrants into political organizations has indirectly communicated to these populations that their voices do not matter in American government. Sarath and others of his generation grew up with the contradictory messages of American democracy in school while simultaneously witnessing the marginalization of their relatives in daily life. For many of them, the histories of the Black liberation movement became their inspiration to find value in their own power even when others did not.

Sarath's shared experiences with PrYSM members manifested in his influence on articulating the group's values, cultural practices, mentorship, family, and the idea of returning to one's "roots." His ability to articulate for himself what his life story has necessitated in a social justice context has given him the tools to motivate and mobilize working-class youth in Providence. While at Brown, Sarath and his classmate Kohei Ishihara interacted with local youth in gay clubs and gatherings with the small gay community in Providence. As they immersed themselves in the local queer community, they began to build local networks of LGBTQ+ young people and college-age SEAA. Simultaneously, they were politically developing their understanding of identity formation, community organizing, and social movements under the mentorship of professors in American studies and Gender and Women's studies. Sarath and Kohei recruited their friends to form PrYSM, a group that would focus on youth empowerment equally between students and non-students. There was no other organization that focused on youth organizing, LGBTQ+ issues, and issues concerning Asian American Pacific Islander (AAPI) and immigrant communities in Providence with a progressive analysis. Founding member Ammala felt that at first, people "didn't know what to make of us, but the youth were attracted to the culture of the group, the kind of hip, party place, but also something more, like a family."

Figure 2.2: Sarath Suong at an anti-deportation rally 2013
(Courtesy of PrYSM Archives)

Developing an Organizational Identity

As PrYSM developed a core leadership of six college-age youth over the course of that year, they realized they needed a focused articulation of their group identity. They decided to hold a series of retreats to form the core values of PrYSM's identity:

Family. *We call ourselves a family; and it means that we all expect to love and support each other. It means we have to work out conflicts and arguments under the context that we are all brothers and sisters.*

Love. *We believe that activism, social service, and change needs to be directly linked to compassion and love.*

(Ghetto) Roots. *Is a term to describe the value we place on organizing on the streets—in homes, and in the heart of the community; it* *means not joining the traditional confines of the non-profit industrial complex; it means finding solidarity with the most oppressed.*

Movement. *We believe that institutional change needs to be in the hands of the people. We believe that people's dreams and hopes need to be part of this change. And we believe that if we make connections between people, families, gangs, organizations, communities, and cities, we can create a movement.*[95]

These organizational values reflected the members' conscious choices to manifest a new political approach to understand how they wanted to build social movement. The cohesion of family is often a cultural value attributed to the success of Asian societies in dominant American narratives to explain the model minority. PrYSM re-appropriated models from gang culture and LGBTQ+ resistance to reconstitute the concept of family among its members. Its alternative family allows for the organization to operate beyond the bureaucracy of a social service or social movement model to meet the holistic needs of its members with unconditional love and acceptance for who their intersectional identities as SEAA working-class, queer youth.

PrYSM's critical analysis of institutional enforcers charged with regulating the bodies of SEAA and other poor youth of color put them in a position to create an inclusive environment for marginalized youth in Providence. Over the next two years, PrYSM developed four main components to operationalize their values: a GED certificate program; a women's support group; the Southeast Asian Queer leadership (SEAQuel); and an organizing core trained to lead campaigns and do PrYSM's political organizing work, including the campaign against detention and deportation.

The centralization of women and LGBTQ+ youth signified the most dramatic change from SEAA organizations that emerged in response to refugee resettlement. The limitations of power for women and LGBTQ+ individuals had often constrained their ability to set an agenda that spoke to their varied subjectivities. Patriarchal structures within existing organizations seldom privileged leadership by SEAA women, who instead held tokenized positions with little power. In short, there had been only marginal inclusion of openly LGBTQ+ individuals and topics. When SEAA community groups did gain positions of power, the male leaders often ignored the specific priorities of SEAA youth, women, or LGBTQ+ people. Entire SEAA populations have been subordinate to the invisible, dominant male perspective. Funders and potential ally groups do not question the possible intersectional differences among SEAAs and engaged with these gatekeepers as their sole insight to the communities.

The campaign against detention and deportation offered the political opportunity to change this dynamic. PrYSM's campaign allowed for family members—often women—to be experts and provide leadership on forced removal. The General Educational Development (GED) certificate program, which included daycare for students with children, offered the most economically disadvantaged community members the chance to apply for better jobs, trade schools, and higher education. Students in the GED program formed the women's group, which worked with SEAQuel to provide safe spaces for members to share stories, develop a collective identity, build community, and develop their political consciousness centered on gender and sexuality.

Family Constructed and Reconstructed

The concept of family as a core value for a mostly queer and female organization has profound meaning in the culture of the group. The notion of reconstructing family emerged organically, but PrYSM founders interpreted it through the lenses of LGBTQ+ formations of surrogate families and gangs.[96] In *A Dream Shattered*, Long suggests that culturally conflicted youth become assimilated to gang culture to protect themselves from existing gangs that control the streets of their neighborhoods and to create a sense of family missing in the home due to the stresses of immigration. Aihwa Ong refers to the discourse on Cambodian youth involvement in gangs as not only a form of assimilation but also an assertion of masculinity and romanticism. She argues, "For Cambodian kids, African American gangs, more than any other ethnic grouping (including the Vietnamese), represented the iconic figures of street glamour and working-class masculinity."[97] She cites the generational differences within families and the desire to "be American" as determining factors in Cambodian youths "self-fashioning as Cambodian-American *BoyZ in the 'Hood*."[98] This dominant narrative, similar to that of scholarship on African Americans, assumes that disintegration of the nuclear family unit led directly to the downward socio-economic mobility of the 1.5- and second-generation in their attempts to reconstitute family in gangs and "counterculture."[99] Conversely, the LGBTQ+ movement has long espoused the reframing of families beyond the nuclear family because of the history of rejection LGBTQ+ individuals faced from their families for their sexuality and as a challenge to conservative movements against gay marriage.[100]

PrYSM founders adopted both the gang culture and the queer movement's conceptualization of the family to support members in an alternative space of non-judgement, where youth could freely express their various identities. PrYSM found inspiration mainly from the Combahee

River Collective (CRC) of the 1970s, who were "a small group of black lesbian socialist feminists" who started as the Boston chapter of the National Black Feminist Organization in 1973, before breaking away due to what they saw as the national organization's homophobia.[101] PrYSM founders pointed to the CRC's statement about their political stance as the foundation for the youth group's mission: "We believe that the most profound and potentially most radical politics come directly out of our own identity, as opposed to working to end someone else's oppression... sexual politics under patriarchy is pervasive in Black women's lives as are the politics of class and race."[102] PrYSM's leaders wanted to create the safe space that CRC claimed to be for Black lesbian feminists like scholar-activist Barbara Smith: "It was the first time that I could be all of who I was in the same place. That I didn't have to leave my feminism outside the door to be accepted as I would in a conservative Black political context. I didn't have to leave my lesbianism outside. I didn't have to leave my race outside."[103] Many PrYSM youth like youth leaders escaped to PrYSM as a refuge from a difficult family and socio-economic environment. It provided support, understanding, opportunities for development, and a sense of control over the structural oppression bearing down on their lives.

Love as Justice

This philosophy of justice was not unusual within the social justice movements of the past, but it was not always articulated as a spiritual or religious path. In her study of the African American, Chicano, and Asian American Movements in Los Angeles in the 1960s, Laura Pulido notes that many of the activists emphasized "the importance of creating social change from within as well as without."[104] bell hooks claims that the decentralization of the discourse of love and spirituality with the emergence of the Black Power movement of the 1970s created "the absence of public spaces where that pain could be articulated, expressed, shared, meant that it was held in—festering, suppressing the possibility that this collective grief would be reconciled in community even as ways to move beyond it and continue resistance struggle would be envisioned."[105] As a grassroots youth group unbound to funding mechanisms, PrYSM took lessons from previous generations of lesbian Black activist writers and entwined it with its members' own cultural practices.

PrYSM members shared what justice would mean to them in the context of the history of war in Laos, Cambodia, and Viet Nam, and for individuals facing deportation. Sarath responded, "If I could meet Pol Pot, I would want to know why he chose to do what he did—what he was thinking. I would want to know exactly what happened. I would want him to apologize.

I think that would give people a sense of closure. Right now, there's this big hole in our history, in our understanding of ourselves as Cambodians." For members of PrYSM, this willingness to forgive also translated to their loved ones who had been entangled in the criminal justice system and were facing deportation.

Since its founding, PrYSM has been a space where its members' views of themselves shifted as they developed politically, through their shared conversations, and the staff's commitment to creating inclusive safe spaces. LGBTQ+ youth in PrYSM saw the centrality of love and inclusivity as an opportunity to explore their identities. Former youth member, Heng, remembers constantly asking Sarath, Kohei, and Paul about their sexuality and gender expression. He appreciated the fact that they always welcomed his eldest sister, who identified as lesbian, to PrYSM events where others had rejected her. PrYSM's culture gave him the chance to adhere to his religious beliefs simultaneously with the values of gay liberation: "Other movements understood identity politics as endorsing the creating of communities of similarity. In contrast, the gay movement focused on freedom of individual expression, making it hypocritical to exclude any form of gay political expression."[106] PrYSM represented one of the few spaces where local youth felt accepted unconditionally for their intersectional identities, and relieved them of the burden of performing heteronormativity in order to conform to other aspects of their identity, such as religious affiliation or ethnicity.

PrYSM members incorporated traditional concepts from their cultural and religious identities as Khmer and Laotian people into how they advocated for justice and dealt with conflict and injustice in social movement spaces. They evince what hooks advocates as critical to dismantling hegemony:

The absence of a sustained focus on love in progressive circles arises from the collective failure to acknowledge the needs of the spirit and an overdetermined emphasis on material concerns. Without an ethic of love shaping the direction of our political vision and our radical aspirations, we are often seduced, in one way or the other, into continued allegiance to systems of domination—imperialism, sexism, racism, classism.[107]

As members consistently repeated to me over the years, PrYSM's continued growth and its ability to attract disenfranchised youth grew from its success in incorporating values of love and acceptance into its political mission and day-to-day operations.

Family and Love Expressed through SEAQuel

Sarath led the first LGBTQ+ Southeast Asian youth group in the country, SEAQuel. Because so many PrYSM members had originally bonded through their LGBTQ+ networks, SEAQuel immediately became PrYSM's most popular program. Though it started at roughly the same time as the women's program, SEAQuel had three times as many members, created a name, and developed a culture, a regular meeting schedule, and a decision-making process. While the populations for each program differed, with the women's program being largely young mothers and women with compounded responsibilities and SEAQuel being composed primarily of young men, it also speaks to how gendered roles in their ethnic communities impacted the effectiveness of the programs within PrYSM. SEAQuel had regular meetings and drop-in hours on Friday nights, when teenagers would rather be out socializing.

The drop-in hours became an alternative to the bar scene for underage SEAA queer youth who were not allowed into the bars. Armstrong explains that spaces such as "gay bars and other subcultural institutions were important for developing a group consciousness and the beginnings of a more public identity. Bars were certainly the most public aspect of submerged private communities."[108] Those spaces became the site of coming out for youth and signified more than a space to socialize. One former youth shared, "Coming out was not simply a way of describing the public revelation of sexual identity; it was also an organizational and political strategy built upon the logic of identity politics."[109]

The overall sense from PrYSM's leadership was that SEAQuel would potentially dominate the identity of the group as it intersected with the group's deportation work. Sarath expressed his feelings about the program:

> I'm so proud of SEAQuel. I've wanted to do this for so long, and now it has so much excitement. It's going so well, and everyone's full of ideas. For a long time we had been working on the deportation campaign, and it was a decision we had made as a group. But it was a hard decision for folks because for some of them, they were like, "Why do we want to show solidarity with people who would beat us up on the street for being gay any other day?" So it was hard, but we decided to take it on because of the bigger picture, of the larger political statement we were making. And it was a false assumption that only straight thugs were getting deported. But now it's cool because I feel like we were work on things that really are a priority for the LGBT community. Not like other LGBT groups that are mostly white and middle-class.

Sarath stresses that the politicization of members did not stop at "coming out" spaces as it did for other, middle-class and largely white LGBTQ+ organizations. Rather, the intersections of class, racialization, and sexual orientation were not mutually exclusive. PrYSM youth faced ostracization by their families and communities, and older men in their own community targeted them for violence because they did not conform to their gender assignment. SEAQuel youth simultaneously were 1) swept into the daily racial microaggressions of police harassment of youth of color; 2) entangled in the Gang Intervention Unit's efforts to enter them into the expanding gang database; and 3) navigated the school-to-prison pipeline that released them into a cycle of poverty stemming from their criminal records.

SEAQuel's organizing efforts against the criminalization of poor youth of color, regardless of sexual orientation, set itself apart from mainstream liberal gay activism that has so often marginalized and excluded poor BIPOC. Hanhardt, in analyzing the attempts of white, middle-class LGBTQ+ communities to dis-identify from "criminality" in the movement for hate-crime legislation, points out:

> *The antiviolence movement was the first model of gay activism to receive public and corporate monies, and it was following these initiatives that other forms of LGBT politics entered the streams of nonprofit and private funding... the threat of violence has functioned as a sort of moral bookend to queer deviance that promises redemption, if only for some. The dual insistences that the lesbian or gay man is not the criminal and that antigay violence is the act of the criminal.* [emphasis added][110]

The intersectionality among SEAQuel youths' identities gave them the capacity to express the group's core value of unconditional love in coalitional movement-building across the diversity of PrYSM members and allies. Through local coalitional organizing with Caribbean immigrant families, PrYSM built its analysis of the school-to-prison pipeline for youth of color, which it integrated into the analysis and campaign work of the Southeast Asian Freedom Network (SEAFN) discussed in subsequent chapters.

Roots and Movement: The GED Program Tries to Shift from Survive to Thrive

Regardless of the efforts by the state to integrate the new immigrants, the reality of the economic structural demise of the middle class, privatized housing that led refugees into economically depressed neighborhoods, and the dissipation of resettlement resources over time without sustainability plans left the younger generation of childhood arrivals with less chance of economic integration than had been touted as inevitable linear process of assimilation.[111]

In response to members' need to increase their economic opportunities, PrYSM volunteer Paul Pasada developed a GED preparatory course. Paul had worked part-time at a local, government-funded social service agency providing GED preparatory classes and shifted his expertise to developing the GED program at PrYSM. Between 2003 and 2004, roughly 15 students had taken the course, and about 75% took the G.E.D. and passed. More than 50% were female members of PrYSM who had children. Sotheavy expressed her gratitude for the program:

> I wanted to finish school, but I had the baby. Now I can get a better job—if I pass the test! (laughs) Most places you can't really take your kids there, but here it's ok. We can bring the kids; we bring food. It's like family…. We help each other learn, and we can ask the guys anything.

Paul admitted he wanted to improve the pedagogy to reflect more popular education methodology that would politically engage students, but the need for the students to pass the exam outweighed the desire for politicization. The circumstances of the women's lives required them to be in a state of financial security before they could even consider organizing. The GED program was critical to building PrYSM's reputation as a caring member of the community outside of their perception as radical youth activists. The GED program helped the group slowly become part of the community infrastructure as a resource for economic mobility.

It was not the case, however, that all of PrYSM's GED students delayed becoming politically active. Several of the women in the GED program and anti-deportation campaign tried to jumpstart a women's program within PrYSM. Bora describes their inspiration:

> PrYSM is just so dominated by men! They're great and we love them, but Ammala and some of the other women wanted to start a women's program that talked about things only women go through. A lot of the PrYSM girls are moms, and some are single moms. They recruited me, and we've had a few meetings, but we haven't really done much yet.

As Bora's last statement implies, there was no vision or objectives set forth for the women's program. There was no formal structure to the women's weekly meetings; they shared food and talked about their lives and issues facing working-class SEAA women, particularly single working mothers. Yet the group was difficult to sustain as its members—single working mothers and young women who were expected to fulfill traditional gender roles at home—had unpredictable schedules. Membership in the women's group ebbed and flowed as its leaders went in and out of active participation over the next ten years. Despite the challenges of holding meetings and maintaining steady leadership, the women's program built PrYSM's reputation in the community and helped bolster people's loyalty to the organization, planting the roots for the movement-building work to come that started with the conversations in the G.E.D. program.

Toward a New Southeast Asian American Activism

The values that the founding members created are critical to understanding the ways in which they operated within the organization and it shaped their choices for programming, campaigns, and fundraising throughout the group's evolution. Having said that, the founders were very clear about the idealism and naiveté. Their sheer passion for social justice and determination to wield a better world drove their success. Kohei reflected on her experiences:

We really had no idea what we were doing. We were just a bunch of college kids who were radicalized by what we were learning in school. We became friends with other local youth in the gay community, and that's how we began to hear about the problems people were facing here—as LGBT youth, from the police, of not having money. Some of us got together and decided we'd try to apply what we were doing on campus and with gay activism in the working-class neighborhoods right here.

The organization's first actions addressed the new gang database used by local law enforcement. The database policy was so broad that it allowed the police to label any group of youth seen together in any situation as a gang, including such unintended scenarios as walking home from school. PrYSM identified the practice as police harassment and strategized ways to combat racial profiling. The group's first major victory was to facilitate a truce between rival gangs, encouraging them to fight the targeting of youth with the database and oppose deportation in their community. The reality of the heightened stakes of deportation reminded the gang leaders that the shared danger in the state apparatus aimed at criminalizing and dividing their families outweighed their differences. One of PrYSM's founders, Chase, explained the thought process that resulted in the truce:

We started talking with the gangs because each side had people related to our people. We realized that the database was catching all kinds of kids in the mix—kids that weren't even in a gang. And then there were all these rumors that they were gonna send people back [to Cambodia]. We had to organize.

Chase's comments reveal the embedded relationship the gang members have within their own communities as they took account of the impact of the gang database on the youth in Providence overall. They saw themselves as protectors and leaders of their communities. The young men believed that their actions should be contained between their own gangs and the police, and that the sweeps of people through the database were unjust in the way they criminalized innocent people.

Over time, the SEAA queer youth recruited by PrYSM became the dominant group within the organization. And since no other organizing group for SEAA youth existed at that time in Providence, they embodied PrYSM's collective identity and organizing priorities. Allies from other ethnic groups remained active members of PrYSM, but the target population had narrowed, and with it, the mission and vision privileged the specific experiences and needs of SEAA youth. With the threat of deportation for these Southeast Asian refugee childhood arrivals, moreover, PrYSM's work on racial profiling and police harassment took on added significance locally and nationally.

*Figure 2.3. Anti-deportation Protest with PrYSM Youth and Kohei Ishihara, 2003
(Courtesy of PrYSM Archives).*

Impact of Funding on Organizational Culture in PrYSM's Early Years

PrYSM chose to make one significant shift since 2016 in order to re-conceptualize its priorities. PrYSM decided to diversify its funding portfolio such that it would not be solely dependent on large philanthropic foundations. They made this decision after reflecting on the role of funders on their organizational culture and priorities over time. To achieve their goal to maintain autonomy in their internal processes and political strategies, the leadership committed to relying on fiscal practices that aligned with their political vision and values.

As a grassroots organization without non-profit status, PrYSM staff felt the flexibility to grow organically with the priorities of the membership in their nascent years. However, as Kohei Ishihara's Executive Director role became more complicated with increased funding, revealing the tensions between class and sexuality within the group. On the one hand, his racial and sexual identity made it easy for him to resonate with youth sense of not belonging to a confined identity. It gave Kohei currency to enter and to stay in the organization. On the other hand, Kohei's class privilege married with his passion and vision for PrYSM shifted the culture of the organization in critical ways.

As funding began to flow into PrYSM from outside organizations, its staff made two major changes that created an organizational identity that was more structured and recognizable to funders: the adoption of a 501(c)3 status, and an increase in paid staff. Between 2003 and 2004, Kohei convinced the board of directors and staff that PrYSM should apply for the official non-profit tax status to secure more funds for its emerging programs. Until then, it had secured small funds for its meager budget of $50,000 from local donors and grantors using a local ally organization as its fiscal sponsor.

At that time, Sarath ran SEAQuel and Paul ran the GED program. Ammala helped members to start developing the women's group. Other founding members had removed themselves from the daily operations of the group and served mainly as allies or board members. Kohei, in charge of the administrative and operational concerns for the group, commanded a bird's eye view, and no one doubted his reasons to register as a non-profit organization, especially with the national media attention they received from their anti-deportation campaign in 2002.

The process of becoming a non-profit organization took nearly a year to be approved by the federal government. By 2005, PrYSM officially gained 501(c)3 status, allowing it access to large grants and the potential for exponential growth. Over those 12 months, PrYSM secured a $300,000 budget from major philanthropic foundations. Kohei continued as the E.D., applying for and managing grants in addition to supporting youth members.

PrYSM's staffing suddenly changed from mostly volunteers to five full-time employees, including Kohei. A young, single Khmer American mother from the GED program, Sophie, became their membership coordinator, and Mimi, a Laotian lesbian youth, was hired as the SEAQuel coordinator. Sarath transitioned to national coalitional work. Paul stayed on as the GED instructor, and another Brown affiliate, Jane, was hired as the organizing coordinator, in addition to youth and individual campaign coordinators who worked on stipends.

Kohei's newly official, salaried role meant that he needed to hold staff accountable to their new positions as paid employees. To him, it meant regular staff meetings, documentation of progress, coming to work on time, and absolutely full workdays. It fundamentally shifted the sense of unity and passion for the "ghetto roots" of their work, to a sense of responsibility to perform as a "job." It required a new language of engagement as deliverables to the funders rather than campaign goals and tactics and, at times, it increased accountability to the funder over the priorities of the community. Years later, Kohei recognized how his class privilege impacted this new structure:

> *I pushed everyone so hard because I didn't have to do anything but think about PrYSM, 24 hours a day. I didn't have family to take care of or bills to pay for my parents. The Southeast Asian staff and volunteers always had crises with their family or relatives, and they had to pay bills, so sometimes they were working multiple jobs. It's a privilege to organize and work—overwork—for low pay in a nonprofit.*

In the three years after becoming a federally recognized non-profit, the organization disintegrated in critical areas. Kohei's demands as the E.D. overwhelmed the staff, who eventually quit. In the vein of championing the staff, Paul challenged Kohei's authority, and soon the youth members took sides, leading to large membership attrition with Paul's departure. Additionally, founding members, who themselves were working-class young adults, began to suffer from burnout in addition to personal life transitions that drew their attention away from the daily management of PrYSM.

While the introduction of major funding and resources did not lead to the organization's disintegration, the sudden shift in culture, expectations, and professionalization had ripple effects that forced the leadership to regroup and think about what kind of organization it wanted to be. In the end, PrYSM's leaders chose to "return to a radical political vision of social change rooted in a love ethnic and seek once again to convert masses of people, black and nonblack" as they realized "a culture of domination is anti-love. It requires violence to sustain itself. To choose love is to go against the prevailing values of the culture."[112] Though they remained a 501(c)3, PrYSM chose to re-commit to their core values and instead sought out alternative fundraising options that would allow them to remain consistent with their values and internal culture. They believed they could reject the patron-client relationship while creating financial sustainability independent of the nonprofit industrial complex. By 2005, the organization had solidified its identity as an LGBTQ+, working-class youth, social justice group, both locally and nationally. PrYSM's presence in coalitional and national spaces proved critically significant to disrupting normalized narratives of SEAA youth, negotiations, and expectations of a population often tokenized in the world of policymaking.

CHAPTER THREE
Intersectional Leadership: Bringing Our Full Selves

Dr. Martin Luther King, Jr. was talking about a radical revolution of values, and that radical revolution of values has not been pursued in the last forty years...people have isolated these struggles from each other. They have not seen the parts for one whole, of a radical revolution of values that we all must undergo. (Grace Lee Boggs, Interview with Bill Moyers, 2012)

By 2010, many of the original PrYSM members developed other interests apart from their participation in the group, had new responsibilities that took time away from the group, or had moved away. Most maintained supportive relationships with the organization but transitioned out of their core roles within PrYSM. Several people became board members, including Sarath, Ammala, and one former youth member. Kohei resigned due to internal conflict from the demands he made of staff in his role as executive director (E.D.) to meet the expectations of the funders; he also felt exhausted from years of overwork and sought to be near relatives in California due to an illness in the family. Sarath wanted to go back to school and move onto the next stage of his life, but he also wanted to leave PrYSM in a good place before leaving. He said, "PrYSM always intended for there to be a transition in leadership to the youth who went through our programs and are from Providence. It's been harder than I thought, and there are things I want to do for myself, too, like finish school." Like so many other activists who founded organizations during the post-9/11 period, Sarath struggled with physical and emotional fatigue and a dissonance between his desire to achieve a sense of normalcy and establish work-life boundaries, economic stability, and personal growth. Sarath had become embedded in the organization's identity, a fact that also made it difficult for PrYSM to grow.

Activists often refer to Sarath's experience as "founder's syndrome," where a "cult of personality" consumes an organization such that it becomes synonymous with its founder. A founder often struggles with the mixed emotions of letting go of the organization, and this tension precludes them from taking on smaller roles or allowing for the group to evolve with new staff/members. Fellow members of the group, moreover, tend to have difficulty paving an organizational identity separate from the founder. For these reasons, Sarath's attempt to slowly transition out of PrYSM was a positive decision for both him and the organization. His decision underscored the intentionality that PrYSM set forth to mentor a new generation of youth leaders into the organization by the end of 2016.

In this chapter, I delve into the process of collective intersectional identity formation in PrYSM through their peaks and shifts in political conscientization and leadership development of youth members and staff. In particular, I highlight the ways in which the multiplicity of identities manifest in the organization, and how group members must constantly negotiate privileges and historical oppressions. To begin, I unpack Kelley's reference to "infrapolitics,"[113] or the internal politics that center individuals and organizations to focus on the specific periods of social movements between major campaigns to understand the daily, more mundane character of social change beyond the "spectacle" of political protests.[114] The chapter focuses on the attempt by PrYSM founders, particularly Sarath, to transition leadership that is inclusive of both LGBTQ+ and women while still meeting the original political vision of the group and the fiscal and bureaucratic responsibilities of a non-profit organization. The pressures of poverty and immigration status burdened many SEAA youth organizers as they worked to meet the demands of social movement work. The youth members' internalized perceptions of gender roles posed barriers for young women to rise within the programs and assume leadership roles. The organic development of the transition of leadership—and the emergence of young women members—gave rise to PrYSM's most successful endeavors to date, the local Community Safety Act campaign.

Overall, PrYSM members embraced heterogeneity and intersectionality despite efforts by outside groups to categorize them into singular identities; they performed fluid identities that crossed imposed labels.[115] They defied the assumption that they had to choose topics and boundaries specifically connected to their collective branding. Yet as much as PrYSM always intended to uplift the young women they served, they struggled to retain female members and mentor them into leadership positions. As with some of the most famous women activists in the Asian American Movement (AAM) of the early years, Yuri Kochiyama and Grace Lee Boggs, the young women leaders in PrYSM found their political identities in the campaigns that brought together the intersectional experiences of race and class.[116] Until 2016, the internal dynamics between members and staff prevented the solidification of a strong gender justice agenda, or even the active pursuit of funding to develop the women's program. Like the generation before them, PrYSM had unintentionally created a masculine-dominant organizational culture,[117] even though they challenged heteronormativity, rejected assertions toward an AAPI gay masculinity and even queer inclusivity from a cis-male-dominant perspective, and included cis-females in the group.[118]

This chapter examines the leadership development and politicization of members and staff through the story of three main characters who embody the ways in which these themes unfold within the infrapolitics of PrYSM. Heng was one of PrYSM's early members whose story is not dissimilar to many queer and low-income marginalized youth who found themselves amidst the sanctuary in PrYSM. First, Heng's story represents the ways in which transformation and unconditional love of the self-evolved into a desire for transformative social justice in the world around them that embodied PrYSM's values outlined in the previous chapter. Chanravy's experience as the first cis-gender female director of the largely gay male group forefronts the gritty, internal obstacles even within social justice organizations, in this case at the intersection of gender and sexuality. Finally, in the current generation of youth leaders, like Linda and Steven, we see unapologetic youth members who demand a seat at the table without hesitation. The development of these three individuals tracks PrYSM's internal growth to nurture new leaders and the concurrent impact their efforts have had beyond the local terrain of Providence.

Heng's Story

Heng was one of PrYSM's first youth who they committed to developing as an organizer. Heng's personal story of growing up in one of the poorest and hyper-policed neighborhoods in Providence both resonates with the structural experiences of many PrYSM youth and was unique in his sense of isolation and distance from his co-ethnic community. The space of PrYSM helped youth like Heng find an authentic self-love for every aspect of his identity, understanding of his family's life experiences, and integration into the Southeast Asian American and queer communities on his terms.

Family Resettlement

Heng's family escaped Cambodia as refugees from Cambodia in the early 1990s, during the third major cohort of refugee migration as a result the American War in Southeast Asia beginning in the 1970s. His family was among more than 250,000 refugees from Cambodia who had lived through American intervention in Viet Nam and the Cambodian border, auto-genocide of the Khmer Rouge that killed one-third of the population, and the treacherous escape through the jungle to the border refugee camps in Thailand only to spend years in squalid conditions to wait for third-country resettlement. His father had been a child soldier until his escape to a refugee camp in Thailand, of which Heng did not know the name. His mother had witnessed her aunt's suicide and his grandmother died in his mother's lap as a child, leaving his mother orphaned. Heng's mother became a child beggar until she reunited with her cousin by chance in the Thai refugee camp; and this same camp is where Heng's mother met and married Heng's father. Her cousin's father, who had fled to the United States first, found out about the whereabouts of his four children and Heng's mother when Viet Nam invaded Cambodia in 1979 and eventually sponsored their immigration to the United States.

Heng's extended family originally resettled the West End, a low-income neighborhood of Providence, with other Southeast Asian refugees because of the cousin's father's sponsorship to Rhode Island. With six children, Heng's parents soon decided to move to Lower South Providence, or the Lower South Side, where the ethnic mix was 50% African American, 30% Hispanic, 3.3% Native American, 4% Asian, and the remaining 12.7% Euro-American. The median income in the Lower South Side was about one-third lower than the West End, and just half of Rhode Island's median family income.[119] Heng's family of eight lived in a six-bedroom house subsidized through federal Section 8 housing, next to Black and Dominican neighbors. In turn, this context shaped the children's self-perception. According to Heng, none of the children identified as Khmer, even though they knew it was their ethnic heritage and they had had enough Khmer language comprehension to accompany their parents to government agencies to translate for them. Rather than self-identify as Khmer, they tried to fit in with the Caribbean and Black neighborhood kids. The circumstances of Heng's family's historical trauma and struggle to survive in the United States fundamentally impacted Heng's personal trajectory and ethnic identity formation, as well as the struggles within his family with PTSD and poverty.

Heng's story magnifies the contradictions of refugee resettlement in Rhode Island and the impact PrYSM has had on local youth's lives. Sarath, Kohei, and other PrYSM staff provided the support network for Heng as an adolescent youth member to overcome structural and personal barriers in his life to transition his gender expression from female (Lili) to male (Heng) in college, and to build a career as a grade school teacher and LGBTQ+ advocate.[120] His story is emblematic of how PrYSM's early organizational culture and priorities offer an approach to social justice organizing that rejects the established non-profit structure as well as a strictly structural intervention for revolutionary change espoused by Asian American radicals of the 1960s that I discussed in Chapter One.

When the System Breaks Down

Heng's family's resettlement in the U.S. involved the contradictions of the hyperghetto in refugee resettlement. Heng recalls how he and his siblings grew up in an abusive household with an alcoholic father:

I thought he drank because he was sole provider. I found out later it was because he was a child soldier in Cambodia. He worked 7pm–7am putting signs on the Boston buses. We feared him because he beat us. He would call our names and then beat us in that order. I always just thought, "How could I make him not hit me?" I thought my mom was weak. Whenever he beat us, she would go into her room. Afterward, she'd say to us, "Don't get him mad next time." They told me I needed to learn to be a silent girl. So I became very silent. I was popular, a straight-A student, but very shy, quiet.

Rather than addressing his father's need for mental health care and his chronic abuse, the family dealt with their collective needs in resettlement by burdening the children—especially Heng—with the responsibility of performing the roles of obedient, dutiful children.

When Heng was still in elementary school, their father left the family, which led their mother to spiral downward both financially and psychologically. She needed mental health care and wanted traditional Khmer remedies, but the state agencies and insurance companies refused to pay for anything but Western-trained mental health providers and treatments. Health providers tried to resolve Heng's mother's problems with medication. At one time, Heng remembers counting 51 bottles of prescription drugs for his mother in the house. Thus, even when Heng's mother, the sole adult caregiver and provider in the family, did engage in positive help-seeking health behavior, the system's lack of culturally competent policies failed to address her needs. The state's demand for Heng's family to comply with its bureaucratic system and Western-based approaches left little room for refugees to advocate for themselves because their perspective on topics such as medical treatment was fundamentally disregarded in the first place.

Consequently, Heng's mother would try to alleviate their financial difficulties by gambling. As the oldest child left in the home, Heng thus felt a strong sense of responsibility for his younger siblings and newborn niece. As an elementary school child, he began to assume the role of the default provider and protector for the family by searching for cash-based jobs, paying the bills on time, and caring for his siblings and niece. But Heng fell into a deep depression as a result of his profound sense of responsibility and the lack of control in his life. By the age of eleven, he had attempted suicide and had been institutionalized three times. He had completely lost faith in the system that was ostensibly supposed to protect his family but in all its surveillance miserably failed them.

During this turmoil, Heng found a father figure in a man involved with illegal gang activity. Because Heng was good at math, the man paid Heng to do his accounting and became Heng's first employer. Eventually, Heng was coerced into delivering drugs, but the man "always supported me in going to school and stuff because he needed me to be smart and to keep a good reputation." He worked for the man from ages eleven to fifteen, even while Heng was a Jehovah's Witness and a member of PrYSM. At this young age, he did not understand the danger and consequences of his involvement with this man. There was no contradiction in his youthful mind because he was gainfully employed to contribute to his family, and thus this was a good, spiritual act that simultaneously would help alleviate his socio-economic conditions that PrYSM tried to advocate for on the policy level. To note, throughout Heng's time as a drug courier, no adult, including teachers, counselors, and PrYSM staff, noticed changes in Heng's life severe enough to intervene. And his mother asked no questions when he gave her the money to pay for rent and brought food home.

He had perfected performing the roles expected of him from adult figures. As the Cambodian refugee Ra said in Tang's book, *Unsettled*, "The refugees always pass through somebody's hands . . . somebody is always in charge."[121] Yet, in this case, Heng's governmental handlers and adult mentors saw only what they wanted to see: the performance of the successfully assimilated refugee child. Heng's ability to perform to the expectations of the adults in his world gave him a sense of power—they rewarded him for the role he played in that context with money, approval, and a sense that he had "solved" his own issue of being a "problem child" to a "rehabilitated child" on their terms. Heng's double consciousness allowed him to speak and act in ways that were legible to adults such that he would be recognized, and the adults, including the political organizers, wanted to hear that their programs were successful. Heng allowed them to perpetuate the patron-client relationship such that it justified their programs rather than fundamentally addressed his needs. At that age, however, Heng still felt that both the Jehovah's Witness temple and PrYSM served deep emotional needs for a safe space and a feeling of belonging.

Searching for Family

The experiences of war and refugee flight left many families torn across physical and emotional planes, and the silenced trauma sometimes manifested in isolation, mistrust, and violence. The role reversals across gender and generation within family units could leave children taking on adult roles while also feeling like they had somehow lost their own sense of family. For many queer Southeast Asian American youth in PrYSM like Heng, moreover, these tensions became compounded.

Once he assumed the role of caretaker, Heng was always looking for opportunities to improve his family's economic situation. He and his younger sister, Duong, joined PrYSM for the youth stipend when Heng was fourteen:

We were walking by Classical High and we saw a flyer for a $200 stipend for youth organizing. We didn't know what youth organizing was, but we wanted the money. We went to this really creepy office on Broadway, and I kept thinking, "Only white people to do this . . ."

Their assumption that civic engagement belonged only in the category of whiteness in America was typical of many youths of color who have been socialized to think the political process does not involve them as youth, immigrants, and racialized bodies. Despite their initial reservations, Heng and Duong quickly became excited about PrYSM. They never wanted to go home after meetings; Heng recalled how he and Duong would ask Kohei for things to do after the youth program ended. Kohei soon realized their desire to spend more time at the organization's office. He always prepared tasks for them to do after the program and made sure to drive them home so that they would arrive safely. They began to feel more secure at the organization than in their own home, and by extension, Heng and Duong were willing to invest more time and responsibility into the group. Heng confided, "Kohei was the only man I trusted, solely because he was gay and loved me. I called Kohei my gay dad and Sarath my gay uncle. [They] never left my side at PrYSM. I always felt safe because they were always nearby." Kohei, Sarath, and Paul, a Filipino staff member, validated Heng's sense of self and believed in him. The unconditional love Heng felt from Kohei, Sarath, and Paul is indicative of their willingness to be open and honest with him while offering him a sense of belonging without judgement. In no uncertain terms, Heng came to see them as "family."

Heng's comment reflects the complicated ways in which his identity manifested in PrYSM. After Heng and Duong joined PrYSM, they pushed the organization to expand its dialogue and priorities to address issues that intersected with all youth of color, not just SEAA. Because they did not identify as Southeast Asian or Khmer, Heng recalls not wanting to organize in Southeast Asian communities:

Sarath, Kohei, and Paul kept saying, "You're Southeast Asian; your community needs you. You should be working in your community." I never felt comfortable in PrYSM as a Southeast Asian. I never considered myself Cambodian, and I didn't speak [the language]. I kept saying, "Kohei, we gotta work with DARE" [the local organization for Black and Caribbean youth], and so he started joining coalitions with them. Duong and I were always so excited when we were in coalition with Black and Latinos, and we'd always sit beside them and join them in breakout groups.

When Kohei started hiring youth from the West End who spoke Khmer, Heng's sense of self and perceived sense of value in the group was put into question. He remembers:

I got jealous. I told [Kohei] he won't need me anymore and he's going to like them better because they can help him translate . . . . They had to pull me aside and talk to me because I was being mean to the West End kids. I didn't know how I was acting, but I guess those feelings about not being Cambodian enough came out.

Heng took much of his frustration out on Becky, a girl who was fluent in Cambodian. After Kohei, Sarath, and Paul talked with Heng, and emphasized his worth within the group, he tried to reconcile with her. Becky taught him about Cambodian culture and how to cook. In addition, Heng and Duong did not realize this at the time, but they helped PrYSM further integrate into the multicultural social justice community of Providence by their willingness as SEAA youth to reach beyond the boundaries of ethnic, or pan-Asian, to multi-racial organizing. Even though PrYSM founders had felt this way, their members had to drive this vision for it to be effective and embedded in the group's long-term identity. The inter-ethnic coexistence, marriages and social environments within which the PrYSM youth live make organizing activities potentially both more challenging within their co-ethnic communities and with more possibilities for coalition-building. Ultimately, Heng found security, a stable family environment, and a sense of control in his life in PrYSM. He quickly became a successful community organizer and developed a sense of ownership over the PrYSM space despite never embracing a Southeast Asian or Khmer identity.

Performing the Good, the Ghetto, and the Radical

Heng felt he was living multiple, compartmentalized lives. No one at school saw any signs of neglect at home, and no one, including his religious congregation or PrYSM staff, had any suspicion that he was doing anything illegal. Heng performed the role of the model minority Asian student at school, excelling to the point that he skipped a grade in middle school. Thus, he performed his role so well that his teachers overlooked the fact that he and his sister Duong came to school dirty and hungry. At home he took on the filial duties of a traditional Khmer daughter by caring for his younger siblings and contributing to the family income. He occupied the contradictory positionality of what Nikki Jones refers to as the double-bind of the "good and the ghetto" for young women.[122] He convincingly appeared innocent—in contradiction to the racial and class stereotypes that attract police surveillance and brutality—while acting street smart during drug exchanges so as not to be exploited. At the Jehovah's Witness temple, Kingdom Hall, Heng pursued his religious studies with a passion, acting out the role of a misguided soul in need of salvation.

Heng also perfected his role as a social justice organizer. Although the rhetoric of social justice was distant and theoretical to him, even when it reflected his life, he understood what social movement actors and funders expected of an organizer, and he learned social movement vocabulary without believing in it. He also found the fascination activists had with Black radicalism confusing. Growing up among Black and Latino friends and dis-identifying as Khmer, Heng viewed privileged East Asians in national coalitional spaces "pretending to be Black" as a means of trying to legitimize their place in the movement. Their performativity of masculinized, hip, political radicals who "grew up in the hood," only accentuated their class and ethnic privilege and ultimate *in*authenticity compared to his relationship to Blackness from his childhood. He understood that the Asian American Movement had modeled itself after the Black liberation struggle since the 1960s,[123] and in particular, Black masculinity, which could be deemed resistance identity.[124] He did not see the behavior of privileged youth as a radical gesture that "reconfigures identity for a progressive political agenda," but instead an appropriation of Black culture influenced by mainstream media's valorizing of Black hypermasculinity. He was particularly cognizant of the extent to which masculinity had been conflated with strength and power, and with it, the disidentification with queerness, which requires one to "thrive on sites where meaning does not properly 'line up' in regard to gender."[125] Heng thus saw the expectation of his identity as an organizer to be interwoven with that of race, class, and gender expression. He felt that the hypermasculinity stereotypically associated with Black men— and that young AAPI organizers performed in social movement spaces— contradicted the simultaneous emergence of AAPI queer organizing, which at the time often focused on creating supportive spaces for people to freely "perform their queerness" however that might look for them.[126]

By the time he was fifteen, Heng's worlds began to collide. The congregation started to pressure him and Duong to stop interacting with their oldest sister, who was openly lesbian, and with PrYSM, because of their gay staff and members and their political activism. The man for whom he ran drugs was starting to pressure Heng, at the time a young woman, to contribute more profit to the business beyond accounting and drug delivery.[127] Heng had reached a crossroads in which he had to choose between his biological, religious, economic, and political families. At age 16, he graduated early from high school and, with Kohei's help, went to college to run away from his boss and escape his life in Providence. Heng's various biological and chosen families met his basic needs of income, stability, and safety. However, he eventually realized that unconditional love, forgiveness, and faith were fundamental to his idea of family. Heng understood the limits of his religious affiliation with the Jehovah's Witnesses and their unyielding desire for him to reject his PrYSM family because of their sexual orientations. In the end, Heng chose his PrYSM family and continued to volunteer for them during his vacations from college.

Heng's Search for Justice Through Forgiveness

One of the unique characteristics about PrYSM's developmental process is how it embeds the cultural practices of Buddhism as almost a natural element of political development. In fact, pervasive in PrYSM's youth development is Sarath's philosophy of love and forgiveness as an articulation of justice without compromising the fight for equity and human rights. The integration of cultural identity and political analysis and action defines the organization's collective identity and intersectional leadership.

In college, he felt free for the first time and began to express himself as lesbian. Yet he felt "something still didn't feel right." By his sophomore year, he decided to change his identity and found a physician to guide him through the medical process of physically transitioning from Lili to Heng. Heng's gender transition allowed him the freedom to be his authentic self for the first time in his life. Slowly, his parents accepted his decision, and he began to rebuild his relationship with both of them, first by forgiving them, and then by learning about their own childhood traumas.

Heng reflected that his time at PrYSM gave him strength to explore his identity in multi-faceted ways: "I think the reason why I loved being at PrYSM was because I was always jealous that the guys got to express their love—who they were—so openly in PrYSM." In essence, Heng is talking about forgiveness as acceptance, for his family and for himself. This is a lesson he learned not in the religious space of the Kingdom Hall, but in the political space of a SEAA LGBTQ+ youth group.

When Heng was about to leave for college on a full scholarship from a highly competitive national foundation, Kohei shared with Heng the recommendation letter he had written for him. He called Heng a ninja and said the pen was his sword. Heng found Kohei's words deeply validating and admits, "When I was in PrYSM, I was an amazing organizer, but I did things because I wanted to solve other people's problems. They had an issue, and I wanted to make it disappear." Organizing was cathartic for Heng in that he felt he wielded power and control over other people's problems that he could not control in his own life.

Now a teacher, Heng sees himself as a positive male role model for his mostly Black and Latinx students, many of whom who do not have father figures in their lives. He tries to validate them the way Kohei, Sarath, and Paul did for him, using Kohei's ninja metaphor. He also understands social justice more deeply, as a vision for societal change rather than a means to alleviate one's personal problems. Heng uses his experience of gender transitioning to help young people searching on the internet for information about gender transitioning and encourages them to be true to themselves however it makes sense to them. Heng's ability to overcome his personal obstacles illustrates the best of what PrYSM had to offer in its first years, in all its complexity as a youth group focused on SEAA marginalized youth who went from struggling to survive to fighting for individual transformation and institutional change. Heng's story illustrates how PrYSM's organizational values created a sense of home for many marginalized local youth that became an entry into political consciousness and activism. Yet in those first few years, the unprecedented success of PrYSM could not overcome the uneven commitment from funders, who encouraged the youth group to show "winnable" individual cases in order to generate continued investments from donors to fight the deportation issue. PrYSM reached the moment of truth about how it wanted to engage with the non-profit industrial complex, which inadvertently changed the entire culture of the group through the formalization of roles and expectations. After starts and fits, it eventually chose to stay committed to its members' needs over funders' demands.

Developing Female Leadership

Over the years, Sarath's role changed from organizer to Executive Director to Board member. As the organization grew and the founders aged, they began to leave for various reasons. The dedication to PrYSM took a full-time commitment, and it often prevented them from pursuing their own personal growth and goals beyond the organization. They slowly transitioned into various roles such as Board members, advocates, and donors for PrYSM. Secondly, the founders always had the vision that PrYSM would one day be led by local Southeast Asian American youth, and preferably, from their members. Sarath's main purpose for staying on PrYSM's board was to support their new Executive Director (E.D.), Chanravy Proeung, a local young Khmer American woman.

Chanravy grew up in one of the first Khmer refugee families to arrive in Providence. Her family migrated to Providence in the early 1980s to reunite with her aunt, a local entrepreneur. Her aunt secured space in an abandoned warehouse and expanded her small jewelry-making business into an operation that employed Khmer women and girls, including Chanravy and her mom. They worked long hours to make designer jewelry that major retailers sold for more than ten times what subcontractors could pay workers. Chanravy recalls, "We would go into the department stores and see the jewelry we made, but we could never afford to buy any of it." Regardless, the warehouse became the site of community building for many of the local Khmer families as they had flexible schedules, could bring their children to work, and they kept a connection to their culture through language and food brought at the workplace. The kinship networks that naturally occurred between refugee women in their country of origin became channels for economic opportunity in resettlement and provided the roots for the younger generation to position themselves as community leaders.[128] Chanravy's extended family became staples of the Khmer community in Providence. Chanravy's knowledge of and participation within the local landscape formed the skills that she needed to become PrYSM's ideal candidate for their next leader.

After Chanravy finished school, she was unsure of her next steps in life. She began to volunteer for PrYSM events and activities in her free time and, like younger members of PrYSM, she found herself "a part of a community for people around my age that wasn't available at the other Khmer organizations." Sarath and the board felt that Chanravy represented their vision for PrYSM of building local leadership while also providing intergenerational cohesion through the alliance of the religious organizations, MAA, and progressive political activism. They gradually offered her increasing responsibilities with more compensation. Once she agreed to assume a full-time staff role, they groomed her to transition into the E.D. role by teaching her how to manage and write grants, meet with funders, and facilitate programs. Additionally, Chanravy took on more public speaking roles in order to assume the new face of PrYSM. Sarath knew that Chanravy still had much to learn about running a small but complex non-profit such as PrYSM, so he stayed on the board to ensure her a positive and supportive initiation. He wanted to apply individualized, hands-on mentorship to develop the leaders in PrYSM.[129] However, this mentoring model did not consider the dynamics of trauma, gender, and basic skills training that an E.D. position would require for someone without formal training or experience. It required addressing compounded issues that community members faced on a daily basis, as many of their youth did, in addition to developing their skills to assume the same role for others, forming relationships, articulating strategic approaches, leveraging resources, and planning collective action.[130] A core aspect of this was having the time, motivation, and emotional capacity to work individually with members to develop these skills while addressing the obstacles in their daily lives.[131] Thus, Sarath and the board underestimated the amount of time and dedication it would take to transition Chanravy into an E.D. position that included the multi-faceted responsibilities that both Sarath and Kohei had assumed during their tenures.

Infrapolitics of Intersectional Leadership

Robin D.G. Kelley's call for the need to understand the internal dynamics within social justice communities helps activists learn the landscape of relationships, past and present, and raises the complexities of how intersectional identities manifest in social movements.[132] The infrapolitics of PrYSM highlight the complexities between sexuality and gender as they play out in daily activities. Chanravy's role as E.D. was precarious from the beginning for multiple reasons. While she participated in community organizations most of her life, the learning curve to communicate with funders and be responsible for all the administrative tasks as E.D. was steep. She often felt "like I was just given these things to do without enough instruction." Meanwhile, the diminished funding for youth organizations during her time as E.D. meant that the organization faced more pressure to fundraise to maintain its programs while offering less compensation for youth stipend positions. Without the direct links to elite universities that Kohei and Sarath provided through Brown University, recruitment of the "activist-minded" allies from local colleges slowed. New college students who did volunteer met obstacles in their ability to initially connect with Chanravy the way they had with Sarath and Kohei. Chanravy felt "disconnected from the college student volunteers. I grew up here. How do I explain how to talk to our youth to rich students from other states? The kids coming to PrYSM were my relatives, friends of my relatives. I could talk to them in a way that the people from the university can't." During Chanravy's tenure, the organization decided to refocus its work on local campaigns that would emphasize base-building of local youth in an attempt to highlight her strengths.

Most significantly, the transfer of power from strong gay male figures to a straight woman in her twenties brought its own set of infrapolitics that juxtaposed gender and sexuality in relation to perceptions of leadership and internalized gender roles. Throughout the organization's history, the lives of many of the women in PrYSM have been complicated by the daily expectations placed on them by family and society, a common phenomenon documented about female activists in what Bindi Shah calls the "senses of belonging."[133] In Shah's study of Laotian young women's leadership in the group Asian American Pacific Islander Environmental Network (APEN), the "senses of belonging" have two components: "First, identification, both individual and collective, or membership in a distinctive bounded group, whether place-based or ethnic, racial, national, cultural, or religious; and second, the affective dimension, or emotional feelings of belonging in a space where one does not have to explain oneself, a sense of location."[134]

Notions of integration became complicated based on the group's intersectional collective identity. As one young woman stated, "We belong because these people are our family, we all know each other—from school, from temple, our families, you know.... But PrYSM was always a 'gay boys group' for the most part, and we are okay with that, but it doesn't really feel like home for us." That sense of liminality within the organization represented the "formal and informal experiences of exclusion" where the extension of "[control over] women's bodies is one of the main means of maintaining ethnic boundaries and cultural difference."[135] PrYSM women often struggled to lay claim to the physical space as well as visibility from the elders and their peers. Despite Sarath's efforts to develop leadership and formalize positions for young women, those issues became increasingly obvious during Chanravy's tenure as E.D. in PrYSM. Problems with accepting women in a public, vocal leadership role have plagued the SEAA community, as it did in the AAM a generation ago.[136] The role of PrYSM's gay male leaders sometimes reflected the dominant American hetero-normative perceptions of "women's work," reproducing much of the gender roles in their social environment.[137] Queer male leaders, such as Sarath, Kohei, and Paul, offered an emotional support network to youth, nourished them with homecooked meals, and expressed unconditional love that PrYSM youth often felt they lacked at home. What was seen as a rejection of social norms for the men would be a reinforcement of them if Chanravy continued the practice of "mothering" as an E.D.

There was a cultural expectation of mothering from female members in addition to their gendered labor roles of "cleaning up after the program meetings and keeping everything organized for [male members]" according to one former youth leader. PrYSM's cultural identity had long been portrayed not only as queer-friendly, but also as a space dominated by gay men and transgender people. Chanravy felt that some members thought of her as an intrusion into that safe space, and their collective identity, regardless of their shared ethnic identity and local relationships. During her tenure, SEAQuel, PrYSM's LGBTQ+ youth program, continued regular walk-in times for young people to have a safe space to congregate, but its attendance slowly declined. That growing distance, according to various staff, was exacerbated by PrYSM's lack of rapport with the new, straight cis-woman E.D. Even though local youth saw Chanravy as part of the community, they also did not feel they could divulge their true concerns and experiences with her in the same way as they could with the gay male leaders with whom they identified. Chanravy fell into the crevice of simultaneously assuming an insider status with expectations to behave within the gendered norms as a Khmer woman, and yet she could not gain the same kind of trust and intimacy with the queer-identified youth because she did not necessarily reflect the characteristics they deemed necessary for PrYSM leadership.[138]

Rebuilding a Room of Her Own

The role of women in leadership positions in non-profit organizational settings has not been dissected beyond management models in corporate and other organizations. Women leaders tend to gravitate toward one of two directions—either they replicate the positions of male counterparts as a means to gain equal respect, or they generate new programs and opportunities for other women to revamp organizational priorities and demographics. Part of Chanravy's responsibility as the E.D. included reviving the defunct women's group. With support from Ammala and other former female youth members still tangentially involved with PrYSM, they reached out to young women who had left the group. Chanravy encouraged current members to recruit their female relatives. Her presence as a leader drew women back into the group. One former youth stated, "We wanted her to succeed, so we tried to support her by participating in the women's group." Another former youth shared that it was exciting to "see a woman who grew up like me in a leadership position," and by associating with her as a shared cis-female Khmer identity, they viewed her differently than the men who previously led the organization.

Chanravy also created greater stability and investment in the women's group by more actively discussing its members' needs for attending the program, which she did not feel she could do in the LGBTQ+ programs as a cis-female. The young women came together to talk about the challenges they faced at the intersection of SEAA, women, and socio-economic status. The reflection of oneself in each other created an instant solidarity that nurtured a safe space to be one's whole self, rather than having to identify with only one aspect of their identity. Like Shah's study of APEN and Heng's reflection as a young girl in Providence, PrYSM youth faced the challenges of gendered expectations in the home while having to perform both the model minority in school and the strong woman in social circles to avoid being harassed. PrYSM's women's group simultaneously reinforced and rejected socially imposed gender roles. Shah's analysis of young SEAA women's experiences held true for PrYSM as well:

> *Even though these public arenas embody different cultural constructions of femininity and sexuality than those in immigrant families (Maira 2002), expectations of "good" Laotian womenhood remain…. And given the high degree of poverty and welfare dependency in the Laotian community, these parental pressures to stay at home and attend a local college also reflected an economic decision.*[139]

The youth in Shah's study seemed to experience much more familial stability and a sense of community than the SEAA youth members of PrYSM as most of them still lived at home with family and were not single mothers. According to Shah, "Families can provide strength and resources for adolescent girls of color who experience the challenges of uncertainties, conflicting expectations, and rejection based on color, culture, language, and class. For second-generation Laotians, 'the family' plays a central role in their lives and gives meaning to their ethnic identity."[140] The PrYSM youth frequently lacked familial support, as relationships at home were often fragmented and strained. Following Shah's logic, the impact could attribute to a loss of ethnic identity, or as some of the women in PrYSM assessed, a pressure to conform to gender roles as an essence of one's ethnic identity. In other words, the proper performance of one's ethnicity inextricably intertwined with one's gender assignment.

Regardless, nearly all of the women in PrYSM's women's group reported upholding their familial responsibilities by attending to household chores, caring for younger children in the extended or immediate family, and taking on additional jobs outside of their daily responsibilities as high school students. PrYSM's lack of programmatic structure and vision failed to secure funding perpetuated the barriers for full participation by young women in ways that would fulfill the vision of the women's program. The female leaders and members saw their multiple burdens as the major obstacles to the women's political training compared to other PrYSM programs, and the lack of leadership and financial support to participate only exacerbated the challenges to their potential as movement leaders. The opportunity to participate in non-SEAA-specific training, then, became crucial for women's leadership development.

Transition from Leadership to Gatekeeper

The Organizing Committee (OC) of PrYSM returned to its work on local campaigns concerning racial profiling of youth of color with allies in Latino and Black organizations that would eventually become the Community Safety Act campaign in 2014. Over the next three years, Chanravy developed a local reputation as a strong leader. However, she believed that without administrative and development staff and the support of an active board that could assist with fundraising, she could not be expected to maintain the same vibrancy the organization had in its early years during the height of youth-based funding initiatives. She also was deeply upset with the financial constraints she faced: "I often wouldn't get my paycheck on time, and I had no professional development training from the board or others. I was out on my own to take care of the daily responsibilities." The training and mentorship she received was focused on political development, not the administrative training required to fulfill the daily demands of her position. According to Sarath and other PrYSM members, Chanravy had natural speaking skills to garner support from funders, and she fit the profile of the successfully assimilated youth who shifted into the professional non-profit world.

As tensions grew between Chanravy and PrYSM members, Sarath and representatives from other SEAFN groups noticed that Chanravy vented her frustrations about PrYSM directly to allies and funders, creating moments of animosity between PrYSM and ally organizations. To funders, Chanravy violated the golden rule of non-profit work: to never publicly express discontent about other organizations or individuals. Her vocal, public grievances represented a lack of professionalism to those in the philanthropic community. Rather than identify the root causes and offer technical or conflict resolution resources, funders tend to defund organizations and channel resources elsewhere.[141] Some PrYSM staff believed Chanravy's behavior had a direct correlation to the dissipation of PrYSM's funds, exacerbating the friction between the organization and its first female E.D.

In 2013, the tensions reached a peak level as Sarath, with the backing of the board, rejoined the PrYSM staff as co-director with Chanravy. Chanravy viewed the decision as an invalidation to her aptitude and trustworthiness as opposed to a sincere effort to strengthen her leadership. To Sarath, though, the organization was in dire straits due to inconsistent funding, diminishing youth membership, and Chanravy's public dissatisfaction with PrYSM. While they held the title of Co-Directors, and met regularly to make decisions about the organization, Chanravy felt that the power differential between Sarath and herself were obvious. The youth, staff, and board clearly viewed Sarath as the person who made the final decisions and had the ultimate authority within the organization.

PrYSM had a staff of five people working part- and full-time, and it explored funding opportunities for government-funded projects that promoted public health education to SEAA youth. By 2014, the remaining youth and staff, which constituted fewer than half the members compared to Sarath's tenure, made the commitment to expand the organization's work to make it economically viable and attractive to more youth staff. They re-engaged with an emerging campaign against racial profiling, the Community Safety Act campaign, and with the immigration issues of undocumented youth facing criminal deportation.

The end of 2015 marked a new opportunity for Chanravy—she decided it was time to transition out of PrYSM. Chanravy shared with me that she felt her position had been undermined, her contributions had not been acknowledged, and her trust in the organization had waned. SEAFN played a critical role in alleviating the tension between Chanravy and PrYSM. Doua Thor, who became E.D. of the SEAA national policy group, SEARAC, in 2004, wrote a Philadelphia-based youth group, 1Love Movement, into a grant to conduct public education and organizing on immigrant rights through SEAFN. When SEARAC's next E.D., Quyen Dinh, renewed their funding commitments in 2015, 1Love hired Chanravy as the national organizer to coordinate SEAFN activities in charge of building a national grassroots movement of SEAA youth groups. Chanravy's transition from PrYSM into SEAFN not only gave Chanravy a new start, thus not alerting skittish funders that there was dissension within the organization that could have jeopardized future funding. SEAFN was able to support both PrYSM *and* Chanravy and continue its large-scale work on immigration policy. In this instance, the coalition of SEAA youth-based groups played the role of a mediator to support the cohesion of the movement where the infrapolitics of the movement crossed the lines of gender and sexuality. Other stakeholders, namely the MAAs, AAM, and funders, had failed to mentor and provide the guidance that PrYSM needed during a moment of internal growth, and these young activists had to navigate the tensions by themselves rather than through the support of external resources.

Chanravy's position at SEAFN gave her the mentorship she desired through 1Love's E.D., Mia-Lia Kiernan, who encouraged her and SEAFN to tackle human rights work. Chanravy earned a human rights certificate, and won the prestigious Soros Justice Fellowship which, in non-profit circles, is understood as a key to winning lucrative grants and recognition from funders. Fellows often become gatekeepers for future philanthropic initiatives in their areas of expertise and can open up a plethora of opportunities for historically marginalized communities and grassroots movements. However, the fellowship's structure also perpetuates the neo-colonial hierarchy of power within marginalized communities; indeed, the Soros Fellowship essentially handpicks future leaders and gatekeepers, and trains them to craft a public image that is palatable to the gift giver, without ever relinquishing power to the communities themselves.[142]

Chanravy's challenges as E.D. may very well have been related to her lack of personal readiness for the job. However, they also speak to the way in which her identity as a low-income, Khmer woman from a family impacted by trauma, required particular kinds of support and development that a small organization like PrYSM did not have the capacity to provide. PrYSM's funders at that time, who largely were youth and social justice-oriented rather than refugee-based foundations, did not seem to be able to recognize or offer technical assistance, as the focus for them was on deliverables from youth organizing and campaigns. As activist-author Karen Ishizuka documents, many women from the 1960s and 1970s reduced their roles or even left active movement work to take care of family members, either through direct caregiving or by taking on more lucrative jobs that would sustain the financial needs of their families. Thus, the privilege of staying in the movement and meeting the strenuous demands of long hours for little pay led early AAM activist Steve Louie to conclude that "the larger lesson was that you better include everybody in the room and you better figure out where your blinders are."[143] The lack of critical interventions and developmental guidance by movement elders, allies, and funders speaks the fundamental contradiction within movement politics. It required a masking of the "family secrets" and the performativity of the grateful recipient of the "gift" of donation through the demonstration of deliverables at the expense of opportunities to truly create the conditions for successful leadership from the ground up with individuals who funders want to "save."

A Post-Millennial Progression

The return to a local campaign in 2014 marked a critical transition to a post-Millennial rise in leadership within PrYSM through their programs. It embodies the generational shift in strategy and representation that displayed the accelerated political development of these emerging leaders. The organization had two full-time employees, Steven and Shannah, who played critical roles in both the work with SEAFN and the organization's most challenging work, the Community Safety Act (CSA) campaign through the Step Up Network, the local coalition that organized the campaign of which PrYSM was a member. As detailed in Chapter Six, the Step Up Network's CSA campaign demanded changes in Providence police's gang database, racial profiling, and coordination with immigration enforcement. The coalition's work culminated in the formalized campaign between 2014 and 2016, which gradually involved one of PrYSM's emerging youth leaders, Linda, who had participated in both the young women's program and the organizing circle.

During the course of the campaign for the passage of this Act, a formal CSA working group was formed by the City of Providence. The committee made revisions on drafts of the bill after hosting four internal, closed-door meetings over two months, and eventually would work to implement the Act once it was passed. Shannon, the non-SEAA PrYSM lawyer, resigned from the working group to make room for Linda, who would be the only Khmer American and local youth on the committee. Her new position in the working group was a public condemnation of those in city government who blocked the previous CSA vote. By placing Linda, a directly affected community youth member, among them, government officials were forced to face her, as the embodiment of the potential consequences of their actions. Linda's publicly held position represented a huge step in developing the voice of the youth leadership within PrYSM, and specifically that of women. She reflected, "There has been perpetual violence in our communities by the police, and we have to do something about it rather than letting it continue on."[144] Linda's transition into the council position extended PrYSM's national organizing on deportation issues. Sisters and mothers assumed lead roles as the narrators and liaisons for those at risk of deportation to talk about their situation and its impact on the families. They had the power to engage emotionally with their audiences, and they validated those audiences as valued members of the community. As post-Millennials evolved into leader, cis-women leaders, like Linda, are no longer simply the family representatives and storytellers. They perceive their roles as organizers with the capacity to sit at the table to determine policy and question state practices that undermine the safety of their neighborhoods. While storytelling had been both a tool of organizing to re-humanize communities of color, such as deportees, the people giving personal testimonies had been just that, reduced to storytellers without the skills or knowledge to inform or create policy.[145] The CSA campaign was a milestone for PrYSM in that it engendered the feminist tactic of storytelling to the men, and simultaneously transferred the power of decision-making to a young cis-woman leader.

After heated pressure from community members and the Step Up Network, the Providence City Council put the CSA to a vote at their June 1, 2017 meeting in front of 200 community members led by the Step Up Network. The Act was renamed the "Providence Community-Police Relations Act" (PCPRA) with a vote of 13-1, with only minor edits to the original CSA text. The three-year battle to pass the PCPRA mirrored the ongoing national battle for police accountability in the wake of the murders of Black and transgender people across the country; it was the manifestation of long-standing hyper-surveillance, policing, and criminalization in communities of color within Providence and nationally.[146] The victory symbolized the fruition of PrYSM's foundation and vision, and its accomplishments were due in large part to the organization's post-Millennial leadership in and participation in a multi-racial coalition.

Unlike previous campaign work on deportations—in which the female member of the family provided a compelling narrative—the gender roles reversed for this generation of organizers. The strategic storytelling within the CSA campaign thus retained their control of how and in what context they presented their vulnerabilities, and for the purpose of gaining demands with which their members would be comfortable. For example, youth leader Steven's personal testimony served as the emotional plea to the public, in which the performativity of his masculinity assumed a position of vulnerability and *emasculation* in his confrontation with the police. Linda, on the other hand, became the visible and vocal representative with power at the decision-making table. Her willingness and ability to hold decision-making roles elicited a sense of gender justice that encompassed women's empowerment across the spectrum of issues. As Linda pointed out, "We want to take the mic and let people know we are fierce, that we won't just sit back and let them do whatever." The past shortcomings for gender justice within the space of PrYSM were gradually being remedied, and it represented a new chapter in PrYSM's collective identity formation.

The CSA campaign grounded PrYSM in its original mission of building the local power of SEAA youth to speak out against being criminalized simply because of one's racial and class identification, and it gave rise to one of its most powerful women leaders. This campaign allowed PrYSM youth to find solidarity with other BIPOC through the Step Up Network, and to understand their shared experiences of "othering" by the institutions enacting state violence. Through those shared coalitional spaces, youth of color built inter-racial understanding. They recognized the differences of violence against those within the geography of "Blackness," and they also came to comprehend how the specifically targeted oppression of Black people, as articulated by the #BLM movement, impacted other BIPOC.

The campaign exemplified Cindy Wu's concerns in relation to Asian Americans and Black Lives Matter upon the murder of Philando Castile in St. Paul, Minnesota, by a police officer initially perceived as Chinese. In her essay, Wu reflected on the "resonances between the state violence experienced by African Americans and other U.S. Blacks with the type that Southeast Asian Americans face. The Twin Cities . . . are one of the few places where men of Asian descent are criminalized . . ."[147] She states in another essay that "There is much work that is left to be done not only on the profiling and policing of 'Asian-raced' criminality but also on the criminal justice arm of the government's handling of Asian Americans and Asian immigrants. State violence is chronic. And Black lives matter."[148] The Step Up Network that formed to pass the CSA set the foundation for a new intersectional generation that articulates its humanity across and inclusive of racial and ethnic difference, as well as through finding common cause grounded in immediate conditions of social, economic, and geographic marginalization.[149]

The coalitional and community-based campaign symbolizes the inter-racial and inter-generational potential of this generation of activists to organize with a critical analysis of the state, while communicating and building a critical mass of cross-sectional alliances focused on the daily lives of those within their communities. PrYSM developed a new sense of power within the community that included feelings of self-sufficiency and resourcefulness. They challenged the traditional philosophy that "community development has largely meant the delivery of services and the building of structures, not organizing,"[150] and that "development" included the freedom from surveillance and criminalization of those who live in economically impoverished neighborhoods. It took three years of campaigning for the CSA to pass as a city ordinance, and it was the biggest victory for PrYSM locally in a decade. The tremendous accomplishment heralded a new generation of committed activists.

The youth activists emerging from PrYSM's current membership and other SEAA organizations have articulated their claims to self and collective identity in ways that invoke Gary Okihiro's synopsis of the original purpose of Third World liberation:

> Subjectification understands the subject not as humanism's "I am" but as complex subjects in formation and in constant engagement with society. That recognition emerges not from a trivial, youthful search for identities but from profound acts of power or agency. Self-determination by the oppressed against the forces of colonial, hegemonic discourses and material conditions is the objective of subjectification; the agency of the subject-self drives the movement for Third World liberation.[151]

To achieve the goal self-determination, new generations must continue to heed the "calls for an analysis of the power relations that occur within community-based initiatives."[152] Unless attended to with intentionality, power relations will obstruct the full potential of all of a group's members, beyond the reproduction of conscious and subconscious dynamics of invisibility and hyper-visibility that dominate our communities.

Figure 3.1. PrYSM Youth Leader, Linda, at the May Day Rally, 2017
(Courtesy of PrYSM Archives).

Full Circle Healing

The rapid growth of youth leadership opportunities within PrYSM over the course of two years resulted in the need for unprecedented structure and accountability within the organization. By 2017, they had generated twenty-four staff or stipend positions available for youth or members who had aged out of the youth programs. Some of the youth leadership positions overlapped such that they belonged to more than one program. The responsibilities and personal growth of the staff and youth leaders did not keep pace with the organization's rapid growth. Issues common to many workplaces, such as communication, time management, accountability, and gendered power dynamics, became the cultural norm amongst the staff. PrYSM board members responded by initiating a summer healing process for the staff and youth in addition to an assessment whereby an external consultant would conduct a survey and interviews on the staff and youth's feelings about PrYSM. The process was to lay the foundation to 1) rectify residual gender dynamics that had long been a part of PrYSM, and 2) develop a strategic plan that incorporated a transition of leadership in the next five years.

The staff drew from external allies in the movement to develop what they called a full circle healing process, borrowed from two main concepts. First, full circle healing draws from indigenous traditions that provided the foundation for restorative justice models. It involves creating a circle of trust whereby individuals may share their frustrations or sense of injustices to particular individual(s) who have done harm to them and/or the community. The goal is for the individual(s) to more deeply understand the impact of their actions, and thus inspire more transformative behavioral change driven by empathy. In this situation, there is no perpetrator of bad behavior, but rather an overall sense from youth members of the dissatisfaction with the lack of accountability and mentorship from staff and the E.D.[153] Second, PrYSM used organizational evaluation tools to conduct evaluations of staff, board, and peers to supplement the full circle healing conversations that still retained their core approach to social justice with dialogue, reflection, and renewed action.[154] They held two four-hour sessions per week for ten weeks for staff and members, two three-day camping retreats for staff and members, and two 90-minute surveys for all staff, board, and members. The outcomes for the process provided the vision for next steps back to the board to create a strategic plan for the next few years, and to continue the reflective sessions and the skills training sessions, developed from the healing conversations throughout the year.

The results of the process exposed areas where the organization still needed to fulfill its vision to practice transformative ways of being on the micro and daily activities. The youth felt there was an uneven distribution of labor and that it dovetailed with their roles as paid staff with mostly male staff holding power, and female staff carrying out daily responsibilities, such as cleaning the office. They reported a persistently skewed bias toward political education, which was at odds with virtually no training for mundane organizing work, like public speaking, facilitating meetings, taking notes, and how and what to communicate to coworkers, members, and media. Yet due to patriarchy and ageism, they sometimes blamed themselves for not finding their voice to ask for help, as one youth reflected:

I feel like I haven't put in the effort that I should to become a youth coordinator because when Kate asks if I want to speak publicly I don't volunteer to do so. Also, I get caught up with school all the time so I couldn't make it to CSA meetings but when I was able to I couldn't really understand them and as a youth leader I should've be able to hold myself accountable for not understanding and ask the adults after or during breaks.

Because there were no defined job descriptions and no consequences for not following through on one's responsibilities, the staff and youth leaders consistently reported feeling like they did not know what was within their job descriptions and when they were taking on too much or enabling others to not fulfill their roles. One youth shared in a meeting, "Sometimes you ask me to do things. I know how to protest and think critically, but I don't know how to do basic things like run a meeting."

Finally, they felt that as the E.D., Sarath had been a significant factor in many of the leaders' growth, serving as their support system and their mentor. His increasing absence from the daily work of PrYSM left many feeling like they lost the most important figurehead and mentor for the group. The outcomes of the healing process speak to several major issues at an important juncture in PrYSM's growth. The members' desire for more attention and guidance also can be interpreted as their investment in an organizational identity that had become integral to their personal and political identity as changemakers within and on behalf of the organization. They did not just work at PrYSM or attend its programs for entertainment—they joined this group as a site that could foster their personal and professional growth. Their concerns communicated a sense of pride and responsibility attached to their roles, and it implied that they saw themselves as public representatives for the group. They felt such a part of PrYSM that they made time to attend the healing sessions, were willing to participate in the evaluative process, and wanted the organization to improve rather than simply walking away. The healing process gave evidence of the transformative identities the youth have come to experience such that they wanted to mold PrYSM into the space that could nurture their full potential as political organizers and whole beings. One youth leader summed it up: "I spend hours and hours at PrYSM. I have invested years into PrYSM in making sure the work is done. It's taught me so much that I can't just stop now." The process of transformative leadership development had now reached the stage in which the post-Millennials would determine the future culture and direction of the organization.

The group decided to continue thematic healing sessions to dig more deeply into concerns raised during the healing process. It also decided to plan skills-training sessions with the support of external allies to train youth leaders and staff, so they could feel empowered to take responsibilities they previously had not felt equipped to handle. PrYSM hired an external executive coach to write the job descriptions of every staff and stipend position, in addition to working with Sarath to set boundaries to his commitments so he could balance his time between national organizing and time at PrYSM. In previous generations, issues that presented internal tension often exacerbated conflict and resulted in the fractioning and mass exodus of membership, or departing the world of activism all together.[155] By engaging in a long overdue healing process that was rooted in their values of love and family, PrYSM embraced the desire for new youth leaders to take ownership of the organization and shape it into what they felt they needed to become the new generation of social justice leaders. Though they always embraced PrYSM's original values of love and social justice, the feminist intervention in integrating and valuing their young women leaders marked a turning point for the group. In 2018, the generations of PrYSM women had come full circle as Linda assumed the role of the new Soros Social Justice Fellow that Chanravy had once held. Chanravy went on to found her own multi-racial women's social justice group, Sista Fire, in Providence and mended ties with PrYSM through their support of one another's activities.

PrYSM's evolution as an organization had resulted in its bureaucratization as a non-profit organization. Its formalization of roles, responsibilities, behavioral consequences for paid employees, and dedication toward expansion symbolized this culmination into the non-profit bureaucratic model. PrYSM's SEAFN allies had simultaneously reached a point at which they were becoming non-profit organizations. Typically, the bureaucratization stage of a social movement delineates its stagnation or end.[156] It remains to be seen if this newly professionalized model, within the changing contexts of the philanthropic landscape, enhances the work and dynamics of the organization, or if it perpetuates power dynamics and creative disengagement from the youth, as occurs in other grassroots movements.[157] Throughout the healing process, the organization as a whole could finally come to terms with the reality that Sarath had been waiting for them to accept—the time for a transition of leadership was now. By the end of 2017, a new generation of social justice activists had begun to see itself as capable and willing to accept the role as the new SEAA movement generation.

CHAPTER FOUR
We Will Not Be Moved: Between Having Voice and Having Power

Struggle is part of the course when our dreams go into action. Unless we have the space to imagine and a vision of what it means fully to realize our humanity, all the protests and demonstrations in the world won't bring about our liberation.[158]

In April 2002, soon after Cambodia and the United States signed the Memorandum of Understanding (M.O.U.), I accompanied Thida, the sister of a detainee, to a national conference organized by the Cambodian Mutual Assistance Associations (CMAAs) in Portland, Oregon. The majority of the organizational leaders were middle-aged and elderly men who were first-generation refugees. They represented leaders and representative voices for the Cambodian American community, nationally and locally. At the gathering, the staff from Southeast Asian Resource Action Center (SEARAC), as a conference cosponsor and national representative of CMAA, and other gatekeepers of the Cambodian community espoused two main narratives. The first was a need to make Cambodians in the United States aware of the changes in policy and the potential for deportation. Second, they framed the sense of injustice about the deportation of refugees around the discourse of the Cold War because the Khmer Rouge regime's genocide in the name of Communism still dominates the collective memory of Khmer Americans. In particular, they compared deportation to Cambodia to a "death sentence to a Communist country."

Through my connections with staff at the local MAA in Oakland, California, the Cambodian Community Development, Inc. (CCDI), I was able to encourage them to invite Thida to speak publicly about her brother's detention and deportation case. She had asked me to accompany her to the event. As the only female speaker, and the only one younger than thirty years old, Thida did not feel confident speaking at the conference by herself. Thida shared her brother's story of receiving poor legal advice and being incarcerated as a teenager for stealing a laptop out of the open window of a home. She spoke of the multiple times he had been moved without notice across state lines to various detention centers, some extremely overcrowded and others with poor health conditions.

Thida shared stories of her brother's and family's depression and sense of injustice at what they saw as an overly harsh punishment. She laid bare their frustration that her brother, a refugee child arrival, could be forever punished with deportation to a country he had never known. By sharing her family's story and centering her point of view as a young girl and little sister, Thida reframed the issue—it was not about making an anti-communist argument as much as it was about centering about the human experience of emotion and collective experience of refugee poverty and forced family separation.

At the end of her speech, Thida asserted that the United States became responsible for refugees when it brought them to its shores, and that it was the only country she and her siblings knew, regardless of their formal citizenship. She left the stage nervous, not knowing how she would be received. The next speaker, an older Khmer man who led another MAA, looked straight at Thida as he referenced Martin Luther King, Jr. and maintained that the American Dream included justice and equality through the legal system as well as all other aspects of life. It was his way of retaining his power as an elder while simultaneously showing agreement with Thida as a cross-generational expression of empathy and solidarity. The generational divide on the deportation issue had shifted, and SEARAC's educational and policy position papers that it shared with MAAs changed from their anti-communist framework to one focused on the accountability of the United States to its Southeast Asian refugees. In this moment, the "intergenerational discontinuity"[159] in resistance had potential to re-articulate SEAA relationship to the state that could be agreed upon across generations.

Unfortunately, the positions that MAA leaders took publicly at this stage did not translate immediately into collective action or a shift in direct services for those historically marginalized within SEAA communities. After exhausting social services and legal remedies, individuals and families engaged in other forms of political participation against their deportation orders, such as direct action with grassroots groups like PrYSM. Those groups drew national attention by conducting interviews with the media, addressing political representatives for assistance, and organizing rallies and forums on deportation. As the only national network of organizations confronting immigration enforcement in the post-9/11 climate, the organizations within the newly formed Southeast Asian Freedom Network (SEAFN) represented young people who had been silenced in public discourse.

The emergent leadership among those working-class youth was an opportunity to restart the relationship with MAA elder leaders, many of whom had been in power since SEA refugee resettlement of the 1970s. By legitimizing the decision-making voices of traditionally marginalized subpopulations, external allied organizations had the potential to ultimately shift power dynamics from the older generation of MAA staff to bicultural young leaders. At the same time, PrYSM and other SEAA youth leaders experienced a sense of tokenization in the coalitional spaces that involved pan-ethnic Asian Pacific American communities, particularly in regard to policymaking. This chapter demonstrates the contested notion of who gets to "sit at the table" when stakes are high. In order to understand the dynamics of the coalitional spaces, I explore thick ethnographic descriptions of their development to give context to the specific moments of tension and hegemonic negotiations of power and representation.

Between Having Voice and Having Power

The mobilization against detention and deportation in SEAA communities demonstrates the challenges for marginalized communities to truly gain power, and funders' efforts exacerbated the organic development of sustainable coalitions and power. The strategic storytelling and value systems that the youth in this book communicate through their identity expression play an instrumental role in their political choices as grassroots organizations.[160] Marshall Ganz describes storytelling as "how we learn to exercise agency to deal with new challenges, mindful of the past, yet conscious of alternative futures."[161] The shared stories built empathy and trust among the youth, and thus enabled a national, coordinated body consisting of PrYSM and other progressive Southeast Asian American (SEAA) youth groups with a powerful impact on youth's sense of collective identity and collective action, which then initiated funder interest.[162]

In this chapter I document PrYSM's involvement in the emergence of the Southeast Asian Freedom Network (SEAFN), a grassroots coalition that formed in response to the impending deportation of SEAA. The coalition's organic formation underscores a generational break from the MAAs and co-ethnic elders toward an alignment with the Asian American Left from the 1960s to the 1970s, from which many of these youth groups sought mentorship and inspiration. The valorization of leftist political development is juxtaposed with the marginalization of groups like PrYSM, or between those being nurtured as leaders within the organization and those at risk of deportation.

SEAFN's development illustrates the compounded tensions between the MAAs and the progressive grassroots youth organizations, as well as tensions within these movement spaces amongst organizers and those they claimed to represent. The philanthropic agenda only heightened tensions by forming coalitions while also creating competition for funding.[163] This example documents the beginning of a new generation's approach to garner resources and claim independence from the pressures to perform to the satisfaction of funders and elders alike, in what Karen Ishizuka refers to as "moments of personal awareness that are strengthened through the life-pulse of collective ownership lead to political, social, and cultural activism and have resulted in new identities, agencies, and understandings."[164] PrYSM's participation in SEAFN laid the groundwork for a coordinated body of new leaders to claim authority and autocracy in the way they wanted to express their identity as SEAA as well as the claims they made to their migration histories and as Asian American Movement (AAM) leaders. Although they desired broad-based coalitions and support from AAM and MAA leaders, they saw SEAFN as an opportunity to release from the burden of intergenerational obligations.

Southeast Asian Freedom Network (SEAFN) Formation

Soon after the CMAA conference, the Southeast Asian Resource Action Center (SEARAC) convened a series of conference calls for community leaders and legal advocates to discuss the new agreement between the United States and Cambodia. The goal of the calls was to inform participants of the new policy, how it would affect the community, who would be directly impacted, and what advocacy steps could be taken. The SEARAC calls occurred on a monthly basis over the course of four months. The first call had approximately twelve participants, most of whom were lawyers and policy advocates in Washington, D.C. After some discussion about community awareness and notification of the legal changes, some advocates volunteered to create fact sheets for public dissemination. The call focused on making sure everyone was educated and knowledgeable of the issue enough to share the information with local constituents. Although callers expressed concern and confusion about who was eligible for deportation and the lack of information directly from Immigration Customs Enforcement (ICE), they were not ready to react on a political level. Subsequent calls centered on policy and legal arguments as remedies for the impending deportations.

On the second conference call, SEARAC invited Committee Against Anti-Asian Violence, or CAAAV: Organizing Asian Communities, a grassroots leftist organization out of New York City, to join in. Borann Hem, CAAAV's representative on the calls, shared with participants CAAAV's intention to focus their 2002 leadership training on strategizing against deportation and invited all organizations to send a representative to the training. With each subsequent call, the number of participants dwindled as the conversations moved from education to legal and policy advocacy, with the extensive attention to legal ramifications of the new M.O.U. The language and topics of these calls clearly privileged legal and policy experts. Despite the unintentional exclusivity, the calls served as a place for information-sharing and validating the importance of the issue to SEAA communities.

During the same period, SEARAC obtained statistics from INS (the federal immigration agency that later changed its name to Immigration and Customs Enforcement, or ICE) that estimated the number of people slated for deportation and how many others were at risk. The agency shared only that Viet Nam and Laos were in similar, closed-door negotiations with the State Department. The lack of information from ICE created a growing sense of urgency for action amongst families and advocates at the fear of how broadly the policy changes would impact the community. SEARAC's ability to access information from ICE gave community members some concrete answers, but ICE's inability or unwillingness to offer definitive numbers, timelines, and the criteria or scope of deportations created a generalized, palpable fear in SEAA community organizations across the country who served as liaisons to their constituents.

As part of its Youth Leadership Project (YLP) serving Vietnamese and Khmer youth in the Bronx, which later became the independent organization Mekong, CAAAV initiated a summer institute, called Freedom Training (FT). FT recruited SEAAs under thirty years of age from progressive youth-based organizations across the country. Youth leaders learned about major issues in local SEAA neighborhoods, as well as organizing strategies and methodologies for systemic change. Through FT, they could share information about their communities and bond with one another as people connected through a common historical experience of war and forced migration. Most of the people who had been involved in previous organizing efforts were 1.5-, 1.8-, and second-generation refugees,[165] and Vietnamese, Hmong, Lao, and Khmer from various class backgrounds.

The organizations in attendance at the 2002 FT included six Southeast Asian American youth-based organizations: YLP, in New York, Asian Freedom Project in Wisconsin, KGA in California, PrYSM in Rhode Island, Family Unity in Massachusetts; two MAAs: Greater Philadelphia Cambodian Assistance Association in Pennsylvania and Cambodian American Consortium in California; two grassroots progressive pan-Asian American groups: Asian Americans United in Pennsylvania, API ForCE in California; and SEARAC, representing the only policy-based organization, who sent one Cambodian American college intern. While most staff representing these groups were young SEAA who knew or were related to people at risk of deportation, KGA, Asian Freedom Project (later known as Freedom, Inc.), and PrYSM were the only ones who brought individuals with deportation orders, totaling about half of all FT participants.

The participants in the training were starkly different from those on the SEARAC calls. It was the first time that people directly affected by deportation participated in discussions, rather than just lawyers and policymakers. While the gender distribution of participants was almost even, those with deportation orders were all male. Almost all of the organizational representatives were women, and as a group, they had more years of formal education and organizing experience than the men present. The outcome of the FT was the first national network of youth-based organizations to address immigration enforcement in the post-9/11 period: The Southeast Asian Freedom Network, or SEAFN.

The deportation issue was a natural extension of the local work that PrYSM did in regard to the gang database created by Providence police. They felt compelled to participate in the FT as some of their members were potentially deportable due to past criminal activity, or they had been criminalized through racial profiling tactics of the gang database by local police. Moreover, no one else they knew of in the New England region was working with that population as it intersected with race and ethnicity beyond Family Unity, which consisted of a handful of deportees, not political organizers. FT provided an opportunity to learn technical skills to organize, and as a sense of "home" for like-minded activists.

PrYSM members immediately felt the impact of their attendance on the building of local movements. One person with a deportation order recalled, "I thought we were just doing this thing in our neighborhoods, but for people to come from all over the country to talk about this, just to talk about us..." For Sarath, Kohei, and the other PrYSM founders, FT was also an opportunity to validate and gather support for their work as emerging leaders. Several members told me privately that personally, they felt like they did not know if they were making the best choices as PrYSM's leaders. Ammala and Kohei shared that they would make decisions about the anti-deportation campaign based on their gut feelings and their own research—not from a guidebook, formal training, or mentorship—which carried the weight of individual lives and their ability to fight their deportation cases. As a result, they sought out this gathering as a means to be trained and supported as leaders just as much as to strategize and share information with other organizations. The coalitional space became the horizontal organizing structure where they could learn the tools and skills needed to become effective organizers without the vulnerability of having financial resources at risk to them if they had asked for technical assistance or training from funders.[166] They were able to develop their own culturally appropriate collective identity through storytelling, and it manifested in a virtual, symbolic, and political space that lay the foundation for a collective, rather than hierarchical, movement to prosper.[167]

Freedom Training 2002

Freedom Training (FT) lasted three days and culminated with the formation of Southeast Asian Freedom Network (SEAFN). The first day offered a series of icebreakers and goal-centering activities. Most of the workshops were facilitated by CAAAV staff, but they used a Freirian participatory action approach, wherein groups engaged in creating a power analysis of the stakeholders in the deportation issue, participated in consensus-building processes to devise a national campaign against deportation of SEAA refugees, and determined ways of strategic storytelling that built collective identity with the community and reframed the deportation issue in the media. This combination—visual mapping, group decision-making, and storytelling that make up popular education techniques—balanced the knowledge and power dynamics between organizers and directly affected individuals. That methodology proved key to validating members' lived experiences, while using the stories for the campaign. Through this process and these methods, the youth would develop a political awareness and analysis of their world.[168]

Each organization shared its best practices and the activities that it engaged in related to immigration issues, and the impact of those activities on the local community. The FT group also discussed how each organization was hoping to address common issues around deportation and detention, and what they needed to accomplish those goals. For several organizations, FT was the place for them to learn more about deportation to educate their local membership. The representatives decided that after they debriefed their members about the outcomes of FT, they would collectively decide whether or not to participate in anti-detention/deportation activities with the new coalition. They did agree on the long-term potential of consolidating local efforts into a more unified national vision, voice, and strategy for SEAA in general. By the end of the FT, all organizations voted to be members of SEAFN as a means of fulfilling the larger vision of a progressive platform in their communities that would lay the groundwork for broader movement-building goals.

The goals of SEAFN were multifold. They were dedicated to fighting detention and the deportation of Southeast Asian Americans, and in solidarity with other racialized immigrant groups who felt unjustly targeted by immigration practices and policies. In doing the work, SEAFN set out to create a safe space for individuals and families impacted by deportation. As grassroots activists, they prioritized the development of leadership and organizing skills of marginalized groups within SEAA communities, such as former gang members, queer, women, and youth subcultures. SEAFN was a site to build infrastructure for progressive organizations, with the objective of coordinating future actions or mobilizations at the national level. The network offered an alternative channel for marginalized populations to partake in efforts to create or challenge legislation and policies that impacted them on a national scale, when they otherwise would feel isolated. Given these goals, directly affected community members had the chance to participate in calls, meetings, and decision-making. That decision-making process prioritized collective dialogue and consensus formation.

The second day of the FT focused on specific ways to organize against detention and deportation. We began by sharing our knowledge of the issue in terms of facts and analysis. At the request of the FT planning committee, Ly-Huong Nguyen and I, as representatives from California, co-authored an analysis of the detention/deportation issue that would be used over the course of the next few years by various organizations and individuals (Appendix D).

We identified these key themes as the foundation of our analysis:

- **Illegality of the memorandum of understanding**: We challenge the legality of the contract between the U.S. State Department and the Ministry of Interior, a Cambodian American repatriate whose position does not normally grant the authority to negotiate international agreements.
- **History of U.S. involvement in Southeast Asia**: The historical events and processes of U.S. involvement in Southeast Asia are directly linked to its *responsibility* to accept refugees from the war, and to the significance of refugee migration in the context of (inter) national immigration policies.
- **Attack on youth of color**: Deportation of a large portion of young people in Southeast Asian working-class communities is embedded in an ongoing state of structural violence against urban youth of color through marginalization from schools, racial profiling, inadequate-to-nonexistent basic social services, and culturally insensitive legal systems.
- **Attack on the poor and immigrants**: The attack on Southeast Asian refugee youth as youth of color occurs simultaneously with their class position and "perpetual foreigner" status as Asian Americans living in direct contradiction to the Model Minority Myth. The implicit message in this policy [M.O.U.] is that immigrants carry with them violence and an inherent lack of respect for the American "rule of law," thereby justifying deportation as the antidote to crime in low-income immigrant communities. Moreover, the denial of

basic legal rights to immigrants creates a legal system privileging those wealthy enough to afford private attorneys.

- **INS as a despot**: Since 1996, the INS functions as the government arm that implements immigration enforcement without discretion, claiming its "lack of power" to make decisions. Although as an institution its role is only to implement the law, within those parameters there exist many individual choices and interpretations—in other words, power.
- **International and industrial perspective**: Intersectionality exists between labor demands by U.S. industries and the ebb and flow of immigration policies and arbitrary migrant flows, as well as the prison industrial system—criminal and immigration—as "safety-valves" for these policy decisions and enforcement practices.

Through consensus building, the group decided to adopt all of these points as their platform on the topic of detention and deportation. The unanimous adoption of that platform by SEAFN members illustrates the generational shift in SEAA activism.

Like the generation of Asian American activists before them,[169] they viewed the history of United States involvement in Southeast Asia as one of imperialism. Rather than embrace the Cold War discourse that justifies military coups, bombings, and forced migrations,[170] they re-appropriated the narrative to make claims for American accountability. Instead of viewing the acceptance of refugees into the United States as symbolic beacons of democracy to whom refugees owed the gift of freedom,[171] the Millennial generation of activists diverged from their elders to argue that the United States bore an ethical responsibility for its military interventions in their countries which included mandatory resettlement. To those emerging leaders, successful resettlement was not a gift but a moral imperative.[172]

In the next stage of the training, they created a power analysis of strengths, challenges, allies, and targets to set the foundation for a national campaign. In addition, we shared best practices from those who were working locally against detention/deportation in the San Francisco Bay Area. By that point, PrYSM had held their most successful event to date. Their anti-gang database in Providence had pulled together a critical mass of young community members ready to act when deportation became a reality in the Cambodian community. They convinced former and active gang members to call a truce in order to build an alliance against a potential unjust separation from their families. The truce was highlighted in an awareness-raising community barbeque organized by PrYSM at a local park that previously had been a site of inter-gang violence. More than 300 former and active gang members and their families came to the gathering.

No fights occurred, and eventually some of these members became core PrYSM organizers. To the rest of the member organizations at FT, PrYSM's work provided a model of and inspiration for what was possible in our local communities, as well as the importance of creating space and communication channels amongst themselves. Ironically, while PrYSM went to FT to learn and feel a part of something and find like-minded young people, they were the ones others saw as a model to emulate.

Following organizational presentations, individuals divided into breakout groups to discuss strategies and tactics. They learned that although they had common goals and objectives, our geographic and demographic conditions varied from city to city. Therefore, organizational tactics necessitated flexibility and could not be uniform. This realization of differences in local terrains represented a significant break from the way in which local progressive organizations and coalitions encouraged individual groups to conform to their messaging on immigration reform, which targeted either white or Latino audiences. We realized we had to create our own approach and messaging that resonated both with our ethnic communities and our political philosophies.

That evening, Monami Maulik, the co-founder of the New York Taxi Drivers Alliance, came to speak about her organization's campaign against post-9/11 detention and deportation. As the founder of another organization, Desis Rising Up and Moving (DRUM) (their acronym is in homage to DRUM of Detroit, a radical Black autoworkers' union in the 1970s), Monami talked about how in New York City, South Asian communities endured racial profiling, detention, and coerced "voluntary" deportations, whereby they were convinced by ICE officials to sign documents that they would voluntarily leave the country, She gave insight to their structure and campaign, and their successes and challenges. She emphasized the organization and the community's isolation in New York City and nationally since 9/11; the opacity of ICE; and the obstacles DRUM's campaign faced in finding an individual in ICE to whom they could target their protests in order to have a personification of the bureaucratic state agency.

Immigration policies redefined our communities, not by nationality or migration processes, but by the sweepingly generalized class of "noncitizen." After talking with Monami, many of the attendees realized the difficult task of confronting ICE had been multiplied by the circumstances of 9/11 that netted all noncitizens into the growing dragnet of "terrorists." The critical contribution of SEAFN's alliance with DRUM proved mutually beneficial. At a time when the majority of social justice groups hesitated to publicly support South Asian and Muslim groups, SEAFN stood out not just as an ally against hate crimes, but against the surveillance, racial profiling, and punitive immigration practices that directly led to increased removal of

Southeast Asian, Latino, Middle East and African immigrants and refugees. PrYSM and other SEAFN groups replicated the innovative, individualized storytelling campaigns developed by DRUM through their humanization campaigns of individuals with deportation orders. The inter-ethnic solidarity between DRUM and SEAFN provided the resources to embark on the first national campaign for the Network in the fall of 2002. They seized on the shared stigmatization the young people felt, built solidarity amongst their families, peers, and their multi-racial communities.[173] In doing so, they expanded their potential social networks and coalitional opportunities to create a critical mass against the barrage of anti-immigrant messages and policies in the aftermath of 9/11.[174]

The FT ended with the agreement that its participants signified the beginning of SEAFN, whose first priority of action was to fight detention and deportation at local and national levels. To do this, the groups would continue strategizing and sharing over conference calls, develop a possible collective national strategy and tactics, such as a National Day of Action (NDA), while allowing for local flexibility in how they framed the nuances of their messages and what activities they chose to plan. Although there were strained moments that are indicative of growing pains for any new formation overall, the participants reflected on the weekend as a success in moving toward their vision of building long-term bonds between organizations and communities. The question remained whether SEAFN would be able to sustain a national presence, and whether it would stay committed to its goal of leadership development through popular education and consensus building. SEAFN gathered three more times over the next two years in Providence, Rhode Island, in Long Beach, California, and as part of the SEARAC strategizing conference in Oakland, California. For various reasons, most members could not travel to other cities—gatherings served as a way for them to meet Southeast Asian American leaders from other parts of the country who travelled to their city.

The political camaraderie built during these convenings became critical in coalition building. Tony, a directly affected member who participated in the first FT, said, "We felt really touched that people cared about our situation. People who didn't have anything to do with this came from all over the country to spend their weekend trying to fight this thing with us."[175] The realization that the young people participated in something larger than their local, sometimes tedious, work validated their dedication, identity, and the commonality of their successes and challenges. Yang from Wisconsin felt a unique sense of solidarity:

There are a lot of Southeast Asians, especially from Laos, where we are. But they either don't care about organizing or their work is really about social service. That's how they train the younger people, too. But here we saw people that understood life in America the same we do, and we got to share ideas about how to do things, not just follow what someone else tells us is "the way to do things." It makes more sense to us and to the young people we work with.[176]

The meetings brought together staff, members, and directly affected individuals and their families as part of an "imagined community"[177] beyond their scripted racial, ethnic, or class identities. In that space, a new set of values in how to achieve their goals went beyond deportation itself to the process of empowerment and re-humanization.

Subsequent SEAFN meetings followed similar formats and consisted of one or two representatives from each organization. The gatherings led to separate trips for members within the network; one youth group would visit another one as part of their programming to have the members bond as well. Unfortunately, because of the irregularity of participants at the conference calls and convenings, SEAFN had to revisit previous discussions every time, wasting precious time they had to strategize. That irregularity led to a sense of frustration and some members began to question whether the long-term goals of SEAFN had outlived the short-term focus on deportation. The combination of a perceived divergence from priorities and continual impending personal crises for deportees made it increasingly challenging to build sustainable leadership within SEAFN.

SEAFN soon developed a loose structure encompassing its membership, decision-making process, tactics and strategies, and goals for a national deportation campaign. The Network's membership criteria reflected the organizations that participated in the original FT. SEAFN's work would consist only of Southeast Asian and youth-based organizations and individuals or family members directly affected by detention and deportation. The organizations that gravitated toward the Network tended to be progressive-minded groups with organizing as the central component of the youth programs. Individuals and family members were encouraged to have support from a local organization.

Within the first year, three organizations—Asian Americans United, Asian Freedom Project, and Cambodian American Consortium—discontinued their membership in SEAFN, due to internal restructuring that arose from their inability to sustain revenue and build leadership willing to continue participation. By the end of the year, an Oakland-based, multi-ethnic youth-based coalition, Asian American Youth Promoting Advocacy and Leadership (AYPAL), had joined SEAFN, and began a local, two-year campaign for new immigration legislation. The shift in membership marked a new imbalance between the organizations within the network: from SEAA ethnic enclaves to coastal cities that traditionally had access to more external funding resources from major foundations and donors.[178] That move, ironically, also allowed for the potential for more interaction and rifts between groups and external allies in the competition for membership, resources, and funding.[179]

PrYSM felt that the national presence and inter-organizational bonding that occurred within the space of SEAFN was emotionally and politically important to both leaders and members. Despite little financial resources, they took great pains to participate in every call and meeting, and regularly interacted with the other SEAFN organizations. Gradually, PrYSM became the center of gravity for SEAFN, particularly as youth staff transitioned out of YLP due to family obligations, burn out, or the need to find employment elsewhere. Then, between 2006 and 2008, internal disagreements led to YLP's break from CAAAV to form the group Mekong, leaving PrYSM to be the only stable SEAFN group on the East Coast.

It was critically important to PrYSM that the decision-making process in SEAFN was organic, allowing the new generation of leaders to pave their own way of learning to work together rather than forcing a predetermined process on them, developing a vision and goals, and defining the coalition on their own terms. The freedom of such a grassroots style of operation allowed for more radical messaging and actions than with the MAAs that had been involved earlier. That difference transcended the generational differences of the groups. I argue they were grounded in the lack of involvement by funders during that nascent period similar to how Kohl-Arenas characterized the farmworkers movement of the previous generation:

[Privately funded] programs depended on resources from outside stakeholders. They also focused primarily on how farmworkers could help themselves improve their own behaviors and conditions, without challenging individual growers or the structure of agricultural industry. The revolutionary interpretation of mutual aid to foster self-determination and ownership, and the subsequent union approach, were both replaced by a more traditional charitable model.[180]

In the SEA refugee resettlement context, MAAs had become the benefactors of government and private funding that became focused on individual self-help as a mode of economic survival and social assimilation. In its independence from funding restrictions, SEAFN could be the radical voice similar to the early farm workers movement that Kohl-Arenas describes.

Organizing Tactics and Movement-Building Strategies

SEAA individuals who asked for support from the organizations in SEAFN often faced compounded problems that led them to the criminal justice system in the first place. Unlike PrYSM and other groups in SEAFN, many organizations, from legal to radical grassroots, advocated for the specific kinds of service support for clients. Legal representatives often only had the capacity to provide legal advice and representation. Social services usually could not assist with the legal research into one's case, nor did social work organizations generally create the space for political consciousness-raising activities or leadership development. Policy-based organizations did not require individualized, direct relationships with community members. At that time, none of these categories of organizations that constituted the community infrastructure developed a strategy to integrate these various needs of community members because they did not have it in their mission to develop holistic responses to the systematic disenfranchisement of this subpopulation. Moreover, the philanthropic infrastructure did not promote and support holistic approaches; rather, they preferred issue-based silos to those that would simultaneously integrate political organizing.[181] Building more personal relationships in the community rather than with legal, social service (particularly with MAAs), or policy organizations, youth organizers often mentored and supported individual members through multiple aspects of their lives while trying to engage them in a political analysis to explain their circumstances. Although they were not always successful, their overall approach demonstrates the difference between their social justice-oriented approach in comparison to the service-specific responses of the AAPI agencies and MAAs.

Many individuals and families needed emotional validation as they faced emotional devastation of potential family separation, as some individuals became desperate, suicidal, or financially reckless. It was almost impossible to fight a legal case for a client who was experiencing extreme symptoms. Having the time to be personally engaged in their cases and improve their lives enough to stay out of cash-based economies meant supporting them in finding gainful employment. It meant helping them develop their job search and interviewing skills and supporting them as they filled out job applications. Reaching the goals and objectives of legal, policy, social service, and grassroots organizers alike depended on addressing members' compounded crises which no one group could tackle alone. SEAFN's tactics and strategies thus took on four components at the local level: trust-building through holistic support, humanization campaigns, National Days of Action, and building a local movement.

Trust-Building through Holistic Support

SEAFN was successful in identifying pro bono attorneys, in large part because of their willingness to do much of the leg work in preparing a case, such as obtaining the proper documents, prepping the client for trial, helping the client fill out forms, and helping families understand the legal process in accessible language. The families that reached out to SEAFN usually initially asked only for legal support and were connected to lawyers or legal organizations willing to offer a free consultation and possibly take the case pro bono on the phone. Many times, local organizers from SEAFN groups accompanied individuals to the meetings and assisted in collecting paperwork for their cases. They often became the linguistic brokers between the individual and the lawyer, translating and processing the legal jargon and the spectrum of options for the client. The willingness to walk through the process with the families was critical to building trust and community who had felt forgotten and isolated in their struggles.

Through this process, local organizers began to track the patterns that emerged in the cases. We observed and documented when someone was detained, the circumstances of their immigration arrest, the conditions of their detention and their deportation, and strategies employed by public defenders and pro-bono lawyers. The working relationships that developed between the organizers and community members allowed for organizers to gain from members' perspectives on how to move forward with their individual cases and deportation policy in general.

Drawing inspiration from the DRUM model that Monami Maulik described in the FT, SEAFN also shared information with multi-ethnic and multi-racial allies locally and nationally to build consistent messaging and evidence for legal campaigns concerning detention and deportation. While individual organizations focused on the needs and messaging that made sense in their own communities, they were also able to build broad, multi-racial resistance based on structural and systemic critiques. The holistic support of criminalized community members actually jumpstarted the process of political conscientization and campaign development. In providing critical emotional support for individuals affected by deportation, families also came to trust the community environment in these situations. The analysis of the unique accountability the government had to SEA refugees moved beyond immigrant desires for assimilation to situating ourselves within the course of racial and class-based social justice movements in American history.[182]

Humanization Campaigns

SEAFN mirrored DRUM in building campaigns around individual cases that mobilized the community. The collection of cases helped them identify commonalities that would map possible ways to fight deportation, and the development of leadership of local community members was key to the successful long-term survival of the national network.[183] The goal for SEAFN was to build organizational skills among directly affected individuals through activities such as Congressional visits, public speaking, and independent media and cultural productions. It encouraged people to take control of their cases and create a democratic decision-making process that made sense to them. In essence, SEAFN's emphasis on process was their effort to materialize the vision they had for an equitable society within the campaign against deportation.

Local groups in SEAFN planned deportation outreach and education in community spaces and through organizational programming, such as community forums, immigration clinics, and workshops. Those forums educated community members on the basic concepts of the issue— who was at risk, what we knew of the process, the conditions of those deported, what people facing deportation or who were at risk could do, and what mobilization options were available. Usually, the forums had a lawyer present to answer more technical legal questions. Those events connected organizers to volunteers as well as families and individuals with immigration problems. They also helped people feel less isolated and had more clarity about the process and their options.

The strategic storytelling campaigns challenged the prevailing assumptions that the individuals facing deportation had been isolated from their communities and dehumanized by the singularity of their crimes.[184] The campaign employed stories of "self, us, and now," to individualize and humanize targeted communities such that the relationship between the listener and the protagonist(s) in the stories have shared identities and emotions, eliciting a response to the current issue.[185] Visually and narratively situated, those targeted by deportation as part of SEAA families had already suffered the long-term trauma of war, even while giving agency through storytelling to the individuals and their relatives. The approach helped gain both media and philanthropic attention through the strategic use of directly affected members' stories as parents, spouses, and children of genocide. In the context of immigration debates, the internalized images of the criminalized "alien" or the "deserving" refugee had to be contradicted with the first-person stories that humanized the targets of enforcement policies.

National Days of Action

Between 2002 and 2006, SEAFN coordinated four National Days of Action (NDAs), whereby member organizations held concomitant events to conduct outreach and educate their respective communities on detention/ deportation. The first NDA occurred on November 8, 2002. The events were planned over a series of conference calls within the network and decided upon by consensus. Although they were intended to be collaborations to express national solidarity and strong opposition to deportation policy, no single organization or set of criteria was enforced by all organizations. Each organization had the flexibility to promote its materials and hold events as deemed appropriate for its community. In short, the events' national scope legitimized local organizations, but did not override or impose upon the particularities of local communities.

Developing sustainability in a social movement means building a base of community members and leveraging external and internal resources. SEAFN felt the urgent need to draw attention to the issue impacting their communities and collectively decided to kick off their local campaigns with marches and rallies in each of the eight member-cities. Because most SEAFN organizations already had a membership base and cross-sectional alliances with different movements, finding people to participate in a rally was not difficult and they were able to access additional resources for sound systems, city permits, police liaison, printing materials, and speakers from different communities who could speak to the shared oppression they faced with the police, prison, and immigration enforcement agencies.

On the day of that first NDA in 2002, ten cities participated: Providence, Bronx, Philadelphia, Lowell, Madison, Long Beach, Stockton, Oakland, Davis, and Washington, D.C. The event proved immensely successful in catapulting the issue of deportation into the national limelight, giving SEAFN a seat at the table as an important body for strategizing purposes both locally and nationally, and in giving families an opportunity to share their anger, pain, and frustration with the immigration and detention system. It also marked the first time a national action of progressive political organizing had taken place within SEAA communities across the country. In five locations, the organizations chose to integrate rallies, and all groups chose to have a public vigil, memorializing the sacrifices that refugees made to come to the country and loved ones lost along the journey. The imagery of multiple generations coming together peacefully—highlighting their losses and escape—played into the normative narrative in popular culture about refugee victims.[186] In contrast, the direct actions of the youth groups in major cities legitimatized them with the progressive left circles who often thought of AAPI, and SEAA in particular, as complacent and unwilling to protest. In each location, a major news outlet documented the event, garnering the attention of funders looking to respond to the Bush administration in the post-9/11 context.

The NDA also marked the anniversary of PrYSM's formation, inspiring its members to devote extra time and effort to ensure the NDA's success as it took on personal local significance for them. PrYSM went door-to-door with flyers to encourage people to march with them from East Providence to the ICE local headquarters, where they would hold a vigil for those who had been deported. Afterward, they marched to a nearby park beside the I-95 freeway to rally until 5pm, when they planned to block a major intersection leading to the highway during rush hour. Leaders also asked immigrant community groups, immigrant rights groups, legal organizations, and the local Cambodian MAA to participate in the march and rally.

The Providence social justice community, as well as immigrant families from various Latinx, Caribbean, African, and Southeast Asian nationalities, spent the day together in solidarity. Family Unity drove from Lowell, Massachusetts, to Providence with its own contingent, as PrYSM later did that week for the Family Unity rally in Lowell. Everyone placed a white flower in respect for those facing deportation in front of the doors of the ICE building, and social justice leaders and youth organizers spoke at the rally in the park. The event was highlighted by a Native American ceremony led by Indigenous intergenerational community members. The rally achieved a critical mass, and participants took over the thoroughfare by holding hands in peace, encircling the parameters of the main intersection. About 200 people attended the march and rally, and PrYSM headlined the local newspapers—not only in regard to the rally, but also in respect to their demands for a moratorium on deportations and the release of detainees. The rally solidified the group as the leading voice for the newly formed SEAFN coalition.[187]

Subsequent NDAs fell on the anniversary of the signing of the Memorandum of Understanding, March 22, 2002. After the explosion of news media interest over the next two years, SEAFN decided it needed to refocus on community outreach and base building in order to sustain the direct actions and public pressure for immigration reform. The NDAs thus became more targeted in predominantly SEAA communities with educational and outreach events, rather than large direct actions focused garnering media attention. Each organization held a barbeque or community event with educational materials on hand to continue ongoing awareness within the communities. Those events drew strong turnout and became individual groups' main base-building events as well as one of the main channels through which SEAFN stayed connected to member organizations despite having few resources.

Although SEAFN and its member organizations operated on shoestring budgets for most of the first decade of the network's existence they continued to be one of the few sources of support and healing for many SEAA youth locally and nationally. Their activism empowered a new generation to build a critical mass based on claims of rights and justice across the country, giving "the struggle much of its dynamic, bottom-up character."[188]

Figure 4.1. PrYSM Anti-Deportation Protest 2003 (Courtesy of PrYSM Archives).

Demanding More than a Seat at the Table

In September 2004, SEARAC announced that they had received a small grant from the Four Freedoms Fund (FFF) to organize a strategizing conference to fight detention and deportation policies. FFF began in 2003 as a collaborative project between major funders to target geographic areas with growing immigrant populations. These funders included major philanthropic foundations for progressive causes such as Carnegie Corporation, Ford Foundation, Evelyn and Walter Haas, Jr. Fund, Open Society Institute, and Bill and Melinda Gates Foundation. They provided funding, technical assistance, and capacity building opportunities through meetings and trainings.[189] SEARAC designed the conference agenda and schedule and identified the location, host, and coordinators for each section with Cambodian Community Development, Inc. (CCDI), an MAA in Oakland, CA, where the conference would be held, before it invited SEAFN to the table.

SEARAC divided participants into working groups that would spend most of Saturday in strategizing sessions about what the focus of the anti-deportation work should be. Each group was to then report back to the larger group at the end of the day. Sunday's agenda consisted of the entire group coming together to devise a cohesive national campaign to end the deportation of Southeast Asian refugees. Although SEAFN comprised two-thirds of the participants, no current or former SEAFN members were asked to take leadership roles in planning the conference. Ironically, SEARAC's agenda imitated the work that SEAFN had been engaged in for the previous two years, on media messaging, policy reform, and legal and family services. SEAFN members felt that they had been asked to attend and participate in a conference for the benefit of extracting more information and knowledge without having any real power in the process or resource sharing. SEAFN did not know that a FFF program officer was invited by SEARAC to be on site to decide whether to fund SEARAC to lead the anti-deportation campaign nationally for SEAA. SEAFN representatives did not know beforehand that their presence also had the performative role to demonstrate a "united front" between SEARAC and SEAFN.

Tensions Break Out

On Saturday afternoon, after breakout sessions, the conference reconvened over lunch to watch a PSA. Porthira Chhim, representing CCDI, was scheduled to present a five-minute public service announcement (PSA) that he developed. No other media productions were screened even though SEAFN had created two other videos and had their own training materials on how to speak with media. Prior to the conference, the announcement had already been accepted and scheduled to air on local television, with possible national exposure. The ad depicted the life story of a young man whose face and real identity were used. It followed the same narrative that SEAFN had used in its educational video for workshops but failed to protect the individual's identity. The young man walks down the street as his mother tells the story of how he came to the United States in a voiceover. He walks into a citizenship class and acts as if he is speaking to the group. There is no sound of what he is actually saying or doing throughout the PSA, but the message at the top of the screen is that the viewer must choose to retain *deserving* immigrants in the United States.

The PSA immediately brought a storm of verbal protests in the room. Representatives from PrYSM asked why the funding Chhim had received had not been shared, and why the project had not been more collaborative when Chhim was well aware that SEAFN had been creating its own documentary and videos for more than a year. An AYPAL staffer wondered why a broader media strategy was not discussed with SEAFN in the context of the creating the PSA. I posed the question of security for the person in the PSA because it had included complete disclosure of the subject's identity, home, and family, even though he was under immigration probation. A YLP representative expressed frustration that the PSA was being screened at the conference with the goal to use it in place of SEAFN videos for educational trainings. Several people raised concern that the message encouraged a division between "good" and "bad" immigrants, which SEAFN's campaign against deportation had clearly sought to deconstruct. The probable consequence of such a message allowed for legislation that would encourage the artificial and arbitrary delineation of what constituted acceptable behavior, thus "deserving" of immigration relief, on the basis of common values by the increasingly conservative immigration courts.

Chhim's responses to the criticism exacerbated the tensions. First, he pointed out that SEAFN never contacted CCDI when it made videos, without acknowledging that CCDI showed no interest in SEAFN's deportation work until FFF showed interest. When he told the staffer from AYPAL that SEAFN was too irresponsible to partner with, he used the example of their tardiness to the sessions that morning. In fact, SEAFN communicated the need for an emergency internal meeting early that morning to address sexual misconduct within one of its member organizations. Finally, Chhim argued that the term "deserving" did not imply good/bad dichotomies and would not be interpreted by audience as such. The question and answer period closed without public commitment on whether to use the PSA and encourage its broadcast on public television stations. The rift over this video resulted in broken trust between SEAFN, SEARAC, and CCDI and displayed itself in the presence of the program officer who later chose not to fund the movement. The movement risked dissolution as a result of the competition for resources, differences in political ideologies, and factionalism that had torn apart many social justice movements before them.

Parting Ways

The conference peaked during Sunday's sessions in the CCDI office lobby, where an all-women volunteer crew of staffers and the board of directors' wives served lunch. The meeting that Sunday extended into the afternoon, but most participants had to leave earlier in the afternoon to make it back for work on Monday morning. As a result, the major decision-making for the group's future programming—the final stage of the conference agenda—would be left only to local representatives. After summarizing each group's conclusions from the breakout sessions, the final meeting was used to compile all of the ideas from the previous day and come to a consensus on the next steps. However, it became clear early on that decisions on how to move toward a national campaign had been preconceived. In fact, none of the session summaries made conclusions about how to proceed with a national campaign. Rather, the SEARAC/CCDI proposal to advocate for an immigration policy that re-instated the 212(c) waiver, which narrowly allowed very minor criminal cases to be judicially reviewed, was the only proposal offered for the remaining participants to vote on.

The proposal did not come from any of the session discussions and instead seemed to be predetermined by SEARAC. The East Asian American legal scholar who devised the proposal openly pressured SEAFN to adopt his policy plan in the moment, condescendingly stating that he had been "waiting for years for the community to take action." The SEAFN representatives reacted with silence. They had been put in a situation where they were asked to conform and vote immediately on a plan that they 1) had no part in developing, 2) had virtually no opportunity to discuss, and 3) did not even help the majority of their members who faced deportation for more serious crimes. They felt they could not present any challenge because they were in the presence of a funder who had the power to expand their work, and because the person pressuring them was a leading elder AAM activist to whom they had an intergenerational obligation.

With the FFF program officer bearing witness, SEAFN representatives said they would have to discuss the proposal with their members and could not decide immediately. If they agreed to the legal scholar's policy proposal, they would jeopardize the process of community empowerment through consensus-building that defined their political project. Moreover, their members would most likely oppose the narrowness of the 212(c) waiver that would alleviate very few cases and uphold the good/bad immigrant binary. The legal scholar then framed their hesitancy to imply that SEAFN was the barrier against progress on the issue and they were acting like irresponsible youth. Like Chhim's reaction to critique of his video, this scholar responded to the youth's resistance by imposing stereotypes about urban youth of color on them. SEAFN ultimately declined to state a position at the end of the session but agreed to review his proposal with their members back home. The tense session ended the conference and was the last real collaboration between these groups for the next few years.

Lessons Learned

The Four Freedoms-funded conference elicited two conclusions about SEAFN's relationship on a national stage to existing power brokers of policy. SEAFN continued to struggle to navigate between the local culture of their constituents, their progressive allies in movement coalitions, and national policy strongholds. The upshot of the conference was that SEARAC revealed their model for a national campaign against deportation: the appropriated structure and strategy from SEAFN that had been built over the course of the previous two years. The fact that SEARAC accepted SEAFN's model validates the influence of SEAFN on immigrant rights organizing, not solely by groups like SEARAC, but by also prominent funding sources. In the end, unlike grassroots formations of a generation ago,[190] FFF played a significant role, both positive and inadvertently obstructive, in how honest and organic coalition building could develop its priorities, namely how it viewed positive collaborations and failed to support the development of the movement, such as not offering technical assistance on decision-making, coalition-building, and youth organizing. In other words, giving them the tools and guidelines to better facilitate the process and plan the conference could have changed the direction of the philanthropic approach to funding as well as the direction of the national work in the immigrant rights community.[191]

The conference marked the beginning of the end to any cohesive effort by this generation of SEAFN to launch a cohesive campaign among groups against detention and deportation. It also was the last time SEAFN convened nationally although individual groups would maintain relationships of varying degrees of intimacy. Each organization's participation in immigration reform also changed. They shifted back to a strategy of building local campaigns that focused on preventative interventions to keep members out of the prison industrial complex. The return to its grassroots prerogatives gave new life to the work of SEAFN and allowed it a moment to regroup away from the national spotlight. Although the increased attention attracted funding opportunities and forced collaborations for which it may not have been ready, it also creating tensions that potentially would have negatively impacted the movement overall.[192] SEAFN struggled with funding for its national efforts, and no one organization had the capacity to sustain the network. By 2010, it had in effect become defunct.

SEARAC's New Leadership, New Directions

In an interview with Max Niedweicki, the former executive director of SEARAC, he shared his opinion of Southeast Asian American youth organizations and what he thought were the main obstacles in mobilizing for immigration reform. He responded, "It's hard to advocate for policy changes at the national level [in D.C.] when at the local level the groups you're supposed to represent are calling for the overthrow of the government....We can't make allies with Congressional representatives when people are protesting their local offices." Niedweicki was referring to local SEAFN campaigns that targeted regional ICE officials, calling on them to re-interpret immigration laws. The only actions addressed to Congressional representatives by SEAFN organizations were to encourage its members to hold personal meetings with Congressional staff to educate them on the impact of deportation policies. The meetings were held inside Congressional offices without media present. No one demanded an overthrow of the government. The legislative visits were exactly the sort of activity that SEARAC summer institutes trained their participating organizations to do, and those trainings then inspired SEAFN's decision to include this in their repertoire of contention. But Niedweicki conflated the nuances of the various kinds of political participation and campaign strategies and tactics into a narrative that also fit into his biases about SEAA youth and about progressive social movements. The example of SEARAC's then Executive Director's response emphasizes the contradictory relationship with the MAAs that the youth organizations had to overcome when they entered inter-generational and inter-ethnic coalitions.

Toward the end of 2004, new leadership shifted SEARAC's direction and approach. A young Hmong American woman from Detroit, Michigan, Doua Thor, was hired to lead SEARAC in its efforts to be more responsive to its member organizations and to lead the organization into the new millennium. Thor soon held community gatherings of member MAAs and stakeholders in various cities throughout the country to hear from the membership what they needed from the umbrella organization mandated to represent them at the national level.

SEARAC adopted a clear stance against Southeast Asian deportation for the first time because of Thor's political orientation on the topic. It also made a dramatic shift in its public position by citing U.S. immigration law and practices as a critique of the deportation policy. It proactively educated its membership organizations by offering fact sheets and toolkits to discuss the topic through its partnership with the Asian American Justice Center (AAJC) and with PBS/ITVS and the filmmakers of the documentary *Sentenced Home*, Thor made a commitment to support the work of SEAA youth groups by backing 1Love Movement, a group in Philadelphia. SEARAC funded the group's projects and operations, and heavily promoted 1Love Movement's anti-deportation efforts. By extension, 1Love Movement shared those resources with other groups that had formerly been part of SEAFN. The relationship between Thor and 1Love Movement helped SEAFN re-emerge and helped PrYSM sustain its ongoing anti-deportation support for families by funding a staff person.

As the political tension surrounding criminal deportations and enforcement increased under the Obama administration, policy and philanthropic organizations shifted toward more conservative agendas, including supporting the DREAM Act,[193] immigrant integration, and citizenship/voter registration drives. Funders expressed concern that PrYSM and others in SEAFN did not create the successful and measurable outcomes that funders could tout to their donors. For PrYSM, the loss in funding resulted in the shift back to a local emphasis that meant refocusing on its women's group, SEAQuel, and organizing against school-to-prison pipelines in Rhode Island.

Navigating Power

PrYSM found legitimacy through channels outside of the traditional SEAA leadership: directly affected community members, a network of like-minded Southeast Asian groups throughout the country, and East Asian American-based groups from within the AAM. They developed campaigns based on resource mobilization within the community, as well as outside the main pillars of community infrastructure. The mentors within AAM and the immigrant rights movement played critical roles in validating their anti-deportation work in ways that the MAAs were hesitant to do. That support allowed them the opportunity to spark the interest of potential national funders, and they helped set the stage for more progressive voices concerning detention and deportation in the post-9/11 period. As progressive funders became attentive to SEAFN, the movement involving immigrant rights, policy, and legal organizations also gained traction.

Regardless of the symbiotic relationships that were cultivated between the youth groups and the MAAs, the increased public attention for these groups did not equate to increased power in setting the agenda and garnering resources directly for the youth groups like PrYSM. Some MAAs and AAM leaders made assumptions about the behavioral characteristics of SEAA youth leaders that aligned with common stereotypes of urban youth of color as being irresponsible, uncooperative, and lazy. These narratives became their justification to exclude them in decision-making processes or be equal partners for major funding opportunities. While the choices by funders and by the MAA and AAM leaders may not have been ill-intentioned, the impact of their choices left SEAA youth groups like PrYSM marginalized. The intergenerational and class tensions persisted to the detriment of the family members who sought both immediate assistance and long-term policy solutions to their separation. SEARAC's transition in leadership to a 1.5-generation refugee Hmong woman shifted its relationship with SEAA youth groups and expressed a more amicable view toward advocacy and activism. In turn, its willingness to engage in a broader repertoire of tactics influenced local MAAs to do the same.

In this chapter, the particular evolution of the relationships at play devolved from a promising network of youth groups that could collaborate with long-standing policy and MAA partners. However, the dissolution of the coalition with the MAAs and SEARAC, and of SEAFN itself, by no means ended the efforts to renew commitment to a long-term vision to better the lives of SEAA communities by PrYSM. Rather, it represents the renegotiation that is a necessary part of intergenerational transference of leadership and power. The Millennial leaders had come to realize their potential voice free from the intergenerational burdens thrust upon them. Now they needed to learn how to translate their new political voice into a movement of their own.

CHAPTER FIVE
#RefugeeResilience: The Turn toward Glocal Activism

The longer I'm here, the more American I feel.[194]

I visited the Returnee Assistance Project (RAP) just as it opened to receive newly exiled Khmer Americans in Phnom Penh. While staying at this "guest house turned transition home," I met virtually all the first three cohorts of deportees. One day, Kimho Ma, perhaps the most well-known of the people exiled thus far for his role in the Supreme Court case that dissolved indefinite immigration detentions, accompanied me to the notorious Toul Sleng prison. Toul Sleng was a school that became the site of torture and murder of over 12,000 civilians during the Khmer Rouge in the aftermath of the American War in Southeast Asia. As we walked through the bare classrooms where only the tools of torture remained, Kimho reflected on his transgressions as a formerly affiliated gang member, sharing that his biggest regret was that the government no longer discerned between those who "deserved" to be deported like himself, and those who were involved in petty, non-violent crimes or crimes of poverty to survive. Somehow, there was a sense of responsibility—a sense of grief—of what he viewed to be a "loss of life" because of him. He showed remorse and accountability for the Khmer Americans who shared his fate. Simultaneously, he felt a sense of anger and rejection, of being the "stepchild" of America's war, as a Khmer refugee, and as a refugee child that the country neglected, turned its back on, and then blamed for growing up the way he did.

The ironies of the moment surfaced the stark contradictions. He had left school after having a promising future as a University of California, Davis student who could neither remove himself from his past nor afford to move forward with his dreams. He revealed his sense of pain, frustrations, and guilt at a site that had once held promise only to be desecrated by state-instituted violence, of which the United States infamously chose not to intervene because of its "compassion fatigue" from the war. He stood alone amongst the ruins of war, with no sense of how to engage in a process of unraveling the internalized racist views the world had shaped in his mind, and no channels to right the wrongs of history and of his own story.

Figure 5.1: Ferguson, MO, Solidarity Rally, 2014 (Courtesy of PrYSM Archives)

The Global and the Local: Progressions in Transnational and Diasporic Activism

The evolution of anti-deportation activism has integrated it into the Asian American Movement (AAM) while members of SEAFN positioned themselves as leaders and representatives for the SEAA community rather remaining on the margins. In the process, they have also deepened diasporic ties with the deportees in Cambodia, creating an historic global-local, or "glocal," campaign to end deportation. Embodied in PrYSM are a new generation of SEAA activists, ones who have crossed borders internally and externally to tell their stories on their own terms—even at the risk of public repudiation of their marginalized status in SEAA communities—as formerly incarcerated, as former gang-affiliated youth, as women, and as LGBTQ+. And rather than conform to a prescribed performance, these SEAA activists returned the gift of freedom to their ethnic and movement elders by demanding their democratic rights to self-determination to shape SEAA identity and agendas that were important to them. Their approach to transnational organizing attempted to achieve horizontal instead of hierarchal social movement in both the way they coordinated with individuals in Cambodia and their fundraising choices.

The historic, transnational coordination between 1Love Cambodia and SEAFN catalyzed a new generation of activists in the SEAA community beyond the anti-communist movements of the older generation of activists discussed in Chapter One.[195] The use of international law as the justification for the "right2return" were fraught with relations of power that were never unpacked during the course of the campaign by #Right2Return organizers. As Elora Chowdhury documented in her study on the Bangladeshi women's movement, the dynamic of those with U.S. citizenship making decisions and informing the public narratives of the victims of gendered violence in Bangladesh was ineffective at empowering anyone *but* those involved with the U.S. women's movement.[196] Consequently, the power relations between the movement actors in Bangladesh and the United States evolved into a co-dependent relationship whereby power dynamics magnified rather than shifted.[197] In contrast, SEAFN 2.0's concerted efforts to highlight the voices of directly affected individuals, as well as their commitment to educate exiled Khmer Americans at training workshops in Phnom Penh, gestured toward a consciousness of power relations. As they put it, it was a means to "give voice" to those rendered invisible in the immigration process. Unfortunately, while supportive of the campaign, in informal conversations with deportees in Cambodia and with network members in the United States, it became clear that many members outside the SEAFN 2.0's leadership lacked a firm grasp on the complex language, laws, and processes of the U.N. and international human rights.

Ultimately, the well-intentioned vision by the network leadership and its actualization begs the question whether the politics of power between classes, defined by income, education, or citizenship, had been moving a campaign forward without actually empowering the people it was supposedly "liberating." I asked how 1Love Cambodia felt about the SEAFN 2.0 organizers trying to work with them. According to Borom, the relationship was positive overall:

> At least we're at the point where something is being done, something is being talked about. I tell [SEAFN], the power struggle is not with White America, it's in our own community. Now you have a younger generation [of SEAA] who want to push for equality and we can see them coming up and more people understanding. Intrinsically, they have a lot more compassion [than the previous SEAA generation]; their hearts are in the right place. They're not willing to accept the status quo. They're willing to fight for it. And they are searching for their roots when they come here, so that shows they care. I don't get arrogance from them like a lot of the NGO people who come here.

SEAFN 2.0 activists gave 1Love Cambodia the tools to organize, but they had the capacity to listen and be allies rather than situate themselves at the center of the campaign. At the same time, Borom made it clear that many deportees had mixed feelings about returning to the United States: "Our goal is different from the people in the U.S. We want to stop the bleeding [of deportations], but we're also realistic about returning. I have kids here now, and I wouldn't want them to go through the judgement and racism that I did in the U.S. In Cambodia, they are loved." Borom recognized the simultaneity of transnational justice through his personal experience of deportation, but his political conscientization simultaneously made him critical of the American Dream and the reality of what it meant to be a racialized immigrant child in America.[198] In the end, the campaign did bring a new, powerful dimension to the movement by organizing the diasporic SEAA in Cambodia who had been disenfranchised as refugees in the United States.

A New Generation: SEAFN 2.0

In August 2013, Vietnamese American Youth of Louisiana, New Orleans, or VAYLA-NO, a youth group formed in the aftermath of Hurricane Katrina in the district of New Orleans East primarily for Vietnamese American youth, received funding from the Kellogg Foundation to convene progressive Asian American youth groups from across the country for a racial justice gathering in New Orleans. Core members of the original SEAFN were invited to the gathering, including KGA, PrYSM, Freedom, Inc., and Mekong. Chanravy, on behalf of SEAFN, helped plan the event by working closely with VAYLA's Executive Director, Minh Nguyen, and a small group of people from California and New York.

In the meetings, Chanravy and Minh were the only individuals representing SEAA groups. Searching for social justice mentors, Minh sought out leadership in those East Asian-based groups. The groups have long histories of radical left positions and political campaign successes that they have passed on to a new generation of leaders within their own membership. Organizational leaders have positioned themselves as mentors and resources for emergent SEAA youth groups, thus filling the gap left by many MAAs. Chanravy expressed her frustration during the planning process, which she felt had been taken over by an East Asian-dominated agenda. She added that she had to fight for SEAFN groups and SEAA allies to even attend.

Over the course of the weekend, the Southeast Asian and South Asian American youth groups privately expressed that they felt increasingly estranged from the conference planning process and discourse. They felt that middle-class, college-educated, East Asian groups, mainly from the San Francisco Bay Area and New York City, were dominating the agenda, and the conference culture. To many of the youth leaders, the workshops became intellectual, abstract musings on social justice that did not relate to their personal lives or current challenges they and their members were facing as real crises. The persistent discussions on the need to recognize intersectionality in the movement became convoluted as representatives from the Southeast Asian and South Asian American youth, many of whom also identified as LGBTQ+, felt that a queer intersectional identity was being used to rationalize and flatten the class and color privilege held by many of the people in the room. To PrYSM and other SEAA organizers, the claims to a marginalized identity based on intersectional identities of gender and sexuality allowed those with class and ethnic privilege to try to speak for all present, including SEAA youth, while ignoring the power dynamics of those in attendance.

While the SEAA leaders at the conference believed they benefitted from the legacy of the Asian American Movement (AAM) from the 1960s and '70s, they raised concern about harkening back to the East Asian-dominant period in AAM that perpetuated the narrative of the "gift" of social activism to refugees—the gift that came with the unavoidable strings of indebtedness. These early AAM activists bestowed their legacies to a younger professionalized generation of nonprofit-based activists.[199] Consequently, the Millennial and post-Millennial SEAA activists felt they could again reproduce the roles of benefactors of the gift of AAM that they could accept with terms but never fully own.

By the end of the weekend, though, the SEAA contingents felt disempowered by the dynamics of the conference and seemed to have little desire to continue working with the other organizations. A PrYSM youth organizer recounted, "We are always being used by Asian Americans to organize, but they never actually give us power even though it's about us." When meeting socially over meals and at their hotel, they decided to communicate their frustrations. They first visibly separated from the larger collective and began small group meetings. On the last day of the conference, participants were asked to divide into teams and write on butcher paper what they had gleaned from the weekend's events and their next steps or goals in organizing for a new Asian American Movement. The SEAA group purposefully formed one breakout group, with the exception of VALYA-NO, who acted as the host organization and focused on implementing the logistics of the gathering. At the end of the session, instead of speaking, the SEAA groups stood together and raised a colorfully decorated sign to announce the re-formation of SEAFN. The banner featured a sun in one corner and a river running across the page. The organizers wrote messages of their past, their resilience as refugees, and accomplishments by famous SEAA along the river in addition to inspirational figures from American social movement history. For example, they drew a Sriracha hot sauce bottle and a raised fist, and other iconic symbols of the Black Power, Chicanx, and Asian American left movements from the 1960s. While the map did not include the intricate details of migration, it was clearly an homage to the SEA migration journeys, reminiscent of traditional Hmong quilts that narrate Hmong migration and cultural history. At the center of the sign were the words, "Southeast Asian Freedom Network 2.0" to signify a separation from the body of organizations at the conference. A new generation of SEAA organizers was born.

The gathering ended with a tense subtext that while there were opportunities for solidarity, SEAFN 2.0 demanded any coalition be inclusive of SEAA perspectives and on their terms, not simply in their names. They were confident that they had the means, skills, and determination to organize independently. After the conference, the groups in SEAFN made concerted efforts to support one another's fundraising events and used those events, among others, to have national meetings and periodic phone meetings. SEAFN 2.0, however, learned from the original SEAFN's mistakes with the Four Freedom Funds experience and took control of their campaigns from the beginning.

The groups who attended the Kellogg-funded meeting eventually formed a broad coalition of leftist AAPI organizations engaged in movement-building activities, called Grassroots Asians Rising (GAR), and SEAFN 2.0 groups overlapped with GAR. Yet, SEAFN 2.0 symbolized a severing from the burden of indebtedness that they had been carrying across generations, within and beyond the refugee experience, which had attached itself to the experiential sense of statelessness—essentially, of not belonging.[200] Rebellious intergenerational breaks are common to social movements as part of their growth cycles. Younger activists tend to take more radical positions than their elders based on the freedoms they gained from previous victories, and SEAFN 2.0's unwillingness to compromise their power unequivocally rejected the reified and sacrificial refugee victim. In short, they had to end the relationship with AAM that reproduced the patron-client power dynamic, as "both life necessity and legitimate reason to kill—that is, the refugee patriot both reconfigures race safely through asylum, through multicultural gesture, and through incorporation into an existing interior of freedom's empire [and simultaneously] a biological threat."[201] SEAFN 2.0 had become a viable threat to an antiquated mentality that could not see them as anything other than victims. Their resolute claims to their own authorship of social movement history in general, and Southeast Asian American history in particular, still respected the complicated political histories of conflicting perspectives. But more than that, they rejected the hierarchal relations that they believed those in power took for granted. After a series of meetings with GAR leaders, SEAFN

2.0 negotiated for representatives from their staff assume leadership roles within GAR as a condition of their continued involvement. Their freedom to imagine, articulate, and lead their own future planted the seeds for the transnational movement they envisioned.

Figure 5.2. SEAFN 2.0 Banner at Racial Justice Gathering, 2014
(Courtesy of PrYSM Archives, Truesta Photography).

SEAFN 2.0: Seeds of A Transnational Movement

SEAFN 2.0 members felt that they had previously been driven out of the policy discussions on immigration reform by MAAs and AAM policy groups and yet held the role of first responders to immigration crises locally. SEAFN 2.0 decided to regain control of the debate by developing their own multi-pronged campaign. By the time SEAFN 2.0 started, Quyen Dinh, the new SEARAC Executive Director who replaced Duoa Thor, had to develop trust with SEAFN 2.0, which had come to expect resources from SEARAC that Thor offered them during her tenure. Dinh was emotionally impacted as a student on the University of California, Berkeley campus during the height of SEAFN's original campaign between 2002 and 2004. While a strong advocate for the cause, she felt she had to curtail the funding to SEAFN 2.0 to align with the fiscal resources available to SEARAC when she assumed leadership. This led to initial tensions between SEARAC and SEAFN 2.0, but unlike the relationship with SEARAC two leaders before her, Dinh, Sarath, and other SEAFN leaders were able to reach an agreement on how to best collaborate in ways that gave resources to SEAFN 2.0 to continue. Under the leadership of both these SEAA 1.5-, 1.8-, and second-generation women, SEARAC has actively campaigned against immigration enforcement and the deportation of refugees at the policy level and in individual cases. SEARAC also assisted SEAFN with financial support for the new campaign, a central component of which included independent media productions that would air on social media video sites, challenging dominant frames of debate on immigration.

In 2015, SEAFN organizations and the filmmakers of *Cambodian Son*, a documentary about life after deportation for exiled Khmer American poet Kosal Khiev, offered community screenings of the film in cities across the country. The screenings rejuvenated audiences' energies, helping them to refocus their priorities on the school-prison-deportation pipeline. SEAFN 2.0 decided to update their media materials and create new productions using social media. Unlike the first SEAFN attempts to produce independent videos, SEAFN 2.0 members have become better-trained in media technology and creating media campaigns by non-SEAA ally organizations. The post-Millennial generation activists also have the advantage of their extensive experiences with and access to social media. While SEAFN 2.0 youth had been documenting their activism on Facebook and other sites, the footage of SEAFN leaders testifying and actively participating in the United Nations (U.N.) international conference in 2015 sparked the concept for a new digital social media strategy for the anti-deportation campaign.

While the new media strategy was originally conceptualized in tandem with the goal to humanize the deportation issue to international and domestic policymakers, its main achievement was the burgeoning social media following and common ground among SEAA young people. The use of social media gave SEAFN unprecedented power to articulate its own narrative and strategically frame the issue based on storytelling.[202] SEAFN 2.0 launched its social media video campaign in the fall of 2015, led by 1Love Movement in Philadelphia. SEAFN members traveled across the country to fifteen major cities in thirty days, and then to Cambodia with SEAA populations to interview everyday people and community organizers in the SEAA community focusing on one theme: the history of refugee migration and resettlement as a result of war as just cause to oppose deportation. The films employ first-person perspectives, and make known SEAA experiences with hip-hop beats and rhymes—originally written for each specific video—that represent their collective generational cultural identity.[203] Created with hand-held cameras and edited on home computers, the eight-minute, youth-made videos were released once a month from October 2015 to April 2016. The videos humanized the campaign to end deportation by creating the personal immigration and resettlement narratives of child refugees directly impacted by U.S. immigration policies. They represented the "street ethnography" that Schlund-Vials describes in Khmer American rapper PraCh Ly's work, as one who evokes "cultural facts and cultural truths that correspondingly facilitate alternative routes to refugee reparation and Cambodian American rehabilitation."[204]

The videos offered a resurrection of the refugee youth who had hitherto been invisible except to be upheld as the potential of the American Dream personified. That resurrection was the production of Americana looking back at itself in its racial diversity, imperial residue, and the discursive power of democracy in action.[205] The activists used social media platforms to circulate the videos with the following demands: 1) ending the deportation of refugees from the American War in Southeast Asia; 2) allowing those already deported back into the United States; and 3) renegotiating the terms of the M.O.U. with Cambodia to replicate those established with Viet Nam, whereby only those who have entered the United States after 1996 are subject to removal. Through online platforms, they leveraged the sites where their own generation had found political education, identification, and avenues toward political action.[206] The new media campaign generated enough attention online in the United States and amongst the exiled Khmers in Cambodia that SEAFN 2.0 felt they could escalate their campaign. On the fortieth anniversary of SEA refugee migration to the United States, SEAFN 2.0 released a full statement with these campaign demands framed in the language of the United Nations Universal Declaration of Human Rights.

#RefugeeResilience, #EndDisplacement, #Right2Return: A Human Rights Campaign

After the newly formed United Nations put forth the Declaration of Human Rights in 1951, Black civil rights activists presented to this body's petition, "We Charge Genocide," to ask the international body to protect against the state-sanctioned human rights violations of Black in the United States.[207] Social movement activists have increasingly returned to the U.N. as an international platform for shaming the United States on its domestic policies, including incarceration and immigration enforcement. Allies in the immigrant rights movement, such as DRUM, the National Network for Immigrant and Refugee Rights (NNIRR), and others, have testified at U.N. gatherings on the state of U.S. treatment of racial minorities, immigrants, poor people, imprisoned people, and youth. Through these movement networks, three SEAFN 2.0 members—Chhaya Chhuom of Mekong, Naroen Chhin of 1Love, and Chanravy Proeung, hired as SEAFN staff through funding from SEARAC from 2014 to 2015—were invited to meet with U.N. representatives and share the experiences of unjust detention and deportation of SEAA who came to the U.S. as refugees. As guests of the U.N., their testimonies and the documentation of their trip brought a gravity and legitimacy to SEAFN 2.0's campaign. The real-time recording set a new standard in the use of media for political organizing within the SEAA community. The activists sustained public interest in their activities via video diaries, candid shots of each other speaking to the camera about their impressions, and the dissemination of the videos on YouTube and Facebook. The videos added humor, a sense of community and friendship, as well as fun to the frequently overlooked, mundane work of organizing. They went beyond humanization campaigns of the targets of deportation; they humanized and made relatable the stereotype of the "angry activist." What had seemed like stilted and obscure political activism now became legible and familiar to a new generation of young people.

In preparation for the trip to the U.N. annual meeting in Geneva, Switzerland, SEAFN 2.0 further developed a multi-pronged campaign based on the U.N. Declaration of Human Rights (See Appendix E for full statement):

- **Universal Declaration of Human Rights, Article 26. Right to Education, & Article 7. Right to Equality Before the Law.** Most Southeast Asian refugees were resettled into inhumane conditions in impoverished neighborhoods, making us vulnerable to poverty, crime, violence, structural disadvantage, racism, discrimination and profiling. Many young people fell through the cracks in an under-resourced education system unfit to meet their needs, leaving only 65% of Cambodian-American youth graduating from high school. Many enter into a highly functional and highly funded School-to-Prison Pipeline. Law enforcement agencies in cities across the country began coding Cambodian communities as "gang infested" and we were surveilled and profiled for arrest and incarceration. Over-policing of our community led to racial profiling, police brutality, and high incarceration rates, higher than any other Asian ethnic group in relation to the size of our population.

- **Universal Declaration of Human Rights, Article 10. Right to Due Process, Article 16. Right to Family Unity, & Article 9. Right to Freedom from Arbitrary Arrest, Detention, Exile.** In 1996, the US passed the Illegal Immigration Reform and Immigrant Responsibility Act (IIRIRA) and Anti-terrorism and Effective Death Penalty Act (AEDPA)... Deportation for "aggravated felonies" also became permanent with no right to return, and was applied retroactively, leading to international human rights violations regarding proportionality of punishment, double jeopardy, and fairness under the law.

- **Universal Declaration of Human Rights, Article 21. Right to Democracy.** On March 22, 2002, the US signed a Repatriation Agreement with Cambodia and began deporting Cambodian-Americans. As such, the creation of such agreements must be done through transparent, open, and democratic processes that prioritize the will of the people and insight of directly impacted communities...

Based on these articles of the Declaration of Human Rights, SEAFN 2.0 set forth a list of campaign demands that allowed for a re-articulation of the M.O.U. between Cambodia and the United States. They argued any new M.O.U. agreements between Laos and the United States should resemble the pilot program with Viet Nam that only allows immigrants post-1995 to the United States from Viet Nam—not refugees—to be deported. It would also allow what SEAFN referred to as the "right to return."

The "right to return" (#Right2Return) campaign would allow anyone deported to Cambodia to petition for return based on the new M.O.U. SEAFN 2.0 argued for a family hardship protection in individual deportation cases that considered the contributions and hardships one's deportation had on family members. The group's leaders articulated their demands as follows:

REQUESTED ACTION

We call for immediate recourse to begin to rectify over five decades of U.S. human rights violations that have torn Cambodian families apart from Cambodia to the U.S., and back again:

1. We call for an immediate suspension of U.S. deportations to Cambodia.

2. We call for an open review process of the U.S.-Cambodia Repatriation Agreement, which includes and prioritizes democratic oversight and input of impacted communities in the US and Cambodia.

3. We call for amendments to the Repatriation Agreement that tailor its impacts to consider the individual and community experience of U.S. human rights violations and will protect those with these experiences from deportation.

4. We call for amendments to the Repatriation Agreement that ensure humane, just, and fair structures of support for impacted families and individuals in the U.S. and Cambodia, including economic stability, human and social services, employment infrastructure, visitation rights, and the right to return.[208]

SEAFN 2.0 used the attention it received on social media from the U.N. trip to build an audience for #Right2Return #EndDisplacement with these requested actions. With images, videos, and a solidarity letter for supporters to sign quickly spreading across the internet, SEAFN 2.0 members developed a fundraising approach that the previous generations of SEAA activists did not have access to—they extended their reach beyond the non-profit industrial complex. Each video, post, and letter offered the audience an opportunity to contribute to or volunteer for the campaign; the individual organizations, as well as SEAFN 2.0 as a network, and all were committed to shifting power relations with their funders. They actively sought funding from progressive funders committed to their organizing philosophies and strategies. The U.N. demands and the actions related to them outlined were posted on all SEAFN 2.0 webpages with a link to 1Love Movement's campaign page, SEAFN 2.0's public Facebook page, and later included in their video campaign.

As a bridge between the UN trip and its multi-city tour, SEAFN 2.0 released a statement in commemoration of the fortieth anniversary of the end of the American War in Southeast Asia (See Appendix F for full statement):

TODAY, marks 40 years since our country was taken over by the Khmer Rouge revolution. It was revolution that was rooted in political theory, but not liberatory action. Revolution built on communist ideology, but practiced through dictatorship and mass murder. Revolution that promised life, but led to the genocide of our people. Revolution that cherished our homeland, but led us to displacement.

TODAY, as SEAFN reflects on the deep resistance and resilience of our community, we also commit to recognizing the historic root causes of our experience. We know that French colonialism, and U.S. imperialism and militarism bear responsibility for creating the conditions that led our country into the Killing Fields. We experience this oppression through continuous cycles of violence from one side of the world to the other, from war to displacement to poverty to incarceration to deportation. We are the collateral damage and human cost of colonialism, imperialism, and militarism. And we know that we will continue to carry the weight of all of this systemic violence for generations to come, and that we must heal through determined resistance and resilience.

We must continue to break the cycle of isolated trauma, and ground ourselves in collective healing, and actions rooted in our historic experience and our current conditions. And we have already begun. Our revolution has been our survival and our determination to re-build and re-center our lives, our families, and our people. Our revolution has been our resilient creation of new pathways for us to experience family, love, healing, and community. As we continue to struggle with the impact of intergenerational systemic oppression, we are building a new foundation that honors our humanity and dignity.

TODAY, our revolution honors our ancestors, our history, and our struggle. Our revolution is about action rooted in love.[209]

There is a clear shift in these statements, compared to the time SEAFN started in 2002, to centralize the history and perspectives of Khmer refugees in the United States, even while half of the network is Lao, Hmong, and Vietnamese. What has not been clearly expressed when SEAFN members discuss their frustrations with their East Asian American counterparts, though, is whether those statements represent an underlying tension within SEAA in progressive coalitions, or whether the emphasis on the Khmer experience is a purely strategic position given their centrality in the anti-deportation campaign.

The campaign, however, diverged from being generally inclusive of the Southeast Asian refugee experience, as with the early MAAs, to centralizing the perspectives, needs, and leadership development of Laotian and Khmer communities. The campaign points to the needed discussion of the historic privileging of Vietnamese and Hmong Americans in refugee narratives and resettlement projects. Post-Millennial claims of the particular disparities for their co-ethnic communities demand attention. Their interpretation of intersectional identity thus allows them to navigate between simultaneously claiming a SEAA experience while recognizing the differences and contradictions within ethnic-specific positionalities. Over the next year, SEAFN 2.0 representatives continued to attend the U.N. conventions and traveled back to Cambodia. Through their own social networks, they were able to establish and build upon existing relationships with exiled Khmer Americans, eventually forming 1Love Cambodia, the sister organization to Philadelphia's 1Love Movement in Phnom Penh.

1Love Cambodia was founded and led by exiled Khmer Americans, including a relative of the Executive Director of 1Love Movement, Mia-Lia Kiernan. Their trips to Cambodia included popular education workshops with some of the deportees, where they shared their stories and developed a critical analysis of how their individual narratives fit into the larger analysis of the U.S. historical involvement in Southeast Asia. Borom, one of the 1Love Cambodia organizers, remembers:

Mia-Lia and her friends narrowed down about seven or eight of us, and since she's related to one of the guys [through marriage of a relative], she had a lot of legitimacy with us. She gave us a lot of structure; we each had formal roles, like I was head of policy because I like to be behind the scenes. Wicked is the spokesperson, Sophea organizes the other deportees because she's good with people. [Mia-Lia] knew our traits and gave us our roles like that. She channeled our energies and gave all of us a lot of hope again.

For almost two years, the SEAFN 2.0 contingents traveled back and forth to Cambodia. On average, they recruited between twenty and thirty deportees to the meetings. Gradually, their communications extended to online interactions between the physical visits, and the diasporic relationships led to a transnational campaign that built consistent messaging and narratives and issued demands through the group's social media videos. The exiled Khmer Americans—physically in Cambodia and figuratively in the hyper-ghettos of the United States— forged a diasporic American refugee identity beyond borders.[210]

As with many other efforts, the transnational campaign appealed to an international governing body to address the concerns of what it considered to be a basic human right of mobility. That strategy seems perfectly logical for historically marginalized people who feel they have no influence with their own governments and that those governments are in fact the perpetrators of violence. Scholars have also questioned the ways in which activists depend on legal systems to justify human rights, given those same governments have been used historically and contemporarily to uphold colonial and neo-colonial domination.[211] Samera Esmeir uses what she calls "juridical humanity" to build on Hannah Arendt's concept of "juridical personhood"—rights conferred at birth to every human. Arendt suggests that to remove those given-by-birth rights is dehumanize the person such that it justifies the total domination of the individual as "non-human." Esmeir argues that juridical humanity is the product of that collapse of the human into the juridical person: "The overlap between the juridical person and the human, unlike Arendt, is not assumed here to be ontological but is articulated as a historical force, one that chained the human to the juridical and worked to foreclose other scenarios for the human."[212]

In essence, relying on a judicial system to define the inherent rights of humans is to rely on systems of hegemonic power to confer *human-ness,* and by the same token, also render a person more vulnerable to dehumanization by the very system ostensibly created to protect the embodiment of what constitutes humanity. Thus, Esmeir explains, "The inhuman emerges as having been preserved in the human. The human, in turn, materializes as the excess that remains in the law, and is therefore produced by it, after the expulsion of exploitative practices that the law declared inhuman."[213] In employing the international body of law as a strategic rallying point for their campaign, SEAFN 2.0 subversively used the arm of state power against itself. In other words, they upended an international arm of U.S. hegemonic power by employing its very moral and conceptual universal rights. They condemned both American immigration policy in the contemporary moment as well as the root causes that uprooted migrants in the first place—in this case, American militarism and intrusion into their homelands. However important the theoretical debate of legality and its problematic role in defining humanity, SEAA youth used international law "for the practice oppositional politics [that] is squarely situated both in and against these relationships of power in [their] challenge to the duplicitous forms of domination and affirmation."[214] SEAFN 2.0 understood the stakes of their campaign on families at risk of deportation. They viewed U.S. immigration admissions and enforcement policies as an extension of historical imperialist tendencies that were masked as domestic policy. The youth organizers manipulated the international stage to assume a counter-hegemonic stance that at once aligned with the democratic values their co-ethnic elders held dearly as part of their new American identity, while publicly holding the United States accountable for its failed policies at the cost of human life as its movement elders had done during the Viet Nam war.

SEAFN 2.0's ability to transform its campaign against detention and deportation from local and domestic foci to a glocal one adds to the trend of social movement emphasis in immigrant rights as technology and resources help build the transnational ties, skills, and resources between deportees, their families, and immigrant rights activists. The transformation of the movement inevitably changed the narrative framing of their campaign as well as targets and allies within the campaign. The claims to a diasporic identity had to be coalesced with the claims for rights within the United States, and the human rights approach helped them do this. They then had to reconsider their power analysis of allies and targets of reform from the perspective of international politics, to which they clearly drew from the history of progressive AAM groups that viewed the United States as an empire rather than a benevolent savior with gifts.[215] Thus, the Cambodian government became an ally in this campaign to pressure the American government to end deportations of refugees.

Inhuman Conditions of Deportation: 1Love Cambodia and DHS

Once 1Love Cambodia formed their own organizational structure, they participated in SEAFN 2.0 as leaders of the anti-deportation campaign. They met with Julie Chung, the U.S. Deputy Minister at the U.S. Embassy in Phnom Penh, and she invited a representative from the U.S. Department of Homeland Services (DHS). The deportees explained how the conditions of deportation constituted human rights violations under the Convention Against Torture (CAT) because DHS did not send medical records or medicine were not sent back with the deportees, rendering roughly ten percent of those returning at high medical risk. Moreover, deportees reported that many of the medicines they needed were not even available for sale in Cambodia. The DHS representative claimed they no longer deported people with serious mental or physical ailments. Unfortunately, their advocacy did not go beyond this exchange of information with the DHS representative at the meeting in Cambodia since DHS was unwilling to admit to any wrongdoing, citing that they just implemented the laws set in Washington, D.C. The global-local—or glocal—diasporic campaign appealed to the Cambodian government to revisit the M.O.U. that allowed for Khmer refugee removals from the United States. Mia-Lia had an aunt who worked in the Cambodian government, and SEAFN 2.0 and 1Love Cambodia members used her aunt's access to encourage government officials to form a task force that would review the M.O.U.. By summer, the SEAFN 2.0 delegation returned to Phnom Penh and secured a private, closed-door meeting with the task force, which, according to the delegation, consisted mostly of high-ranking military officers.

Prior to the meeting, SEAFN 2.0 taped a video diary submission in which members expressed their anxiety about it. The meeting was the pinnacle of what the network had been fighting for over the past fourteen years; internally, they did not envision talks moving past this point in the governmental hierarchy. According to Steven Dy, PrYSM's representative on the trip and organizing director, once inside the meeting, the Cambodian task force welcomed them, referring to the delegation as "blood" and "family." The task force spent most of the meeting quietly listening to the personal stories of deportation and the delegation's requests. Most of the meeting was conducted in Khmer, which allowed the exiled Khmer Americans in 1Love Cambodia to take a lead role as their language skills were far better than that of the network delegates.

Steven reflected, "It was so scary going into the meeting. All these military men with stripes and things all over their chests. I mean, I kept thinking they could kill us any minute if they wanted to and nothing would happen to them." His comments reverberated the common fears passed on intergenerationally from SEA refugee elders about the possible risks of political participation based on their first-hand witness of war atrocities. After sharing their stories, the delegation framed their argument against the M.O.U. They described it as a human rights violation that 1) is part of a long-standing history of human rights violations by the U.S., and 2) has a negative impact on U.S.-based Khmer families, not only because of the moral issue of family separation that traumatizes the refugee family members who fled war, but also the U.S.-born children torn from their parent. They argued that it perpetuated the financial burden on U.S.-based families who had the obligation of sending remittances to help sustain the Exiled American while they struggled at the U.S. Federal Poverty Level at home.

Consequently, the delegation asked for the task force to encourage the Cambodian government to put a moratorium on deportation by refusing to issue travel documents to those awaiting removal in the United States, and to renegotiate the M.O.U. with the United States to resemble that of Viet Nam's, whereby no one who had arrived in the United States as a refugee from the Viet Nam War would be eligible for deportation. The video diary of the delegates released after the meeting revealed a relieved and ecstatic group. As Mekong delegate, Chhaya, approved, "It could not have gone better!" However, even though the task force was empathetic to the youth organizers' cause, it made no promises beyond a commitment to continue to review the details of the M.O.U. By the presidential elections of November 2016, the Cambodian government was publicly advocating for a renegotiation of the M.O.U. with the United States. By the time Donald Trump took office, the United States began to renew visa and trade pressures with Viet Nam, Laos, and Cambodia in order to force them to accept deportees. Yet all three countries have since succumbed to the political pressure and began to receive deportees.[216]

The transnational movement built from the organizers' social networks is a profound statement on the potential of social change by local communities who have been historically marginalized and viewed as victims and in need of paternalistic charity. SEAFN 2.0 and 1Love Cambodia's attempt to help families stay in the United States confirm Asian American activist Grace Lee Boggs's assertion: "Community self-reliance and an economy rooted in human solidarity rather than amoral competition has become especially prominent in some Asian and Latin American countries.... We are creating a revolutionary alternative to counterrevolutionary and inhumane policies of the U.S. government, but we are not subversive."[217] Their fight for families to stay in the United States was an ironic testament to the structural marginalization they experienced as refugees. The decision to target their transnational, or glocal, campaign from the U.S. government to the Cambodian government represents their attempt to recognize and decenter the history of U.S. imperialism in Asia and its ongoing grasp to maintain global hegemony.

Expanding the Movement: #ReleaseMN8

In the United States, PrYSM became involved in building a national campaign for a group of SEAA in Minnesota that expanded the geography across movements, nationally, and transnationally. Members consisted of directly affected individuals and their families who were released, incarcerated, and exiled to Cambodia. Members of the families also were members of unions, connecting them to the Asian Pacific American Labor Alliance (APALA) and the labor movement. Some identified as multiracial, thus broadening the critical mass of the movement and the external resources, attention, and support network for SEAFN 2.0.

In October 2016, the United States issued deportation orders for thirty-four men and Cambodia issued travel documents for them to enter Cambodia while simultaneously requesting a U.S.-Cambodian commission to engage in bilateral talks with the U.S. to revise the M.O.U. by the end of the year. After those thirty-four cases, Cambodia declared a moratorium on issuing any further travel documents until the M.O.U. was amended. While negotiations about the U.S.-Cambodian M.O.U. were debated, two disparate situations emerged. Almost half of the deportees lived in Lowell, MA, which has the second largest Cambodian American population in the country behind Long Beach, CA. Some of the directly affected families in Lowell tried to garner support for the campaign against deportation by organizing informational town hall meetings at a local MAA, Cambodian Mutual Assistance Association (CMAA), along with a former attorney who worked with SEARAC. PrYSM leaders frequently traveled to Lowell to support their efforts but SEAFN's national involvement gradually dissipated to supporting only those families facing the deportation of a loved one, rather than organizing a collective response. The Lowell contingent did not have the needed infrastructural stability of staff and financial resources or the social networks within the community or from its leaders to build a campaign of any meaningful response to the deportations.

In contrast, the #ReleaseMN8, a local campaign in Minnesota, burst onto the national stage. Within the group of thirty-four people slated for deportation, eight of them were men from the Twin Cities in Minnesota. They had the support of the community in a way that the Lowell families had not, as they were active contributors and participants in both the SEAA communities and other intersectional spaces. Knowledge about their case became well known enough that they were called the Minnesota Eight, or MN8. With union members amongst the families, and the support of experienced local SEAA organizers, these families built a successful online campaign, #ReleaseMN8. Even with the network of SEAFN 2.0 to advocate nationally and pool resources, the local infrastructure of progressive activists connected to broader movements in government, AAM, and the labor movement made a definitive difference in the #MN8 compared to Family Unity in Lowell.

In the end, five of the MN8 were deported over the first half of 2017, but with legal advocacy from the James Bringer Center for New Americans at the University of Minnesota and the National Lawyers Guild, two were released under supervision by August 2017. The remaining member, Chamroeun Phan, remained in detention much longer. Chamroeun was a young father, and, like many others facing deportation, was born in a refugee camp in Thailand in the 1980s. His only conviction in 2009 had been from an altercation—Chamroeun caused $1000 worth of damage at a bar he frequented, leading to a one-year conviction. Chamroeun's case and the #MN8 movement exemplify the strategy that emerged from deportation cases since 2004, when juveniles were tried as adults and criminal cases were vacated to gain immigration relief. The immigration judge ruled he was eligible for a stay of deportation and the bar owner declined to press charges and testified on Chamroeun's behalf. Yet, his criminal record would always make him vulnerable based on the 1996 immigration rule of mandatory removal for any criminal conviction of 365 days or more. Chamroeun's sister, Montha, was active in bringing attention to her brother's case. She expressed her family's gratefulness that people all over the country and SEAFN 2.0 were able to support her brother as he stood silently with tears in his eyes: "I don't know how we could go through this without the families here to support each other, and SEAFN and lawyers to help us. Having him out and back with us is a gift from God. Now we just want to give back and help others." On more than one occasion, Chamroeun shared how he was "touched that so many people on the outside, people we didn't even know, fought for us, cared about us."

Additionally, Ched and Jenny have been central to the #MN8 campaign, including the advocacy for Chamroeun's release, by keeping the momentum of the local movement alive with their communication with families, connection to local activists, and willingness to garner national attention and support. In addition to the existing support from SEARAC and SEAFN 2.0, as active union members, they gained support from other local unions, the Twin Cities Latinx immigrant rights advocacy group Mijente, APALA, and the Asian Prisoners Support Network (APSN). After MN8 were slated for deportation, Jenny used her union organizing networks to start reaching out to different groups. The legal organizations Minnesota Immigrant

Rights and Action Committee (MIRAC) and James Bringer Center were the first to respond with legal advice for the families.

The families tried to submit stays of removal themselves, and when that failed, MIRAC asked them, "What do you want to do?" Jenny recalled, "We just looked at each other for a minute and agreed: 'Protest.'" They started to plan a series of protests in front of their senator's office, and in the process, they met other organizations that helped train them. Mijente, a Latinx group that formed out of the prison abolition group #NotOneMore, explained that they had to educate and train the politicians, many of whom were relatively new to politics and were unaware of Southeast Asian refugee history or even deportation. "If you don't say anything, they don't know," Mijente leaders cautioned. The families also learned that under the Obama Administration, there were ways to navigate the system through narrative framing and advocacy at the local ICE headquarters. Mijente and another local group, Navigate, sent field organizers to train families on creating campaigns and narratives about their families using social media.

The national civil rights organization #BlackLivesMatter (#BLM) also was involved, training the families and SEAA community about how to organize a rally, and instructing them as to what their rights were as well as direct-action tactics of marches, rallies, and sit-ins. #BLM also provided security and liaisons to the police and DHS at rallies. Jenny recalled, "We never organized a rally before, and it was so empowering to see the #BLM organizers standing up to the police. They tried to tell us we had to stand here and we couldn't do that, and the #BLM people just walked up and said we have a right to be here." According to Ched and Jenny, SEAFN 2.0, including PrYSM, SEARAC, and the National Immigration Lawyers Guild built a national presence by heavily utilizing social media and connecting the families to local and national reporters. As a trainer from the group Media Alliance told them, "An action didn't happen if it's not in the media." For post-Millennial activists, social media attention was critical to a successful campaign, and they were much more astute with these resources to reframe the narrative than previous generations of activists. Jenny agreed: "With social media and with the media training, we feel we are the ones in control. We have power in our stories and we now know our rights with reporters—that we can schedule interviews on our own time, we can get their questions ahead of time, and we can review the stories before they go out."

Figure 5.3: Anti-deportation meeting flier, 2015 (Courtesy of PrYSM Archives)

Counter Frames of ICE: Reclaiming Community Narratives of Detainment

Like PrYSM and SEAFN before them, SEAFN 2.0 and #ReleaseMN8 framed the stories by first mapping the narrative of ICE, and then creating counter frames to respond to ICE. For example, when DHS issued statements about undocumented immigrants being criminals, the activists reframed that narrative by posting stories and photos of the men with their families. Ched pointed out the importance of convincing his mother and her peers to join the campaign: "They felt helpless, and they're scared things would get worse if they speak up. It was heartwarming to come out [of detention] and see the families come together." Ched's sentiment reflects how the prison system isolates those incarcerated from their communities, and the effective response to that kind of oppression.

Social control through isolation in the institutions of mass incarceration has extended to the incarceration of immigrant detainees, who are often integrated into the general prison population. Tanya Golash-Boza defines immigration detention as an all-encompassing entity:

Despite the centrality of due process and habeas corpus protections to legal frameworks in the US, the current system of immigration detention violates these procedural protections in three critical ways: 1) Detainees bear the burden of proof; 2) the state can deny bond hearings; and 3) the judge and jailer are sometimes the same. DHS justifies the detention of noncitizens as a measure necessary to ensure they appear at immigration trials and leave the country when ordered to do so.

Under US law, immigration detention is not considered incarceration. Erving Goffman (1961) described prisons as 'total institutions' insofar as they have these four characteristics: 1) inmates are obliged to sleep, play, and work in one space and cannot leave; 2) inmates are required to live with other inmates, and they all have to do the same things; 3) the day's activities are tightly scheduled according to specific rules; and 4) the various aspects of prison life are supposed to fill the official aims of the institution.[218]

Golash-Boza's definition describes the detainment experiences of the MN8 as well as the majority of the 400,000 immigrants who pass through U.S. detention centers annually.[219] Members of the MN8—and many more, based on reports from many SEAA detainees and deportees over the years—witnessed a pervasive depression and helplessness that many claimed was the most grueling part of their incarceration. Detainment was a dehumanizing process. Overpopulation, being forced to sleep on cold, concrete floors, malnourishment, and being subjected to sexual abuse and racial slurs hurled by guards exacerbated detainees' feelings of despair.

Since 2002, PrYSM and other SEAFN groups tracked these conditions of detention with the coordination of the families of the incarcerated individuals. The "phone trees" amongst detainees to get messages to their families were critical to sharing information with loved ones. Family members then shared the messages with lawyers and advocates like PrYSM and MN8 in order to keep track of detainees and have information about their conditions. During their detention, the MN8 coordinated to send messages to their families based on whoever had access to a phone first. Knowing that families and communities were fighting for them on the outside, the eight men collectively decided to organize the other SEAA in their detention center. According to Ched, they did so in a variety of ways, from connecting the men to legal organizations, giving the men guidance on how to submit paperwork to prevent their deportation, and generally trying to keep everyone optimistic by talking through possible scenarios and staying in touch with their loved ones through phone trees.

As soon as Ched filed his stay of removal request, the MN8 were transported to another detention center six states away. ICE's automated locator system, in which a computer system interacts with the family rather than an actual ICE representative, was the only way for families to find their loved ones. Additionally, the information to families and lawyers always lagged behind their actual status; the automated locator system updates only *after* individuals enter their new facility or have been removed from their current facility. The detainees would be moved or even deported by the time the system had updated. The MN8's families learned of their deportation when one of their family members happened to call the facility asking to deliver a bag of clothing, letters, and photographs—one suitcase is all that deportees are allowed to take with them—and was told the men had already been processed for removal and were in transit. The family member then used the phone tree to send this message sent throughout the MN8 men and their families, which allowed the person's family to track their whereabouts and travel to his detention facility to say good-bye and provide him with some belongings. Otherwise, ICE would not have even informed the families of their impending deportation, and they would have been deported with no belongings nor any communication with their families. This legal strategy dovetailed effectively with the political framework that connected the prison industrial complex with the immigration system and its violations against human rights.

The MN8's example above represents the psychological warfare that DHS imposes on those in its detention centers, as well as the delays and continual shifts in policy that result in confusion and constant changes to one's location and status. After his release from detention, Ched compared his sense of liminality to paralysis:

I'm not healing, I can move on and manage my days but my body and spirit won't really heal. I want to write the last chapter. We're constantly in trauma & crisis mode because we are working with other families who have someone deported or still inside. In this political climate, is there a time to heal? At first, everyone seemed really happy that I got out, but I could tell they're still hurt that others didn't [get released from detention]. Our strategy now is to focus on local governments to write individuals to at least slow the process, but it just seems like people just don't care anymore. They think we're disposable, and we want to tell them we're not. But no media story about families is changing minds under [the Trump] administration. We don't want to do anything with DHS headquarters anymore because we don't want flag our cases. There's nothing humane about waiting around to be deported by one judge with a flip of a file.

The emotional turmoil individuals like Ched have experienced has been examined in the literature on undocumented communities. Cecilia

Menjívar referred to "legal liminality" as "'grey areas' between the dichotomies of legal categories" that undocumented immigrants endure.[220] This term characterizes how childhood arrivals, facing the uncertainty of the immigration system, "must navigate between systems of educational attainment, state surveillance, and family responsibilities or expectations upon entering adulthood."[221] Liminality creates what Roberto Gonzales refers to as "arrested development" of one's transition into adulthood, as some believed their assumed trajectory into adulthood would be stymied by their legal status, thus preventing them from the full rights of adulthood.[222]

In interviews with deportees, many reacted to living in prolonged liminality in self-destructive ways. There are no government safety nets in Cambodia. One of the deportees assessed: "Every person has a different way that they deal with deportation. Seventy-five percent are struggling because you're on your own. Some people turn to the dark side; some people have kids back in the U.S. and are hurting." The one organization set up to assist them, Returnee Integration Support Center (RISC), is funded by the U.S. State Department via a USAID grant and run by Cambodian officials using a MAA social service model. Like some MAAs during refugee resettlement in the United States, however, many of the deportees claim that RISC engages in favoritism and does not always serve those in the most need. Many deportees do not seek out social services, and some developed depression and suicidal tendencies. Others reacted by spending all their money and in engaging in risky behaviors, as if they were about to enter a lifelong prison term.[223]

Borom, one of the 1Love Cambodia members, felt that the women deportees, who now make up ten percent of the over 600 deportees, tend to have more issues with depression since they often have children back in the United States. They keep to themselves and rarely interact with the rest of the deportees. Ched and Jenny exhibited their frustration about the same fears as they communicate with the five men of the MN8 who have already been deported. Tears welled up in Ched's eyes when he talked about having to contain his emotions to stay strong for his family, including his inability to protect and plan for his family. In comparison, they found the most comfort in organizing because it gave them a sense of control and had the potential to positively impact their future in that they felt more empowered.

The MN8 offer insight to the continued, systematic control of this generation's interactions with state control and their resilience in the face of increased surveillance and discrimination. Their experiences are not new to marginalized and hyper-criminalized groups but rather part of the evolution of state hegemony, according to Gilmore:

Prisons both depersonalize social control, so that it could be bureaucratically managed across time and space, and satisfied the demands of reformers who largely prevailed against boldly punishment, which nevertheless endures in the death penalty and many torturous conditions of confinement. Most of the modern history of prisons, those officially devoid of rights—indigenous and enslaved women and men, for example, or new immigrants, or married white women—rarely saw the inside of a cage, because their unfreedom was guaranteed by other means (Christianson 1998; E.B. Freedman 1996).[224]

To the extent that refugee childhood arrivals rejected the American narrative of the "gift" of their emancipation, they became threats to the state in their counter-hegemonic resistance. As such, they no longer assimilated to the model minority image as reliable, self-controlled, docile subjects of the state. Rather, they integrated themselves within the intersectional sectors of society considered the ungovernable, and threats to the status quo that constitute social movements today.

In response to the Trump presidential administration's refusal to reconvene talks to renegotiate the M.O.U., on August 10, 2017 the Cambodian government made an official statement that it would no longer issue travel documents to individuals the United States wanted to deport. The Trump administration immediately retaliated by including Cambodia on a list with three other countries—Eritrea, Guinea, and Sierra Leone—that it would no longer issue any kind of visa to enter the country. Many news media political pundits considered the administration's move as an overly aggressive reaction that offered little diplomatic opportunity. Unlike the initial M.O.U. negotiations with the George W. Bush administration, moreover, the Cambodian government had been prepared to mitigate political pressure from the United States by growing its geopolitical alliances with China in terms of economics, trade, and socio-cultural relations. In short, Cambodia had returned to its historical relationships, and in the process, decentered Western influence.

CHAPTER SIX
Freedom from Policing: Organizing During the Rising Tides of Hate and Solidarity

Courage is a state of mind, of fearlessness, of being fearless. And we can be this on a daily basis. It takes courage to step out of your skin, to step out of your role, to step out of the society's roles for you. —Marianne Schnall, interview with Luong Ung, feminist.com, July 2, 2008

During my time as a Director of a youth organization in Oakland, California, I once had a conversation with an Oakland police officer who described his job to me. He talked about how, since his first days of training, they were that if they saw two "suspicious" men, one white and one Black, walking down either side of a street, to always go after the Black man first because the research showed he was more likely to engage in criminal activity. He said this as a matter of fact of the training that officers receive throughout the country, completely oblivious to the horror of how his statement resonated as well as to my unblinking glare. He clearly believed he was protecting the interests of the "community," of which he interpreted to be the business and property owners in the predominantly BIPOC neighborhoods in which he worked. He also did not catch the irony of his next comment, in which he described his days on his "beat" as so excruciatingly slow that he and his partners would jump at the sight of a group of teenagers—whether they be Southeast Asian American, Latinx, or Black—walking down the sidewalk to stop and interrogate them. At any opportunity, they would be identified as gang members in order to justify further "actions," as he put it. This was the stark reality of what the youth I worked with endured on a daily basis. It mirrored the daily harassment, terror, and violence of BIPOC youth in parts of Providence.

Throughout my time shadowing PrYSM, the resounding issue that always stayed with them was the hyper-criminalization of BIPOC youth, including their Southeast Asian youth and families. Their bodies were marked, surveilled, controlled, and imprisoned by the institutions of policing, schooling, neighborhood, and social groups, including co-ethnic spaces and intersectional social movements. It was part of the normative, casual conversation amongst PrYSM members as well as the center of their organizing campaigns. Every youth I met had at some point been targeted by police or had relatives who had been racially profiled while going about their daily lives. After three generations of activists over fifteen years, the issues remained, but something felt different in 2016. A critical mass of new youth activists were unapologetic and uncompromising in the pursuit of justice and freedom from the hyper-criminalization that targeted them for the prison pipeline. It was up to the rest of the movement, and the nonprofit industrial complex, to follow their lead.

The Providence Community Safety Act Campaign

For years, the Community Safety Act (CSA) campaign had been in preliminary discussions in various iterations amongst leaders in communities of color throughout Providence. In 2014, it began to take shape as a coalition of long-time allies, with strong leadership from Shannah, a lawyer working for PrYSM, Steven, a staff member, and youth leaders Linda and Daniel, who attended coalitional meetings on behalf of PrYSM. Those four people were instrumental in working within the Step Up Network coalition of local organizations to create the language of the CSA. Its critical elements included persistent racial profiling and the behaviors of police in interactions with the public, the rights of individuals when interacting with the police, the surveillance and collection of data, the categorizing and sharing of data with other agencies, and police accountability through an external review board that could also redistribute funds toward youth programs.[225]

This campaign marked a substantive difference in the messaging and strategy toward police accountability compared to the Millennial approach of Sarath's generation. The CSA lies in stark contrast to the post-9/11 period from which PrYSM was founded, where reforms to the police system came from the federal government that increased criminalization by bartering much-needed funds to organizations and schools in exchange for access to information about community members. The coalition's proactive campaign resulted from the longstanding community accusations of misbehavior by the Providence police department, fueled in part by the increasing animosity between police and BIPOC communities that had sparked the #BlackLivesMatter (#BLM) movement. While the Millennial activists acted in piecemeal, reactionary ways that tried to contain policing policies, post-Millennial activists who are coming of age during #BLM demonstrate greater willingness to take risks and demand more as rights rather than "asks" to the government. They initially focused on police harassment during routine public interactions, such as traffic stops. The coalition documented anecdotal evidence of patterns of police behavior. They claimed the police pulled over drivers and stopped people who fit discriminatory demographic profiles to intimidate and question them.

Their first category of demands included a prohibition on racial profiling, establishment of policies for video recording by police, the right to privacy from surveillance for youth and immigrants, and the right to know if one has been added to their gang database and to dispute it, and the prohibition of local law enforcement to act as ICE enforcers. At that time, the coalition believed police practices were a form of state harassment that sent an implicit message that poor BIPOC did not have a right to be in their neighborhoods. They argued that stops regularly escalated into intimidation, coercion, or physically dangerous behavior on the part of officers.

The coalition's second category of demands recognized the increased use of technology to systematically criminalize people living within hyper-policed neighborhoods. These forms of surveillance have included unwarranted tracking of social media of individuals and groups as well as the often arbitrary and false labeling of youth of color as gang members in order to potentially increase future sentences and surveillance. As a response to the surveillance that began in the post- 9/11 period, the coalition recognized the increased pressure and incentives for collaboration between local law enforcement and other agencies, particularly ICE.[226] Hence, the surveillance and database of immigrants and youth of color had a profound impact beyond local and national borders and put them and their families at risk for enhanced criminalization and deportation. In addition to the coalition's attempt to counter the expansive power of local enforcement, they viewed the CSA as a potential model for the nation in their demands to have language access hotlines, the right to videotape by witnesses, and create accountability reports and community external review board to evaluate and have input on the police budget.

The provisions put forth by the coalition represent an attempt to introduce counter-hegemonic actions that re-insert the power of the people over state-supported enforcers of injustice toward vulnerable populations. They force the police to be accountable to immigrant communities rather than making it incumbent on immigrants to speak the language of the state. They surveil the state instead of allowing the state to be in control of data gathering and information sharing. Finally, they wanted an accountability checks and balances through the review board, which had been largely symbolic in other cities. They sought to switch the power dynamics with the police department through resource allocation. This set of demands raised the stakes of the conversation around police accountability to more than just a reaction to state violence—they introduced a dialogue to fundamentally shift power and control of the police into the public domain.

Over the next three years, the CSA coalition met continually, coordinated marches and protests, and attended city council meetings. With the campaign, PrYSM youth leaders found a concrete goal on which to focus, and the organizing committee once again became the PrYSM's strongest arm. Unlike the SEAFN coalition's transnational anti-deportation campaign discussed in Chapter Five, the CSA felt within their reach as a relatively more winnable campaign. As Steven said, "Because it's local, it feels more like we have the power to win this." Just as the national political landscape had started to feel overwhelmingly oppressive to many of the youth in PrYSM, the shift to local politics gave them the sense of control and confidence they needed to assume major responsibilities within the organization.

The rise of more vocal and public white supremacist political groups during and after the 2016 presidential elections also pressured politicians to clearly articulate their positions on racially charged issues, such as police brutality. It offered a window of opportunity for which the CSA campaign had been waiting since they began organizing on the issue of police brutality in 2014. That organizing led to the formation of the Step Up Network consisting of Providence-based groups PrYSM, Direct Action for Rights and Equality (DARE), the Rhode Island American Friends Service Committee (AFSC), and Olneyville Neighborhood Association (ONA). In the fall of 2016, the coalition decided it was time to accelerate the movement and made a concerted effort to have individual meetings with local elected officials and to lead public events and demonstrations to advocate for the passage of the CSA in the Fall 2016 legislative session.

For these protests, City Council hearings, and public events, PrYSM brought its youth, including Linda, who also served as one of the leaders for the women's group. Between 2014 and 2016, the coalition continued to have meetings, develop its organizational members, and organize events during legislative sessions. According to Steven Dy, PrYSM's organizing director at the time, "It didn't feel like we were getting anywhere sometimes, like it would never pass. We had no choice. We had to keep going." They had been told in so many ways, over and again, that their voices could never outweigh the power of law enforcement. Their success, however, was not only marked by the extent to which their demands would be met. The campaign emboldened the emerging youth members to take ownership of PrYSM, and they began to represent the organization's vision of intersectional coalition-building across race, gender, sexuality, and class. Just as the deportation issue had galvanized the Millennial generation of SEAA youth into action across racial barriers, hyper-criminalization and state violence enacted by local law enforcement radicalized the post-Millennial SEAA youth. While their journey to build those inter-racial alliances may have been different, their political training and the work of deportation helped them carry on their vision of cross-sectional social justice movements from the 1960s to the present.[227]

At the September 14, 2016, City Council hearing, Steven testified about a childhood experience of police abuse of power. When he was a teenager, he and a few of his friends met up after school and got onto a bus to go to one youth's house to hang out. On the way, they noticed a Black SUV following them and wondered if it was a police car. They reached one boy's home, and soon thereafter, a policeman knocked on the door demanding that they open it. Steven and his friends refused to open the door without an adult present. Instead, they called the boy's mother. When she arrived, the policeman claimed that her son had been seen hanging out with gang members. Steven thought, "Was he talking about us? Were we 'gang members'?!" Although the mother disagreed, she felt pressured out of fear of the police to make all the friends disband. Through this intimidating and hostile encounter with the police officer, the state apparatus had undermined the family unit by taking away the mother's power to protect her child, psychologically embedding a frame of helplessness for both the parent and children.

As soon as the boys walked outside, three other officers appeared from the SUV and ordered, "No one is leaving. Line up against the wall. We are taking your picture." When Steven refused to have his photo taken, one officer threatened to arrest the friend standing next to him. Steven relented. The officer then informed him and his friends that they were going to be entered into the city's gang database, and that "You are all guilty of 'association.'" Steven testified:

I felt trapped…. I wasn't in a gang, and even though I knew what he was doing was wrong, I couldn't do anything about it. That night, I understood the power of the state. I left feeling helpless. Now, I'm a gang member and I was wanted by the police. We were being divided. We were losing a war we never even knew we were in. Today, we have a chance to reclaim some justice.

In his testimony, Steven concretized the daily harassment and criminalization of youth of color. The context of his testimony, within the campaign for the CSA, centralized the role of the state apparatus in criminalizing youth rather than displacing the causes onto the youth or their families. Kwon offers poignant insights on this kind of truth-telling: "In calling the state on its failure to meet its obligation to its young people and on its reframing of youth crime as a social problem to be solved outside of the criminal justice system or prison-industrial complex, young people revealed how the state had withdrawn from its responsibilities."[228] The physical presence of the youth at the CSA hearings intervened in the normalcy of institutions of power to question ways in which power functions when confronted with the realities of its abuses.

After the elections in 2016, the CSA gained a new level of traction with increased commitment to solidarity amongst progressive movements at the fear of increased state impunity through decreased oversight and regulation under the Trump administration. By Spring 2017, the CSA had come as close as it ever had to passage, making it out of committee and onto the council floor. It was only two votes shy of the ten votes needed for a veto-free passage. At the April 1 City Council meeting, more than 300 community members, including PrYSM families and youth, filled Providence City Hall, and the CSA was passed in its first round of approval, with permission to form a CSA working group, which included PrYSM's full-time staff lawyer as the community representative. The vote was touted as a huge victory for the campaign, and members felt a renewed sense of momentum. But they suffered another setback. After pressure from the Fraternal Order of the Police, Providence chapter, the City Council decided to delay the CSA vote and took it off the next meeting's agenda, without any promise of rescheduling the vote. After continued activism on the streets and through the City's working group that included Linda, as the only Khmer American and only local youth, the CSA finally passed on June 1, 2017. It was a tremendous victory for the community and for the post-Millennial PrYSM youth who were now taking the reins of the organization. This victory marked a moment in which PrYSM essentially came full-circle from its origins of fighting against racial profiling and the gang database. It also symbolizes the ongoing struggle for youth to determine for themselves the landscape of freedom, rather than have it contained by the policing of their bodies, creativity, and behaviors at the sites of surveillance, activism, and philanthropy.

Continual Challenges of Intersectionality

The maelstrom of events following a tragic mass-shooting included a turning point for PrYSM. On June 12, 2016, Omar Marteen went into Pulse nightclub in Orlando, Florida, and shot and killed forty-nine people and injured fifty-three more during the club's popular "Latin Nite." Most of the victims were gay and Latinx, and some were undocumented. It horrified the nation, and in many ways, paralyzed LGBTQ+ communities across the country into a state of heightened vulnerability, who were at the time, preparing their annual local Pride celebrations. In the midst of the national vigils for the victims of the targeted attack, PrYSM found itself embroiled in local controversy that epitomized the ongoing challenges it had with intersectional organizing. The Providence, Rhode Island (RI) Pride organizers worked closely with both the mayor's office and the Providence police to increase security at its parade and accompanying events. The same coordinating committee had nominated PrYSM to lead the parade that year. PrYSM was dismayed that the committee, consisting mostly of middle-class whites, would consider working so closely with law enforcement without consulting LGBTQ+ BIPOC. Members of PrYSM agreed that RI Pride's unilateral decision to increase police presence was an affront to PrYSM's fundamental values. The decision represented a disregard for the experiences of BIPOC with the police and was a contradiction to PrYSM's past work against hyper-policing.

The proposed collaboration with law enforcement came right in the middle of the Community Safety Act (CSA) campaign. It contradicted the campaign's demands for police accountability and protection against police abuse of BIPOC, immigrants, LGBTQ+ people, and Muslims. Charlie and Helen, PrYSM's Queer Thursday (QT) program interns, read a statement that PrYSM staff wrote on behalf of the organization at the next RI Pride planning meeting:

> This year, Rhode Island Pride has named PrYSM "Honorary Marshals" for the 40th RI Pride Parade. In addition, RI Pride representatives, in conjunction with Mayor Elorza, supports the over-policing and increased surveillance of RI Pride. According to Options Magazine, RI Pride representatives met on Monday, June 13th, with Providence Police, Rhode Island State Police, the Providence Emergency Management Association, and local business owners, "to review [their] safety plan and coordinate [their] efforts and communication," after the Orlando mass anti-LGBTQ shooting. As a result of RI Pride and Mayor Elorza's blatant disregard of the trauma, histories, and experiences of LGBTQ people of color with state violence, PrYSM rejects the position of Honorary Marshal. PrYSM rejects RI Pride's tokenizing of communities of color. PrYSM rejects RI Pride.
>
> In response to a tragedy where predominantly Latinx and other people of color were murdered, Rhode Island Pride defaulted to encouraging the police and other institutions that perpetuate violence against LGBTQ people of color to violate our communities. It is telling that RI Pride chose to work with local businesses and representatives of State Violence before communicating with the local and grassroots organizations that work to defend marginalized communities every day, and that RI Pride uses for its diversity shots in Pride propaganda.

After they issued the statement, PrYSM immediately received disparaging emails and messages from the LGBTQ+ community on social media.

In response, critics within the LGBTQ+ movement claimed it was a divisive message that could splinter the local LGBTQ+ community at a time when Pride celebrations were meant to create solidarity and cohesion. Sarath expressed his frustration at the lack of empathy and solidarity shown by some white allies: "There [were] racist attitudes in their fear of racism, and then they couldn't even understand how using the police would make BIPOC feel, especially with the police violence with #BlackLivesMatter right now." The PrYSM members and staff felt that as queer youth of color, they were being relegated to a minority within a minority, or an experience of dual domination.[229] They were being figuratively and literally pulled off the stage with the mic in their hands.

Frictions within the LGBTQ+ movement are not new, as Hanhardt documented in the study of the gentrification of New York and Los Angeles by middle-class, predominately white LGBTQ+ community members who moved into low-income neighborhoods of BIPOC. The continual dominance of middle-class white agendas in the LGBTQ+ movement led to ongoing fissures throughout its history as various leaders disregarded LGBTQ+ poor and/or BIPOC in both intellectual and activist spaces.[230] In Providence, the concerns about increased police protection at the expense of refugees and immigrants, Muslims, and BIPOC went unheeded as the perceived safety of the dominant LGBTQ+ community through police protection took precedence over the actual safety concerns of state surveillance and criminalization.[231] PrYSM's intervention in the Pride conversation exemplifies the ongoing issues of how to celebrate intersectionality in the social justice community. The reality of the ways in which it materializes in movement activities, however, must still be contested and negotiated.[232]

Figure 6.1. Former youth members representing PrYSM at Pride, 2016 (Courtesy of PrYSM Archives).

Hate Strikes Home: The Fine Line Between Safety and Security

Between late in the evening of December 11 and early in the morning of December 12, 2016, PrYSM staff entered their program office to find it in eerie and odd disarray. Although the door was closed and locked, someone had clearly entered the office. Perhaps they crawled through the second-floor window of the PrYSM office? Nothing was stolen, and items were not strewn across the room. Someone had taken everyday office items from the desks and drawers and placed them carefully on top of each other, in pyramid-like constructions. Furniture was moved but not damaged. All of the drawers were opened. Above the central meeting table in the office, a noose made of nylon rope hung from the ceiling and knives were stabbed into the table. The historical symbolism of the noose was a clear message that this was a racial and political act, not a random disturbance or attempted burglary.

PrYSM understood that the break-in was not only an expression of hate but also an assertion of domination and power. The staff interpreted the intrusion as a message that youth of color in Providence would not be able to transgress the social boundaries of race, class, sexuality, and immigration status without dire consequences. They felt the intruders wanted the youth to know that they had the power to violate the PrYSM space at will, rendering it unsafe for vulnerable youth. As scholars Mogul, Ritchie, and Whitlock explain:

> The terms bias or hate crime suggest that such violence is motivated entirely by prejudice (presumably irrational) and not informed by historical patterns of dominance and subordination that produce tangible political, social, and economic benefits for the majority groups. Regardless of the terminology used or its targets, there is no question that such violence is abhorrent, structural, and pervasive.[233]

The noose, one of the most violent symbols of white supremacy and masculinized domination against Black lives, communicated to the PrYSM youth that they were seen as racial others and could be intimately physically harmed. The break-in sent a message of power, domination, and the threat of mental and physical violence.

The local social justice community expressed deep concern for the safety of PrYSM members and staff. There were differing opinions on how to ensure such violations did not happen again. Many allies believed in the need to fortify the office with surveillance cameras, alarm systems, security guards, or some emergency response system to alert the police. This was a painful decision for PrYSM youth given their histories with police surveillance and harassment. As one staff person pointed out, "How do we ask the state to intervene in our safety when so often the state is the perpetrator of violence toward us?" Their precarious situation concretized the reality of how their intersectional identities as working-class, refugee, largely queer, youth of color determined the boundaries of their ability to interact with state protective agencies.

In this moment of vulnerability, PrYSM intentionally acted in accordance with their organizational values of peace, love, and justice. After serious reflection and collective discussion among the staff and youth, PrYSM decided to further commit to its core values and did not resort to policing measures. In lieu of surveillance methods, they initiated their own methods of security, such as using group buddy systems whereby no one would be alone in the office, and they registered the break-in with the Southern Poverty Law Center's hate crimes database. They disseminated a statement that introduced PrYSM and explained what had transpired. It then reiterated its commitment to its own core values:

> Ultimately, these tensions reflect broader issues that underlie our campaign for the Community Safety Act (CSA) and the Community Defense Project (CDP). To this end, we hope that this attack will not be seen as an isolated incident, but one which continues to implicate long-standing concerns regarding systemic injustice, racism, safety and policing in our communities.... Calling the police was never an option we considered. PrYSM is inspired by a dedication to decreasing state violence. Rather than engage local law enforcement, who pose a consistent threat to our safety and dignity, as they patrol and surveille our community, we hope to engage community models of safety, based on transformative justice, so that we can start imagining abolition of prison and policing as reality.[234]

To the PrYSM family, the very impetus of the group's foundation was to fight hyper-policing and hyper-criminalization. The thought of using the legal system and technologies of oppression, even in such dire circumstances, felt morally opposed to everything they, and the communities they represented, had fought to reform. It made sense to "call into question and challenge the multiple and interlocking systems of equality that remain, even as formal forms of discrimination begin to fall."[235] They felt alternative protection measures were completely aligned with the way that many people in their co-ethnic and geographical communities would have responded. The notion that the state entities who oppressed or targeted them would then potentially have permission to surveil them under the auspices of protection seemed counterintuitive. With many of the youths' experiences with state profiling, they did not see technology simply as a consumer product, but rather as an extension of social control and the regulation of their bodies.[236]

Rather than close the office to regroup, PrYSM staff and youth leaders chose to open the office for youth and allies to come, process their feelings, and reclaim the space. The organization had always been unique in the ways it prioritized the emotions of one's personal and political experience, thanks in large part to the founders and the break-in highlighted the effectiveness of that approach. When they met the staff and youth tried to stay composed, but several admitted the significance of these events: "It sent chills through me to see our room like this," and "I am scared to be here by myself now." They talked about the fears staff had of being in the space after the break-in, and their desire to overcome those fears while acknowledging them as real and valid. PrYSM met fear and intimidation with love and community. By January, the fears had significantly subsided, and while they incorporated new security measures, daily programming returned to normal. PrYSM's response to the incident represented a turning point for the organization as it had reached a critical moment in its growing interest and reputation with funders. Throughout its fifteen-year history, the organization had been consistent in its radically progressive positions on social issues and its campaigns. Their collective decision to remain true to their vision to reject responding to fear with socially acceptable means of social control, such as surveillance, communicated that they refused to adjust their values to attain the approval of more powerful organizations and funders.

In the aftermath of the office invasion, a new sense of resolve had been embedded into PrYSM's political campaigns, from the ongoing support for those needing legal assistance through the CDP to the CSA and anti-deportation campaigns. PrYSM was not alone. With the unexpected presidential election results of 2016 that resulted in the resurgence of a conservative, white supremacist political agenda, there was a new awakening for the political left throughout the country, including in Rhode Island, to move urgently toward progressive demands rather than compromise with conservatives. Liberal and progressive foundations throughout the country now felt an urgency to fund more groups that train progressive organizers and who were involved in direct action and political protest.[237]

Figure 6.2. PrYSM Internal Meeting, 2016 (Courtesy of PrYSM Archives).

Shifting Winds in Philanthropic World

Between the 1990s into the early 2000s, the philanthropic trend to divide groups and activism by issues created structures of specialization and a fracturing of coalitions.[238] The Great Recession between 2007 and 2009 and increasing racial tensions during the Obama administration necessitated innovation to respond to the crises whereby funders forced organizations to consolidate.[239] Millennial progressive activists sought constructive approaches by finding solidarity in each other's causes to integrate their issue-based movements into a larger social justice agenda for equity, representation, and inclusion in social, economic, and political life. That strategy became a clarion call to funders to help build a more unified movement against the tide of hate speech and a right-wing, nativist agenda that saw almost immediate spikes in racial profiling, hate speech and hate crimes, restrictive immigration policies, and discriminatory policies within the first year of Donald Trump's presidency in 2016.[240] The trend of the earlier decade toward issue-specific funding no longer responded to the intersectional reality of the world.

The rise of public documentation via social media of the murder of black people by law enforcement officials during the Obama presidency and into the Trump administration resulted in growing tensions across the nation, manifesting in the #BlackLivesMatter movement. As backlash against #BLM, reports of white supremacist violence spiked, such as beatings and murders of BIPOC and those who identified as transgender. News reports of nooses hanging from schools, hate speech sprayed on houses, harassment of Muslim youth in schools by teachers and administrators, and racists memes of public officials on social media, were no longer unusual or spectacular but rather almost a normalized story in the 24-hour news cycle.[241]

PrYSM built alliances in support of groups organizing across issues that critiqued the historical structural, economic, political, and socio-cultural oppression of societal subpopulations PrYSM, as a part of SEAFN, PrYSM composed public statements in solidarity with #BlackLivesMatter and attended protests in: Chicago, Illinois; Ferguson, Missouri; Madison, Wisconsin; Minneapolis/St. Paul, Minnesota; New York, New York; Philadelphia, Pennsylvania; Providence, Rhode Island, and other cities. They went on those solidarity missions without seeking additional funds that would detract from the work of their black and brown allies. They built alliances in support of groups organizing across issues that critiqued the historical structural, economic, political, and socio-cultural oppression of societal subpopulations. Those expressions of coalitional, inter-racial solidarity demonstrate the potential of horizontal organizing in social movements that can build sustained transformation.[242]

By the end of 2016, many donors who had been funding liberal causes became more aligned with progressive activist groups like PrYSM and social justice movements. Philanthropists dovetailed with the call for "all hands on deck" against the ultra-conservative political wave sweeping the government in order to demand and protect the civil rights advances made since the 1960s. The organizations that emerged as the gatekeepers to regional funds overwhelmingly consisted of the groups that formed out of the Asian American Movement a generation ago and evolved into 501(c)3 non-profits. The potential power of an individual funder to set the agenda and re-organize the entire political, cultural, and social service leadership of the AAPI population speaks to the geography of power that the movement has helped construct over time. In the process of "staking claims" to social justice, moreover, we revealed its inextricable ties to the monopoly of entitlement.[243] For PrYSM, that funding structure only exacerbated the ongoing dialogue with the longstanding established Asian American organizations about being part of the decision-making and agenda-setting process and of having control of their own resources. In other words, they felt they had to perform the refugee role to appease the MAAs and downplay the tensions that arose in New Orleans from the GAR gathering in 2014. While PrYSM managed to participate in the regional meetings, the group decided that the level of patronage associated with the funding source was not a sustainable relationship. The power dynamics of the patron-client relationship—the funder held firm control of the client activities, objectives, and position—did not align with PrYSM's vision of self-determination. The limited philanthropic dollars that are allocated nationally toward AAPI causes and groups meant that the Coulter

Foundation's substantive investment in the organizational landscape of the Asian American organizations had a huge impact on how the movement would proceed for decades to come. Thus, regardless of their choice to not seek direct resources from Coulter, the funder still exerted a tremendous impact on PrYSM's national and regional campaigns. In both local politics and national responses, PrYSM soon had to make difficult choices in light of the resurgence of white supremacist rhetoric and anti-immigrant policies.

2016 Post-election Priorities

The conservative and white supremacist backlash to the #BlackLivesMatter movement escalated to a national sense of urgency in the philanthropic world. Funders believed that the Trump administration's prerogative to privatize government safety nets would be fast-tracked through the Republican-controlled government. Funding entities shifted their priorities in the "Age of Trump," and began focusing on rapid response initiatives nationwide for vulnerable populations, such as undocumented, Muslim, and LGBTQ+ people, and political organizing.[244] PrYSM initially benefitted from some of those grants as part of the coalitions protecting LGBTQ+ and immigrant populations. However, the funding shift meant resources were channeled into one-time or temporary funding streams explicitly earmarked for rapid response organizing around specific incidents such as hate crimes. Additionally, the philanthropic shift to political organizing instead of ongoing programming work led PrYSM to reflect deeply about its own priorities. It had always been a political organizing youth group, which distinguished it from most other SEAA youth groups in the United States. Naturally, they were in an ideal position to garner funding from that new wave of philanthropic investors.

Nationally, PrYSM had built a reputation as a strong model for the political conscientization of its youth and its approach to channeling that knowledge into youth-led campaigns. As it developed into a non-profit organization, the integration of programming for its LGBTQ+ youth and women's group depended on the ongoing grants of diverse funders and donors. In a somewhat drastic swing, the funding world re-prioritized the political activism it had once shunned for sustainable programs, believing they would produce the goals of governmentality—to construct successful citizen-subjects—and thereby increase civic engagement within the boundaries of upholding the status quo, as discussed in Chapter One.[245] As a result, some of the grants that PrYSM had previously relied on for ongoing programs and general operations suddenly became unreliable income streams. PrYSM had to choose whether or not to once again reframe its programs to better fit the changing priorities of its funders.

The philanthropic organizations' response was well-intended and logical in the critical moment of heightened social tensions and acts of violence toward historically oppressed communities. Had the long-term funding priorities not changed so abruptly, the rapid response strategy would have been a huge gain for many grantees. Unfortunately, the way in which the funders rolled out a new agenda for the Trump era potentially pressured organizations to choose and even re-envision themselves almost overnight if they wanted to continue with the same level of grant-based resources. The fact that monetary decisions tend to happen simultaneously across various funding entities exacerbates the situation, leaving few options for groups like PrYSM, whose main source of financial support came from independent, small foundations. Rather than completely changing its ongoing programs, PrYSM made the choice to further diversify its resources and make a bigger push to secure financial support from individual donors in the local community.

Philanthropy plays a critical role in shaping the leaders, campaigns, and power distribution among organizations to forge the future of Southeast Asian American activism. They not only provide the essential resources for sustainable campaigns and organizational development, they also have the power to level the playing field between organizations that often represent very different constituents.[246] A grantmaker's funding decisions need to incorporate the long-term development of grassroots organizations that represent social change from the ground up if they are to support fundamental shifts of power distribution. To do that effectively, the measurement tools for success in a convener model of resource distribution should include an assessment of the extent to which power brokers and gatekeepers distribute and share resources and power.

Figure 7.1: Sarath Suong at a Movement for Black Lives Rally, 2019
(Courtesy of PrYSM Archives)

The Convener Model Shapes the Landscape of Movement-Building

In March 2016, the premiere Asian American legal advocacy organization in the United States, Asian Americans Advancing Justice (AAJC), organized its bi-annual conference to discuss the major policy and legal topics facing AAPI communities. The conference seemed to have a different sense of urgency to it, and the presence of grassroots organizations that usually did not attend the event was surprising. The conference's main fiscal sponsor that year was the Wallace H. Coulter Foundation, and its President, Sue Van, would be present and conducting private meetings with potential grantees over the course of the conference, including organizations in progressive AAPI coalitions, GAR and SEAFN, which the foundation housed separately from the conference hotel site for the express purpose of hosting private meetings. The influence that the Coulter Foundation had on conference proceedings demonstrates the power of one individual to change the landscape of an entire movement. In the following years, the intentions of the convener model that the Coulter Foundation developed further entangled movement groups in the non-profit industrial complex and perpetuated the historically uneven power dynamics between AAPI organizations. The convener model identifies local or regional organizations to act as a "convener" for all other potential grantees within their geographical area, such as a state or a region of the country. The funder gives a lump sum to the convener 1) with mandates on how to distribute the money, and 2) while emphasizing the priorities of the funder. The convener has the responsibility of "convening" local or regional organizations to create a strategy to address issues on the funder's agenda, and then disburses grants to the organizations they deem appropriate.[247]

As a bit of background, Wallace H. Coulter made his fortune as a groundbreaking scientist who helped develop the field of bioengineering; he was a bioengineer before there was such a profession.[248] He and his brother started their own corporation that led him around the world, including China, where he formed deep relationships within Asia and a general fascination with the region. Upon Coulter's death in 1998, Van, then the company's long-time Chief Financial Officer who also oversaw Coulter's philanthropic foundation, began emphasizing translational biomedical research and making research accessible to the public. In 2010, the CFO began to fund initiatives in AAPI communities, based on her personal interest as a Chinese American and in alignment with Mr. Coulter's love for Asia. The Coulter Foundation entered AAPI philanthropy by providing funding for the 2010 Census outreach efforts in Asian American communities, nationally. Since then, the foundation has increasingly become involved in funding AAPI organizations based on Van's personal connection to her AAPI identity, with limited background or history of the movement or the organizational landscape, according to individuals in personal contact with her.

The information Van gathered in the individual and group meetings at the conference would decide her priorities for the coming years. She had the potential to profoundly shape the course of the organizations funded by the Coulter Foundation directly, and of AAPI movement activities more broadly. They required potential grantees to attend meetings and be available at all times to the grantor, and the foundation offered grantees substantive amounts of money to conduct campaigns based on the priorities of the grantor. They also forced coalitions and hierarchal relationships among organizations based on the convener model of funding. In essence, the foundation potentially would skew activism and organizations into problematic practices for which the non-profit industrial complex has been critiqued as labor intensive, top-down, and funder-generated causes.[249]

The workshops and other conference activities seemed to take a backseat to preparations for the meetings with the CFO. While there was much discussion in the panel sessions about working together, individuals huddled with their respective organizations or coalitions, regarded other organizations as competition for the most-concentrated funds available to AAPI organizations. This competitive marketplace essentially divided and realigned the AAPI non-profit map. Several activists stated that Van's encouragement of new collaborations and redistribution of power among the organizations made them extremely uncomfortable given her lack of knowledge or engagement with AAPI communities and the history of AAPI activism. One PrYSM member noted:

> She doesn't know the history of the movement, but because she has so much money and wants to spend it on us, she can come in and tell us who to work with and what kind of work we should be doing. She is willing to listen because I think she's aware that her knowledge is limited. So everyone is talking in her ear, and we don't know who she is listening to. It's creating all this competition between everyone, even people who are working together.

Individuals meeting with Van told me that she was holding the meetings to ascertain the needs and issues in AAPI communities across the United States, and to decide who would be the regional conveners for the new strategy she devised to distribute funds and stimulate collaboration amongst local groups. These conveners held a new gravity of power to set agendas for the region and disburse resources, thus acting as the new gatekeepers of their communities, and would be arbitrarily chosen based on Van's conversations with prospective grantees. Similar to other philanthropic initiatives, Coulter Foundation forced relationships between organizations through the interview process and reinforced the power dynamics of more established, well-funded groups who were better positioned to be the gatekeepers and sub-grantors of the Coulter funds.

The Coulter Foundation remapped the entire AAPI non-profit landscape through a process that returned to the top-down philanthropic approaches of foundations between the 1980s and 1990s: forcing relationships and propping up gatekeepers with whom a funder feels most aligned. Suddenly, the funder had the power to define major aspects of the AAPI agenda in the United States. The reason for Van's quick ascent to power within this work must be understood by examining the larger issues of philanthropic neglect within AAPI communities. In the United Sates, only one percent of philanthropic dollars went into AAPI organizations and causes. This disparity led directly to the scurry for attention when a funder such as the Coulter Foundation has the potential to offer significant and sustained funds. The opportunity would compensate for the historical omission of AAPIs by funders and reduce the bureaucracy that so many organizations spend to weave together extremely small grants that require a great deal of reporting and documentation.[250] The opportunity to take full advantage of that long-term investment naturally would be attractive to organizations, especially as a foundation on which they could think big about their future.

Philanthropic Role in Movement-Building

While harboring good intentions, foundations tend to perpetuate uneven development within communities by inadequately measuring and misunderstanding the nuanced politics of intra- and inter-ethnic groups. The convener model of funding privileged particular groups and charged them with the subcontracting or resource sharing with other groups, but without troubleshooting for biases and inherent power relations,[251] leading to an amalgamation of resources and representation at the expense of a multiplicity of voices.[252] In response, one remedy would be to include more representation in foundations that reflect the most marginalized members within a community rather than the most palatable ones to the funders' socio-economic class orientation. The intervention of community members into the funding world has the potential to fundamentally change the culture of philanthropy to increase accessibility and deepen the kind of power shifts inherent in the systemic change that progressive foundations aspire to achieve.

The trend toward place-based grant-making should be measured to see if it alleviates some of the power imbalances within ethnic-based grant-making, but it should combine rather than replace ethnic-specific approaches. Place-based grant-making has the potential to identify impacted geographical sites that may improve socio-economic mobility and encourage inter-racial cooperation. In contrast, ethnic-targeted funding increases the potential of funders to ignore class differences. That approach potentially serves more people who live outside of an ethnic enclave without giving back to it. For example, an urban church may serve an ethnic community that has a large percentage of economically stressed members, but the resources provided could mostly be accessed by those who identify with that ethnicity but are more privileged and live in the suburbs. Place-based grant-making might curb the movement of resources out of distressed communities and retain them as sources of economic stimulation for an area, thus benefiting the entire neighborhood. That said, there has yet to be adequate evaluation of that trend to measure its effectiveness. In the interim, a diverse repertoire of funding strategies should be used to support future generations of movement builders. All of these approaches must include awareness of each strategy's impact to create or perpetuate unhealthy power dynamics and must avoid privileging qualitative over quantitative growth for the many identities within any given community.

CHAPTER SEVEN
Generation Rising: Movement is Making the Future Now

Another world is not only possible, she's on the way and, on a quiet day, if you listen very carefully, you can hear her breathe. —Arundhati Roy (from "Confronting Empire" speech at World Social Forum, Porto Alegre, Brazil, January 28, 2003)

Forty-five years since the first mass exodus of SEA refugees in 1975, there remains an ongoing struggle at the sites of power and governance, especially in the courtroom and in Congress. Those spaces have been overlooked in favor of the United States' fixation with its national myth of civilizing refugees and transforming them into model citizens. The voices of refugee communities came to reflect the class hierarchies that developed in the context of resettlement, compounded by the established infrastructure that emerged with the rise of the non-profit industrial complex.[253] After 9/11, mainstream U.S. media framed SEAA urban youth within a set of dangerous discourses that has antagonized youth, immigrants, and criminals.[254] The racialist and classist stereotypes implicit in the term "urban" demonized low-income SEAA youth as a threat to the assumed innocence embedded within the reified image of the refugee victim deemed to be deserving of salvation.[255] Thus, those low-income youth had to navigate between challenging narratives that situated SEAA youth within a black-white binary and their attempts to benefit from problematic narratives about "deserving" AAPI model minority immigrant.

PrYSM, by their very existence, contributed to the history of Asian American resistance in critical ways that subverted those narratives. PrYSM helped form SEAFN, which emerged out of an organic need by community members to stand up for the rights of families facing deportation. Unlike some coalitions at the time, PrYSM was not an externally forced coalition engineered by newly important foundations.[256] PrYSM understood the power of visual images and made the choice to be independent of mainstream media and representing themselves in their authentic intersectional identities that did not conform to the Model Minority aspirations of the previous generation of refugee leaders. The group made the strategic choices in its narrative framing and cultural productions, and more importantly, the decision to prioritize the use of social media tools, "family" meals, and queer club culture to build their base as community rather than using it solely as a campaign tactic to change the minds of the public policymakers. The local and national infrastructure that PrYSM had created allowed them to develop tactics, strategies, and analyses from the perspective of urban, working-class, immigrant youth.

Unlike other national coalitions at that time, SEAFN's flexibility with its messaging and actions allowed member groups like PrYSM to participate in local actions that made sense as to where their own members and local communities stood politically. Coalitions like SEAFN became a source of support to small groups like PrYSM as well, offering emotional support for many organizers who felt isolated in their local environments. In turn, these youth organizations gained the legitimacy to challenge political leaders intent on maintaining the status quo in regard to policymaking. For those very reasons, PrYSM and youth groups like them were marginalized and seen as a threat to national organizing by the established Southeast Asian American organizational infrastructure and in multiracial or pan-Asian American coalitional spaces. Progressive funders played a critical role in re-centering the work of youth groups such as PrYSM, but with potential contradictions embedded in the patron-client relationship characteristic of the non-profit industrial complex that gave rise to what I borrow from Mimi T. Nguyen as "the gift of freedom" that SEAA youth have to navigate in social movements today.

A Generation Rising

In each chapter of *Generation Rising*, the seeds of emerging generations of the Asian American Movement have been articulated in the multiply nuanced shifts in the changing demographics of movement builders. PrYSM's cultural shift into a hybridity of SEA urban American youth identity informed by the political development of the 1960s movements for liberation. The performance of both SEA and urban American youth culture represented both a legacy of social movements of the past as well as a careful critique of those social movements since 2002. PrYSM's framing of detention and deportation is informed by the refugee experience, American imperialism, and human rights. They deployed strategies and tactics that contested the "common sense" winnable objectives of policy-based and Mutual Aid Associations (MAA) groups. Their long-term vision of change prioritized the process of political development and intersectional conscientization of members over the pressure to achieve deliverables spurred by funders.

Social movements have been dismissed as spontaneous acts of spectacle sparked by frustration toward specific conditions expressed in emotively bound reactionary, fleeting grand gestures, such as mass protests or demonstrations. This book demonstrates the politico-historical processes that developed an infrastructure for SEAA-based social movements in

Providence, and later, transnationally through glocal activism with 1Love Cambodia. The convergence of the 1960s anti-war movement and the refugee-led rebuilding of refugee resettlement through MAAs between the 1980s and 1990s became the foundation on which the youth constructed their historical argument against detention/deportation, both within the Southeast Asian refugee communities and as part of a cadre of emergent social change actors in coalitions nationwide.

PrYSM exemplifies the evolution of Asian American Pacific Islander activism in the twenty-first century. Just one generation ago, the ideology of early Asian American activism could be categorized into genres of cultural nationalism, variations of Marxism, and identity politics. In each case, the organizational activities that stemmed from within the movements were a response to the injustices of their environment—whether economic, political, cultural, or social. Early goals to recruit masses into the campaigns that they engaged in were enacted with these pre-existing assumptions about leadership. Strategies and tactics were often molded to fit the ideology of the organizations, or even a "cult of personality" of the founder(s), rather than the worldview of the people they were purportedly trying to organize.

Over time, the existing structures and hierarchical leadership models proved problematic to the building blocks of liberation: rank-and-file members' leadership development and empowerment. Youth members and their transition to leadership in this study represent a new generation of movement actors who enter social movements 1) out of the historical legacy of activism that had aimed to mentor and recruit young SEAA activists, and 2) to pivot away from the 1960's dominant ideologies of revolution that used the Viet Nam war as an anti-imperialist backdrop to negotiate the reality of their co-ethnic refugee communities in the United States. This organic development of a millennial SEAA philosophy toward social movement re-centers what had been the margin of the movement to allow a "third space" of liberating frames and social movement to come to fruition in rejection of a patron-client model that has permeated the nonprofit industrial complex. Consequently, the funding for Asian American Pacific Islander activist groups in the twenty-first century must reflect new generations, while taking heed of the lessons learned from previous decades of funding progressive causes.

PrYSM's emerging SEAA leaders have emphasized process over outcome in the mobilization against detention and deportation, the campaign against local police surveillance and harassment, and youth programming. They attempted to re-conceptualize existing ideologies in practice by challenging themselves and their allies to prioritize accomplishing broader visions for social change within their daily activities and social relations. With the American war in their homelands and subsequent failed socialist projects as their points of reference, the generations of activists since 2002 have molded a vision for the future based on the complex matrix of imperialist and Marxist pasts, and the intersecting identities of class, citizenship, gender, and sexuality within the space of Asian America. In the end, their value system won over the quick campaign wins or funder-driven initiatives that fell hopelessly short of the needs or culture of PrYSM youth. Understanding the particular path from war to resettlement proved critical to framing the argument against detention and deportation and served as a starting point for all of their other work. They attempted to reclaim SEA refugee history, from the neo-liberal narratives to which their parents' generation had assimilated and from the radical Marxism of many of their movement mentors. Their reframed narrative contributed to their ability to weave through the interstitial spaces of SEA refugeeism and Asian American activism in such a way that they performed the rituals of indebtedness to the older generation while simultaneously challenging that generation in their re-imagination of their past and present conditions.

In the aftermath of mass forced migration from war, political persecution, and starvation, the myth of linear assimilation still perpetuates in false narratives of SEA refugee resettlement such that the refugee, not the government, carries the burden of proving they are worthy of "salvation." In fact, the overwhelming evidence of American interventionist practices and policies that precipitated the push and pull forces of immigration to the United States begged the question of American accountability toward refugees in resettlement, given the country's failure to secure Congressional funding to rebuild those countries after peace accords were signed in 1973. The resettlement policy of dispersal and the withering assistance available to each subsequent refugee cohort revealed the threshold of compassion fatigue during the Reagan presidential administration. Resistance to federal attempts at fast-track assimilation proved futile through secondary and tertiary migration patterns, resulting in ethnic enclaves. These enclaves created necessary foundational institutions that have provided political, social, and economic opportunities unavailable in mainstream society; they became the bedrock of political leadership. Ironically, the socio-economic geography of those sites tended to locate the younger generation within the concentric circles of the lived urban experience. Emerging grassroots leadership in SEAA communities thus found themselves in the position to syncretize their demands with the trajectory of the movements in which they participated—in cross-sectional coalitions as well as within their own ethnic and racial identities—because of their shared cultural experiences as urban youth.

The mass mobilizations led by those new generations of leaders marked a legacy of growth from the 1960s and a critical engagement of that historical period through the lens of "refugee children." The MAAs formed to support refugee resettlement are facing a crisis of relevance in their ability to attract 1.5-, second-, and now even third-generation SEAA youth. The MAAs assumed the issues facing the youth could be addressed through cultural preservation and academic tutoring programs that promoted stagnant cultural preservation and assimilationist socio-economic integration as strategies for success. While both types of programs provided services for youth, they failed to affect more transformative change, such as encouraging youth leadership through agenda-setting and decision-making processes that offered a social justice analysis to their circumstances. Moreover, many MAAs ostracized those problematic individuals in the community who did not maintain the image of the model Asian "guest," including many working-class youth whose families came in later refugee cohorts. These programs perpetuated the cycle of placing the burden of success and accomplishment on individuals and families by using monetary and material measurements of success without a critique of systemic barriers and state oppression.

Throughout the 1990s, the youth who grew up in the United States developed a complex identity that embraced their ethnic identities while rejecting the community they felt had rejected them. By the end of the decade, the critical mass of at-risk youth and SEAA gangs—in the face of adverse institutional, economic, and educational neglect and hyper-criminalization—necessitated that youth organizations be established with the mentorship of the older social movement leaders. From these external support networks in Asian American and inter-racial spaces, organic youth leadership emerged such that their bicultural perspectives, values, and programming addressed the issues faced by many youth of color: gang violence, racial profiling, poverty, education, incarceration, sex education, LGBTQ+ identity, and more. The crisis of the deportation issue prompted the few Southeast Asian youth-led groups in the country to assume a central role in shaping the response to the crisis, and for the first time, be the public voices of their own narratives.

The activists in this book rebuked assumptions that they needed outside resources to secure the effective maturation of social movements for oppressed communities. Such thinking presupposes nonexistent networks or limited power within existing networks in movement building. Local PrYSM and national SEAFN campaigns necessitated internal resources that included information gathering and sharing among informal social networks of prisoners, former prisoners, their families, and grassroots youth groups, such as PrYSM, that knowledge of the processes and patterns of detention and deportation could be coalesced in order to develop a strategy to protest detention and deportation. PrYSM's work illustrates the necessity of community-generated campaigns that are focused on building the power of local, directly affected communities. It is undeniable that grassroots organizations took the information gathered from families and transformed it into clear articulations of the issues, needs, and demands for immigration reform.

The tendency of funders to view empowerment and social change with hierarchal visions for change must shift. Such views delineate the targets of change as the communities rather than the structures that oppress them and constrain the receiving community within a discourse of victimology, from which they cannot liberate themselves or achieve liberation without external resources. This approach leads to the distribution of resources creating a cyclical mapping of knowledge production and power accumulation. The informal social networks of concentric relationships between family, prison, gangs, and friends, emerged as invaluable social capital for individuals to get the support they needed to fight their deportation. Those organic networks accessed the few resources available and willing to assist them—local, youth-based co-ethnic organizations. While the organizations existed on the margins of the various institutionalized networks formed by the generation of MAA leaders, they became a cornerstone for coalitional formations post-9/11. Grassroots youth groups such as PrYSM created their own multi-pronged approach to address the needs of their memberships.

Yet, PrYSM simultaneously found their legitimacy through two channels outside of traditional nonprofits: directly affected community members and largely East Asian American groups. They developed campaigns based on resource mobilization of organic knowledge within the community, as well as learned campaign, media, policy-making, and fundraising skills outside of the main pillars of the SEAA infrastructure. The mentors and leadership organizations within the larger multi-racial movements and the immigrant rights movement played critical roles in validating PrYSM's work and other SEAA youth organizers in ways that the MAAs were much more hesitant to do. These allies gave the SEAA youth groups the opportunity to spark the interest of potential national funders and set in motion more progressive demands regarding the issue of detention and deportation. As funders became attentive to media stories that reframed deportation and criminalization, national immigrant rights, policy, and legal organizations also offered increasing support in resources, legal assistance, and policy advocacy and media blasts through list serves and social media. Regardless of the symbiotic relationships cultivated over the years, though, the transference of influence and power to the youth from the "margins to the mainstream" has remained contested and continually negotiated.

Previous chapters in *Generation Rising* illuminate the political process of social movements, the interplay of external and internal relationships beyond a community's engagement with the state and its institutions. The infrapolitics of personal relationships in the form of communal identities facilitated the funding opportunities, strategies, and tactics of the groups in SEAFN. The network engaged both the MAAs and the policy and legal organizations to achieve its holistic goals of redefining the issues and power relations among the different sets of groups. Further analysis explained the dialectical triangulation that has the potential to produce a new movement landscape. The confluence of the internal needs of the changing refugee communities with the upsurge in movement activity post-9/11 created the precise tilting of power that PrYSM and allied SEAA youth organizations were able to leverage to situate themselves as influential voices in the immigrant rights movement and within their own ethnic communities. Whether the sustainability of the movement's efforts to build extends beyond those auspicious moments has yet to be seen.

PrYSM's emphasis on process over immediate reform allowed them to build sustainable infrastructure and community relevance, but not necessarily impact federal policy. The question of who sits at the table for consequential decision-making conversations will most likely persist among stakeholders, including those embedded in the nonprofit industrial complex, such as national policy organizations. While PrYSM was able to monopolize on the power gained through their anti-deportation campaigns, there remained a danger in whether they would be pressured to forsake some of their values to remain stakeholders in broader policy-making initiatives. PrYSM and other historically marginalized groups' demands to participate in policy- making on their own terms cannot be ignored, and the emerging grassroots activists have refused to simply be the storytellers without self-determination. This stand against the tokenization or manipulation of their narratives—of their life experiences—are seeds of change that shift the levers of power. PrYSM's campaigns and programs demonstrated an independent path of cultural production and value systems that both incorporated and rejected various aspects of their co-ethnic and social movement elders. Their strength to adhere to their beliefs regardless of pressure from their co-ethnic and AAM elders prepared the youth organizers to negotiate with funders about their political activities and strategic and tactical choices. Their identity formation played an instrumental role in their repertoire of political acts and positions. Their intersectional collectivity paved the way for them to engage in broader visions for social change beyond singular causes.

PrYSM still has room for much growth, but its leaders have helped to set a standard for a new generation of AAPI organizers. They continue to fight against internalized oppressive behaviors that are normalized within social institutions. In many ways, they have overcome barriers in ideology, ethnicity, and other intersectional tensions to pave a new path of social activism that can no longer be defined through a singular trajectory. PrYSM sheds light on the possibilities ahead for future generations of Asian American Movement organizers who dare to dream. In carving out the "liberated zones" of creativity in which to thrive personally and organizationally, they embody what historian Robin D.G. Kelley sees as "... the time to think like poets, to envision and make visible a new society, a peaceful, cooperative, loving world without poverty and oppression, limited only by our imagination."[257]

Works Cited

Abrego, Leisy J. "Legal Consciousness of Undocumented Latinos: Fear and Stigma as Barriers to Claims-Making for First- and 1.5-Generation Immigrants." Law and Society Review 45, no. 2 (2011): 337–369.

Adams, Tony E., Stacy Holman Jones, and Carolyn Ellis. *Autoethnography: Understanding Qualitative Research.* New York: Oxford University Press, 2014.

Aguilar-San Juan, Karin. *Little Saigon: Staying Vietnamese in America.* Minneapolis: University of Minnesota Press, 2009.

Alba, Richard D., and Victor Nee. *Remaking the American Mainstream: Assimilation and Contemporary Immigration.* Cambridge: Harvard University Press, 2003.

Alexander, Michelle. *The New Jim Crow: Mass Incarceration in the Age of Colorblindness.* New York: The New Press, 2010.

Ali, Anida, and Masahiro Sugano. "Studio Revolt: A collaborative media lab producing motion imagery + performance projects." Accessed January 31, 2019. www.studio-revolt.com.

Ameeriar, Lalaie. "The Gendered Suspect: Women at the Canada-U.S. Border After 9/11." *Journal of Asian American Studies* 152, no. 2 (2012): 171–195.

Ancheta, Angelo N. *Race, Rights, and the Asian American Experience.* New Brunswick: Rutgers University Press, 2000.

Anderson, Benedict R. *Imagined Communities: Reflections on the Origin and Spread of Nationalism.* London: Verso Books, 2006.

Andrews, Kenneth T., and Bob Edwards. "Advocacy Organizations in the U.S. Political Process." *Annual Review of Sociology* 30 (2004): 479–506.

Armstrong, Elizabeth. *Forging Gay Identities: Organizing Sexuality in San Francisco, 1950–1994.* Chicago: University of Chicago Press, 2002.

Armstrong, Elizabeth, and Mary Bernstein. "Culture, Power, and Institutions: A Multi-institutional Politics Approach to Social Movements." *Sociological Theory* 26, no. 1 (2008): 74–99.

Arnett, Jeffrey J. *Emerging Adulthood: The Winding Road from the Late Teens through the Twenties.* New York: Oxford University Press, 2004.

Asian American Center for Advancing Justice. *A Community of Contrasts. Asian Americans in the United States: 2011.* Washington, D.C.: Asian American Center for Advancing Justice, 2013.

Bach, Robert L. *Labor Force Participation and Employment of Southeast Asian Refugees in the United States.* Washington, D.C.: Office of Refugee Resettlement, 1984.

Balboa, Cristina M. "How Successful NGOs Set Themselves Up for Failure on the Ground." *World Development* 54 (2014): 273–87.

Banks, Nicola, David Hulmes, and Michael Edwards. "NGOs, States, and Donors Revisited: Still Too Close for Comfort?" *World Development* 66 (2015): 707–18.

Barkan, Joanne. "Plutocrats at Work: How Big Philanthropy Undermines Democracy." *Social Research* 80, no. 2 (2013): 635–52.

Bartley, Tim. "How Foundations Shape Social Movements: The Construction of an Organizational Field and the Rise of Forest Certification." *Social Problems* 54, no. 3 (2007): 229–55.

Benford, Robert D., and David A. Snow. "Framing Processes and Social Movements: An Overview and Assessment." *Annual Review of Sociology* 26 (2000): 611–39.

Benjamin, Walter. *Illuminations: Essays and Reflections.* Translation by Hannah Arendt. New York: Schoken Books, 1968.

Blee, Kathleen, M., and Verta Taylor. "Semi-Structured Interviewing in Social Movement Research." In *Methods of Social Movement Research*, vol. 16, 92–117. Minneapolis: University of Minnesota Press, 2002.

Boggs, Grace Lee. "Interview." *Democracy Now*, July 13, 2007.

—With Scott Kurashige. *The Next American Revolution: Sustainable Activism for the Twenty-first Century*. Berkeley: University of California Press, 2011.

Bora. "Personal interviews." Oakland, CA.

Borom. "Personal interviews," June–July 2016. Skype.

Brakke, Gray. "Linda Heng interview." *Brown Political Review*, November 4, 2015. Providence, RI.

Braunstein, Ruth, Brad Fulton, and Richard Wood. "The Role of Bridging Cultural Practices in Racially and Socioeconomically Diverse Civic Organizations." *American Sociological Review* 79, no. 4 (2014): 705–25.

Browne, Simone. *Dark Matters: On the Surveillance of Blackness*. Durham: Duke University Press, 2015.

Buchanan, Phil, and Ellie Buteau. *Shifting Winds: Foundations Respond to a New Political Context*. Providence, RI: Center for Effective Philanthropy, 2017.

Buenavista, Tracy L., and Jordan B. Gonzales. "DREAMs Deterred: Filipino Experiences and an Anti-Militarization Critique of the Development, Relief, and Education for Alien Minors Act." *Harvard Asian American Policy Review* 21 (2011): 29–38. http://isites.harvard.edu/icb/icb. do?keyword=k74751&tabgroupid=icb.tabgroup143909.

Bui, Diana. *Cambodian Resettlement in Rhode Island*. Washington, D.C.: Office of Refugee Resettlement, 1981.

Cacho, Lisa Marie. *Social Death: Racialized Rightlessness and the Criminalization of the Unprotected*. New York: New York University Press, 2012.

Cambodian Son. Anida Ali and Masashiro Sugano. Studio Revolt. 2013. https://vimeo.com/ondemand/cambodianson.

Carson, Clayborne. *In Struggle: SNCC and the Black Awakening of the 1960s*. Cambridge: Harvard University Press, 1995.

Castells, Manuel. *Networks of Outrage and Hope: Social Movements in the Internet Age*. 2nd ed. Cambridge: Polity Press, 2015.

Cebulko, Kara. "Documented, Undocumented, and Liminally Legal: Legal Status During the Transition to Adulthood for 1.5-Generation Brazilian Immigrants." *The Sociological Quarterly* 55, no. 1 (2014): 143–167.

Center for Effective Philanthropy. *The Future of Foundation Philanthropy: The CEO Perspective*. Providence, RI: Center for Southeast Asians of Rhode Island, 2016. www.cseari.org.

Chan, Sucheng. *Asian Americans: An Interpretive History*. New York: Twayne Publications, 1991.

Chan, Sucheng, ed., with Audrey Kim. *Not Just Victims; Conversations with Cambodian Community Leaders in the United States*. Urbana and Chicago: University of Illinois Press, 2003.

Chandra. "Personal interview," July 2005. Providence, RI.

Chang, Jeff. *Can't Stop Won't Stop: A History of the Hip-Hop Generation*. New York: St. Martin's Press, 2005.

Chang, Jeff, ed. *Total Chaos: The Art and Aesthetics of Hip-Hop*. New York: Basic Civitas Books, 2006.

Charlie. "Personal interview," December 2015. Providence, RI.

Charmaz, Kathy. *Constructing Grounded Theory: A Practical Guide Through Qualitative Analysis*. London: Sage, 2006.

Chase. "Personal interviews, " 2004–2006. Providence, RI.

Chavez, Christina. "Conceptualizing from the Inside: Advantages, Complications, and Demands on Insider Positionality." *The Qualitative Report* 13, no. 3 (2008): 474–94.

Chawla, Devika. "Narratives on Longing, Being, and Knowing: Envisioning a Writing Epistemology." In *Liminal Traces: Storying, Performing, and Embodying Postcoloniality*, edited by Devika Chawla and Amardo Rodriguez, 97–111. Boston: Sense, 2011.

Chea. "Personal interviews,"2003. Phnom Penh, Cambodia.

Choum, Ched, and Jenny. "Personal interviews," May–July 2017. Skype.

Choum, Chhaya. "Personal interviews," 2002–2006. Bronx, NY.

Chowdhury, Elora Halim. *Transnationalism Reversed: Women Organizing against Gendered Violence in Bangladesh.* Albany: State University of New York Press, 2011.

Collins, Patricia Hill. *Black Feminist Thought: Knowledge, Consciousness, and the Politics of Empowerment.* New York: Routledge, 1991.

Collins, Patricia Hill, and Sirma Bilge. *Intersectionality: Key Concepts.* Cambridge: Polity Press, 2016.

Combahee River Collective. "First Official Statement on CRC Formation." (1973/1995).

Congress, U.S. Illegal Immigration Reform and Immigrant Responsibility Act of 1996. *Division C* vol. Public Law 104-208, U.S. Congress Ed. Washington, D.C.: Library of Congress, 1996.

Congressional Asian Pacific American Caucus CAPAC. Press Release: CAPAC Unveils Immigration Priorities. February 4, 2013. http://capac-chu.house. gov/press-release/capac-unveils-immigration-priorities.

Cote, James E., and Anton L. Allahar. *Generation on Hold: Coming of Age in the Late Twentieth Century.* New York: New York University Press, 1996.

Crenshaw, Kimberlé. "Mapping the Margins: Intersectionality, Identity Politics, and Violence Against Women of Color." *Stanford Law Review* 43, no. 6 (July 1991): 1241–1299.

Daniel. "Personal conversations." Providence, RI, 2016–17.

Dao, Loan. "What's Going On with the Oakland Museum's 'California & the Vietnam Era' Exhibit." *AmerAsia Journal: 30 Years AfterWARd: Vietnamese Americans & U.S. Empire* 30, no. 2 (2005): 88–108.

—"We Will Not Be Moved: The Mobilization Against Southeast Asian Detention and Deportation." Ph.D. diss., University of California, Berkeley, 2009.

—"Refugee Representations: Youth, hip hop, and Southeast Asian Deportation." *Amerasia Journal* 40, no. 2 (2014): 88–110.

—"Out and Asian: How Undocu/DACAmented Asian Americans and Pacific Islander Youth Navigate Dual Liminality in the Immigrant Rights Movement." *Societies* 7, no. 3 (2017): 1–17. DOI:10.3390/soc7030017.

Das Gupta, Monisha. *Unruly Immigrants: Rights, Activism and Transnational South Asian Politics in the U.S.* Durham: Duke University Press, 2006.

de Goede, Marieke. "Ideology in the U.S. Welfare Debate: Neo-Liberal Representations of Poverty." *Discourse & Society* 7, no. 3 (1996): 317–57.

Del Moral, Andrea. "The Revolution Will Not Be Funded." *LiP Magazine*, April 4, 2005. http://www.lipmagazine.org/articles/featdelmoral_nonprofit_p.html.

Dohrn, Bernadine. "'Look Out, Kid, It's Something You Did:' The Criminalization of Children." In *The Public Assault on America's Children: Poverty, Violence and Juvenile Injustice*, edited by Valerie Polakow, 157–87. New York: Teachers College Press, 2000.

Donnelly, Nancy D. *The Changing Lives of Refugee Hmong Women.* Seattle: University of Washington Press, 1994.

Dong, Harvey C. "The Origins and Trajectory of Asian American Political Activism in the San Francisco Bay Area, 1968-1978." Ph.D. diss., Department of Ethnic Studies, University of California, Berkeley, 2003.

—"AAPA Position on Vietnam [from October 1969. *AAPA Newspaper.*14]" In *Stand Up! An Archive Collection of the Bay Area Asian-American Movement 1968–1974,* edited by Harvey Dong, 32–33. Berkeley: Asian Community Center Archive Group, 2009.

Doungsavanh, Ammala. "Personal interviews," July 2005. Providence, RI.

Duiker, William J. *The Communist Road to Power in Vietnam.* Boulder, CO: Westview Press, 1996.

Duggan, Lisa. *The Twilight of Equality: Neoliberalism, Cultural Politics, and the Attack on Democracy.* Boston: Beacon Press, 2003.

Duong, Lan P. *Treacherous Subjects: Gender, Culture, and Trans-Vietnamese Feminism.* Philadelphia: Temple University Press, 2012.

Ebrahim, Alnoor. "Making Sense of Accountability: Conceptual Perspectives for Northern and Southern Nonprofits." *Nonprofit Management & Leadership* 14, no. 2 (2003): 191–212.

Elbaum, Max. *Revolution in the Air: Radicals Turn to Lenin, Mao, and Che.* London: Verso Books, 2002.

Ellis, Carolyn, Tony E. Adams, and Arthur P. Bochner. "Autoethnography: An Overview." *Historical Social Research* 36, no. 4 (2011): 273–90.

Eng, David L. "Out Here and Over There: Queerness and Diaspora in Asian American Studies." *Social Text* 52/53 (1997): 31–52.

Erjavec, Karmen. "Media Representation of the Discrimination Against The Roma in Eastern Europe: the case of Slovenia." *Discourse & Society* 12, no. 6 (2001): 699–727.

Esmeir, Samera. *Juridical Humanity: A Colonial History.* Stanford: Stanford University Press, 2012.

Espiritu, Yen Le. *Asian American Panethnicity: Bridging Institutions and Identities.* Philadelphia: Temple University Press, 1992.

—"30 Years AfterWARd: Vietnamese Americans and U.S. Empire." *Amerasia Journal* 31, no. 2 (2005): xiii–xxiii.

—"Toward a Critical Refugee Study: The Vietnamese Refugee Subject in U.S. Scholarship." *Journal of Vietnamese Studies* 11, no. 2 (2006): 410–433.

—*Body Counts: The Viet Nam War and Militarized Refugees.* Berkeley: University of California Press, 2014.

Fanon, Frantz. *The Wretched of the Earth.* New York: Grove Press, 1963.

Flores, William, and Rina Benmayor, eds. *Latino Cultural Citizenship: Claiming Identity, Space, and Politics.* Boston: Beacon Press, 1997.

Freeman, James. *Hearts of Sorrow: Vietnamese American Lives.* Stanford: Stanford University Press, 1989.

Freire, Paulo. *Pedagogy of the Oppressed.* New York: Continuum, 1970.

Fujino, Diane C. "Who Studies the Asian American Movement? A Historiographical Analysis." *Journal of Asian American Studies* 11, no. 2 (2008): 127–69.

Funders' Collaborative on Youth Organizing (FCYO). *National Field Scan.* New York: Funders' Collaborative on Youth Organizing, 2013.

Gans, Herbert J. "Second Generation Decline: Scenarios for the Economic and Ethnic Futures of the Post-1965 American Immigrants." *Ethnic and Racial Studies* 15, no. 2 (1992): 173–92.

Ganz, Marshall. "The Power of Story in Social Movements." In the Proceedings of the Annual Meeting of the American Sociological Association, Anaheim, California, August 18–21, 2001.

—"Leading Change: Leadership, Organization, and Social Movements." In *Handbook of Leadership Theory and Practice*, edited by Nitin Nohria and Rakesh Khurana, 509–50. Boston: Harvard Business Press, 2010a.

—*Why David Sometimes Wins: Leadership, Organization, and Strategy in California Farm Worker Movement.* New York: Oxford University Press, 2010b.

—"Public Narrative, Collective Action, and Power." In *Accountability Through Public Opinion: From Inertia to Public Action,* edited by Sina Odugbemi and Taeku Lee, 273–89. Washington, D.C: The World Bank, 2011.

Ganz, Marshall, and Emily S. Lin. "Learning to Lead: Pedagogy of Practice." In *Handbook for Teaching Leadership: Knowing, Doing, and Being,* edited by Scott Snook, Nitin Nohria, and Rakesh Khurana, 353–66. Thousand Oaks, CA: Sage, 2011.

George, Alexander L., and Andrew Bennett. *Case Studies and Theory Development in the Social Sciences.* Cambridge: MIT Press, 2005.

Geron, Kim. "Serve the People: An Exploration of the Asian American Movement." In *Asian American Politics: Law, Participation, and Policy,* edited by Don Nakanishi and James Lai, 163–79. Lanham, MD: Rowman & Littlefield, 2003.

Gil de Zúñiga, Homero, Nakwon Jung, and Sebastian Valenzuela. "Social Media
Use for News and Individuals' Social Capital, Civic Engagement and Political
Participation." *Journal of Computer-Mediated Communication* 17, no. 3
(2012): 319–36.

Gilmore, Ruth Wilson. "In the Shadow of the Shadow State." In *The Revolution
Will Not Be Funded: Beyond the Non-profit Industrial Complex,* edited by
INCITE!: Women of Color Against Violence, 41–52. Cambridge: South End
Press, 2007.

Glasser, B. G., and A. L Strauss. *The Discovery of Grounded Theory.* Chicago:
Aldine Press, 1967.

Golash-Boza, Tanya Maria. *Deported: Immigrant Policing, Disposable Labor,
and Global Capitalism.* New York: New York University Press, 2015.

Goldstone, Robert L., and Todd M. Gureckis. "Collective Behavior." *Topics
in Cognitive Science* 1, no. 3 (2009): 412–38. DOI:10.1111/j.1756-
8765.2009.01038.x

Goodwin, Jeff, and James M. Jasper, eds. *Rethinking Social Movements:
Structure, Meaning and Emotion.* New York: Roman & Littlefield, 2004.

Gonzales, Roberto G. "Left Out but Not Shut Down: Political Activism and the
Undocumented Student Movement." *Northwestern Journal of Law and Social
Policy* 3, no. 2, article 4 (2009): 219–39.

—"Learning to Be Illegal: Undocumented Youth and Shifting Legal Contexts
in the Transition to Adulthood." *American Sociological Review* 76, no. 4
(2011): 602–19.

Habel, Estella. *The San Francisco International Hotel: Mobilizing the Filipino
American Community in the Anti-Eviction Movement.* Philadelphia: Temple
University Press, 2007.

Hager, Mark, Patrick Rooney, and Thomas Pollak. "How Fundraising is
Carried Out in US Nonprofit Organisations." *International Journal of
Nonprofit and Voluntary Sector Marketing* 7, no. 4 (2002): 311–24.
DOI:10.1002/nvsm.188.

Haines, David W., ed. *Refugees in America in the 1990s: A Reference Handbook.*
Westport, CT: Greenwood Press, 1996.

Hall, Budd. "Continuity in Adult Education and Political Struggle." *Convergence* XI: 8–15, 1978.

—"Breaking the Monopoly of Knowledge: Research Methods, Participation and Development." In *Creating Knowledge: A Monopoly?* edited by Budd Hall, Arthur Gillette, and Rajesh Tandon, 13–26. Toronto: Society for Participatory Research in Asia, 1982.

—"From Margin to Center? Development and Purpose of Participatory Research." *The American Sociologist* 23, no, 4 (1992): 15–28.

Hall, Stuart. "What is this 'Black' in Black Popular Culture?" In *Stuart Hall: Critical Dialogues in Cultural Studies,* edited by David Morley and Kuan-Hsing Chen, 465–75. London: Routledge, 1996.

Hames-Garcia, Michael, and Ernesto Javier Martinez, eds. *Gay Latino Studies: A Critical Reader.* Durham: Duke University Press, 2011.

Han, Chong-suk. "Geisha of a Different Kind: Gay Asian Men and the Gendering of Sexual Identity." *Sexuality & Culture* 10, no. 3 (Summer 2006): 3–28.

Han, Shinhee. "Asian American Gay Men's (Dis)claim on Masculinity." In *Gay Masculinities,* edited by Peter M. Nardi, 206–21. Thousand Oaks, CA: Sage, 2000.

Hanhardt, Christine B. *Safe Space: Gay Neighborhood History and the Politics of Violence.* Durham: Duke University Press, 2013.

Hein, Jeremy. *From Vietnam, Laos, and Cambodia: A Refugee Experience in The United States.* New York: Twayne Publications, 1995.

—*Ethnic Origins: The Adaptation of Cambodian and Hmong Refugees in Four American Cities.* Thousand Oaks, CA: Sage, 2006.

Heng. "Interviews," 2014–2016. Skype.

Herod, Bill. "Personal interviews," 2002–2004. Phnom Penh, Cambodia.

Hing, Bill Ong. "What Does It Mean To Be Asian American?" In *Major Problems in Asian American History,* edited by Lon Kurashige and Alice Yang Murray, 29–33. Boston: Houghton Mifflin Company, 2003.

—*Defining America through Immigration Policy: An Interpretive History.* Philadelphia: Temple University Press, 2004.

—*Deporting Our Souls: Values, Morality, and Immigration Policy.* New York: Cambridge University Press, 2006.

Ho, Fred. *Legacy to Liberation: Politics and Culture of Revolutionary Asian Pacific America.* San Francisco: AK Press and Big Red Media, 2000.

Hodagneu-Soleto, Pierrette. *Gendered Transitions: Mexican Experiences of Immigration.* Berkeley: University of California Press, 1994.

hooks, bell. *Teaching to Transgress: Education as a Practice of Freedom.* New York: Routledge, 1994.

Huo, T.C. *Land of Smiles: A Novel.* New York: Plume Books, 2000.

Inventos: Hip Hop Cubano. Eli Jacobs-Fauntauzzi, dir. Clenched Fist Productions, 2005.

The Immigration Detention Transparency and Human Rights Project. *Lives in Peril.* Washington D.C.: IDTHR, 2015.

Immigration Policy Institute. "Just Facts: New Americans in Rhode Island." 2011. http://www.immigrationpolicy.org/just-facts/new-americans-rhode-island#.VfW-cy-Priw.email.

INCITE! Women of Color Against Violence. *The Revolution Will Not Be Funded: Beyond the Non-profit Industrial Complex.* Cambridge: South End Press, 2007.

Ishihara, Kohei. "Personal interviews," 2002–2005. Providence, RI.

Ishizuka, Karen L. *Serve the People: Making Asian American in the Long Sixties.* New York: Verso Books, 2016.

Jenkins, Craig, and Abigail Halci. "Grassrooting the System?: The Development and Impact of Social Movement Philanthropy, 1953–1960." In *Philanthropic Foundations: New Scholarship, New Possibilities,* edited by E. C. Lagemann. Bloomington: Indiana University Press, 1999.

Jones, Nikki. *Between the Good and the Ghetto: African American Girls and Inner City Violence.* New Brunswick: Rutgers University Press, 2010.

Kahne, Joseph, Ellen Middaugh, Nam-Jin Lee, and Jessica Feezell. "Youth Online Activity and Exposure to Diverse Perspectives." *New Media & Society* 14, no. 3 (2011): 492–512.

Kahne, Joseph, Nam-Jin Lee, and Jessica Timpany Feezell. "Digital Media Literacy Education and Online Civic and Political Participation." *International Journal of Communication* 6 (2012): 1–24.

Kang, Milan. "Researching One's Own: Negotiating Co-Ethnicity in the Field." In Martin Manalansan, ed., *Cultural Compass: Ethnographic Explorations of Asian America.* Philadelphia: Temple University Press, 2000.

Kelley, Robin D. G. *Race Rebels: Culture, Politics, and the Black Working Class.* New York: The Free Press, 1994.

—*Freedom Dreams: The Black Radical Imagination.* Boston: Beacon Press, 2002.

Khiev, Kosal. "Moments Between the Nights." 2011a.

—"Why I Write." 2011b.

Kibria, Nazli. *Family Tightrope: The Changing Lives of Vietnamese Americans.* Princeton: Princeton University Press, 1993.

Kiernan, Ben. *The Pol Pot Regime: Race, Power, and Genocide in Cambodia under Khmer Rouge.* 3rd ed. New Haven: Yale University Press, 2008.

Kim, Audrey U. *Not Just Victims: Conversations with Cambodian Community Leaders in the United States.* Chicago: University of Illinois Press, 2003.

Kim, Claire Jean. *Bitter Fruit: The Politics of Black-Korean Conflict in New York City.* New Haven: Yale University Press, 2000.

—"The Racial Triangulation of Asian Americans." In *Asian Americans and Politics: Perspectives, Experiences, Prospects*, edited by Gordon Chang, 39–78. Stanford: Stanford University Press, 2001.

Kivel, Paul. "Social Service or Social Change?" In *The Revolution Will Not Be Funded: Beyond the Non-Profit Industrial Complex*, 129–50. Boston: South End Press, 2007.

Kochiyama, Yuri Nakahara. *Passing It On—A Memoir*, edited by Marjorie Lee, Akemi Kochiyama-Sardinha, and Audee Kochiyama-Holman. Los Angeles: UCLA Asian American Studies Center Press, 2004.

Kohl-Arenas, Erica. "Governing Poverty Amidst Plenty: Participatory Development and Private Philanthropy." *Geography Compass* 5, no. 11 (2011): 1–14.

Koshy, Susan. "From Cold War to Trade War: Neocolonialism and Human Rights." *Social Text* 58 (1999): 1–32.

Krummheuer, Gotz. "The Ethnography of Argumentation." In *The Emergence of Mathematical Meaning*, edited by Paul Cobb and Henrich Bauersfeld, 220–277. New York: Taylor & Francis, 1995.

Kumashiro, Kevin K., ed. *Restoried Selves: Autobiographies of Queer Asian American/Pacific American Activists*. New York: Routledge, 2003.

Kwon, Soo Ah. *Uncivil Youth: Race, Activism, and Affirmative Governmentality*. Durham: Duke University Press, 2013.

Lakoff, George. *The Political Mind: Why You Can't Understand 21st Century American Politics with an 18th Century Brain*. New York: The Penguin Group, 2008.

Lam, Mariam Beevi. "Việt Nam's Growing Pains: Post-socialist Cinema Development and Transnational Politics." In *Four Decades On: Vietnam, the United States, and the Legacies of the Second Indochina War*, edited by Scott Laderman and Edwin Martini, 155–82. Durham: Duke University Press, 2013.

Langman, Lauren. "Virtual Public Spheres and Global Justice: A Critical Theory of Inter-networked Social Movements." *Social Theory* 23, no. 1 (March 2005): 42–74.

le thi diem thuy. *The Gangster We Are All Looking For*. New York: Knopf, 2003.

LeCompte, Margaret D., and Jean J. Schensul. *Designing and Conducting Ethnographic Research*, vol. 1. Walnut Creek, CA: Altamira Press, 1999.

Lee, Jonathan H.X., ed. *Cambodian American Experiences: Histories, Communities, Cultures, and Identities*. Dubuque, IA: Kendall Hunt Publishing, 2010.

Lee, Nam-Jin, Dhavan V. Shah, and Jack M. McLeod. "Processes of Political Socialization: A communication Mediation Approach to Youth Civic Engagement." *Communication Research* 40, no. 5 (2012): 669–97. https://doi.org/10.1177/0093650212436712.

Lehr, Valerie. *Queer Family Values: Debunking the Myth of the Nuclear Family*. Philadelphia: Temple University Press, 1999.

Leong, Russell, ed. *Asian American Sexualities: Dimensions of the Gay and Lesbian Experience*. New York: Routledge, 1995.

Li, Wei, and Lucia Lo. "New Geographies of Migration? A Canada-US Comparison of Highly-Skilled Chinese and Indian Migration." *Journal of Asian American Studies* 15, no. 1 (February 2012): 1–34.

Linda. "Personal conversations." Providence, RI, 2016–17.

Ling, Sin Yen. "Personal interviews," 2005. San Francisco, CA.

Lipsitz, George. *Dangerous Crossroads: Popular Music, Postmodernism, and the Poetics of Place*. New York: Verso, 1994.

Liu, Michael, Kim Geron, and Tracy Lai. *The Snake Dance of Asian American Activism*. London: Lexington Books, 2008.

Long, Patrick Du Phuoc, with Laura Richard. *The Dream Shattered: Vietnamese Gangs in America*. Boston: Northeastern University Press, 1996.

Louen. "Personal interview," August 2003. Phnom Penh, Cambodia.

Louie, Steve, and Glen Omatsu, eds. *Asian Americans: The Movement and the Moment*. Los Angeles: UCLA Asian American Studies Center Press, 2001.

Ly, PraCH. "Personal interview," April 2007. Berkeley, CA.

Lyons, Joren. "Personal interviews," October 2002. San Francisco, CA.

Ma, Kimho. "Personal interviews," 2003–2004. Phnom Penh, Cambodia.

Maeda, Daryl. *Chains of Babylon: The Rise of Asian America.* Minneapolis: University of Minnesota Press, 2009.

Maguire, Patricia. *Doing Participatory Research: A Feminist Approach.* Amherst, MA: Center for International Education, 1987.

Maira, Sunaina Marr. *Desis in the House: Indian American Youth Culture in New York City.* Philadelphia: Temple University Press, 2002.

—*Missing: Youth, Citizenship and Empire after 9/1.* Durham: Duke University Press, 2009.

Males, Mike A. *Framing Youth: 10 Myths about the Next Generation.* Monroe, ME: Common Courage Press, 2002.

Marable, Manning. *Race, Reform, and Rebellion: The Second Reconstruction in Black America, 1945–1990.* Jackson: University Press of Mississippi, 1991.

Mao. "Personal interview," February 2003. Phnom Penh, Cambodia.

Marr, David. *Viet Nam 1945: The Quest for Power.* Berkeley: University of California Press, 1997.

Maru. "Personal interview," June 2005. Long Beach, CA.

Massey, Douglas S., and Magaly R. Sanchez. *Brokered Boundaries: Creating Identity in Anti-immigrant Times.* New York: Russell Sage Foundation, 2010.

McAdam, Doug. *Political Process and the Development of Black Insurgency, 1930–1970.* Chicago: University of Chicago Press, 1982.

McAdam, Doug, John D. McCarthy, and Mayar N. Zald. *The Trend of Social Movements in America: Professionalism and Resource Mobilization.* Newark: General Learning Press, 1973.

—*Comparative Perspectives on Social Movements.* Cambridge: Cambridge University Press, 1996.

McAdam, Doug, and W. Richard Scott. "Organizations and Movements." In *The Nature of the Nonprofit Sector*, edited by J. S. Ott and L. Dicke, 257–72. Boulder, CO: Westview Press, 2012.

McBride, James. "Hip Hop Planet." *National Geographic* (April 2007): 100–120.

Medoff, Peter, and Holly Sklar. *The Streets of Hope: The Fall and Rise of an Urban Neighborhood*. Boston: South End Press, 1994.

Meissner, Doris, Donald M. Kerwin, Muzaffar Chishti, and Claire Bergeron. *Immigration Enforcement in the United States*. Report. Washington, D.C.: Migration Policy Institute, 2013.

Menjívar, Cecelia. "Liminal Legality: Salvadoran and Guatemalan Immigrants' Lives in the U.S." *American Journal of Sociology* 111, no. 4 (2006): 999–1037.

—"Educational Hopes, Documented Dreams: Guatemalan and Salvadoran Immigrants' Legality and Educational Prospects." *Annals of the American Academy of Political and Social Science* 620 (2008): 177–193.

Menjivar, Cecelia, and Leisy J. Abrego. "Legal Violence: Immigration Law and the Lives of Central American Immigrants." *American Journal of Sociology* 117, no. 5 (2012): 1380–1421.

McAdam, Doug. *Political Process and the Development of Black Insurgency, 1930–1970*. Chicago: University of Chicago Press, 1982.

McAdam, Doug, John D. McCarthy, and Mayar N. Zald. *The Trend of Social Movements in America: Professionalism and Resource Mobilization*. Princeton: General Learning Press, 1973.

—*Comparative Perspectives on Social Movements*. Cambridge: Cambridge University Press, 1996.

McGarrell, Edmund F., Nicholas Corsaro, Chris Melde, Natalie Hipple, Jennifer Cobbina, Timothy Bynum, and Heather Perez. *An Assessment of the Comprehensive Anti-Gang Initiative: Final Project Report*. Washington, D.C.: Department of Justice, July 20, 2012.

McGarrell, Edmund F., Natalie Kroovand Hipple, Nicholas Corsaro, Timothy S. Bynum, Heather Perez, Carol A. Zimmermann, and Melissa Garmo. *Project Safe Neighborhoods –A National Program to Reduce Gun Crime: Final Project Report.* Washington, D.C.: Department of Justice, April 2009.

Migration Policy Institute. *Immigration Enforcement in the United States: The Rise of a Formidable Machinery.* Washington, D.C.: Migration Policy Institute, 2016.

Minkler, Merideth. *Community Organizing and Community Building for Health and Welfare.* 3rd ed. New Brunswick: Rutgers University Press, 2012.

Mitchell, Tony, ed. *Global Noise: Rap and Hip-Hop Outside the USA.* Middletown: Wesleyan University Press, 2001.

Mogul, Joey L., Andrea J. Ritchie, and Kay Whitlock. *Queer InJustice: The Criminalization of LGBT People in the United States.* Boston: Beacon Press, 2011.

Morris, Aldon. "Reflections on Social Movement Theory: Criticisms and Proposals." *Contemporary Sociology* 29, no. 3 (2000): 445–54.

Morris, Aldon, and Naomi Braine. "Social Movements and Oppositional Consciousness." In *Oppositional Consciousness: The Subjective Roots of Social Protest,* edited by Jane J. Mansbridge and Aldon Morris, 20–37. Chicago: University of Chicago Press, 2001.

Morris, Aldon, and Suzanne Staggenborg. "Leadership in Social Movements." In *The Blackwell Companion to Social Movements,* edited by David A. Snow, Sarah A. Soule, and Hanspeter Kriesi, and Holly J. McCammon, 171–96. Oxford: Blackwell, 2007.

Muñoz, Carlos Jr. *Youth, Identity, Power: The Chicano Movement.* London: Verso Books, 1989.

Murray, Robin, Julie Caulier-Grice, and Geoff Mulgan. *The Open Book of Social Innovation. Report for the Young Foundation.* London: The Young Foundation, 2010.

"My Asian Americana." Studio Revolt [video], 2012. www.studio-revolt.com.

Najam, Adil. "NGO Accountability: A Conceptual Framework." *Development Policy Review* 14, no. 4 (1996): 339–54.

Nakano Glenn, Evelyn. "2010 ASA Presidential Address: Constructing Citizenship: Exclusion, Subordination, and Resistance." *American Sociological Review* 76, no. 1 (2011): 1–24.

Negron-Gonzales, Genevieve. *Hegemony, Ideology & Oppositional Consciousness: Undocumented Youth and the Personal-Political Struggle for Educational Justice.* Berkeley: Institute for the Study of Social Change, 2009. Paper ISSC_WP_36. http://repositories. cdlib.org/ issc/fwp/ ISSC WP 36.

Ngai, Mae. *Impossible Subjects: Illegal Aliens and the Making of America.* Princeton: Princeton University Press, 2004.

Nguyen, Mimi Thi. *The Gift of Freedom: War, Debt, and Other Refugee Passages.* Durham: Duke University Press, 2012.

Nguyen, Viet Thanh. "Refugee Memories and Asian American Critique." *Positions* 20, no. 3 (2012): 911–42.

Nguyen-Vo, Thu-Huong. "Forking Paths: How Shall We Mourn the Dead?" *Amerasia Journal* 31, no. 2 (2005): 157–75.

Niedweicki, Max. "Personal interview," June 2005. Washington, D.C.

North, David, and Nim Sok. *Profiles of Some Good Places for Cambodians to Live in the United States.* Family Support Administration, Washington, D.C.: Office of Refugee Resettlement, March 1989.

Obama, Barack. "Blueprint for Immigration Reform: Building a 21st Century Immigration System." Washington, D.C.: Office of the White House, 2010. https://www.aila.org/infonet/ wh-blueprint- building- 21st-century-immigration-sys.

—"State of the Union Address," February 12, 2013. http://www.whitehouse. gov/state-of-the-union- 2013.

—"Remarks by the President in Address to the Nation on Immigration." November 20, 2014, vol. 2014. Washington, D.C.: The White House Office of the Press Secretary.

O'Connor, Ellen. "Minding the Workers: The Meaning of 'Human' and 'Human Relations' in Elton Mayo." *Organization* 6, no. 2 (1999): 223–48.

Oeur, U Sam. *Sacred Vows: Poetry by U Sam Oeur.* Minneapolis: Coffee House Press, 1998.

Okihiro, Gary. *The Third World Studies: Theorizing Liberation.* Durham: Duke University Press, 2016.

Olivas, Michael A. "The Political Economy of the DREAM Act and the Legislative Process: A Case Study of Comprehensive Immigration Reform." *Wayne Law Review* 55 (2010): 1757–1810.

Omatsu, Glenn. "The Four Prisons and the Movements for Liberation." In *Asian American Politics: Law, Participation, and Policy,* edited by Don Nakanishi and James Lai, 135–62. Lanham, MD: Rowman & Littlefield, 2002.

Omi, Michael, and Howard Winant. *Racial Formation in the United States.* New York: Routledge, 1994.

Ong, Aihwa. *Buddha Is Hiding: Refugees, Citizenship, and the New America.* Berkeley: University of California Press, 2003.

Orellana, Marjorie, Barrie Thorne, Anna Chee, Wan Shun Eva Lam. "Transnational Childhoods: The Participation of Children in Processes of Family Migration." *Social Problems* 48, no. 4 (2001): 572–91.

Ostrander, Susan. "Legacy and Promise for Social Justice Funding: Charitable Foundations and Progressive Social Movements, Past and Present." In *Foundations for Social Change: Critical Perspectives on Philanthropy and Popular Movements,* edited by D. Faber and D. McCarthy, 33–59. Lanham, MD: Rowman & Littlefield, 2005.

Palumbo-Liu, David. *Asian/American: Historical Crossings of a Racial Frontier.* Stanford: Stanford University Press, 1999.

Parenti, Christian. *Lockdown America: Police and Prisons in the Age of Crisis.* New York, NY: Verso Press, 1999.

Park, Edward J. W., and John S. W. Park. *Probationary Americans: Contemporary Immigration Policies and the Shaping of Asian American Communities.* New York: Routledge, 2005.

Park, Peter. "What is Participatory Research? A Theoretical and Methodological Perspective." In *Voices of Change: Participatory Research in the United States and Canada,* edited by Peter Park, Mary Brydon-Miller, Budd Hall, and Ted Jackson, 1–20. London: Bergin & Garvey, 1993.

Passel, Jeffrey S., and D'Vera Cohn. *A Portrait of unauthorized Immigrants in the United States.* Washington, D.C.: Pew Hispanic Center, 2009. http://pewhispanic.org/files/reports/107.pdf.

Pelaud, Isabelle Thuy. *this is all i choose to tell.* Philadelphia: Temple University Press, 2011.

Perez, Debra Joy. "Existing is a Natural Part of Philanthropy: Learning from it? Not So Much." *The Foundation Review: Exit Strategies* 9, no. 1 (2017): 103–6.

Phi, Bao. *Song I Sing: Poems.* Minneapolis: Coffee House Press, 2011.

Piven, Frances Fox. *Challenging Authority: How Ordinary People Change America.* New York: Rowman & Littlefield Publishers, 2006.

Piven, Frances Fox and Richard Cloward. *Poor People's Movements: How They Succeed, and Why They Fail.* New York: Vintage Books, 1979.

Pok, Ra. "Personal interview," March 2005. Long Beach, CA.

Polletta, Francesca. "Contending Stories: Narrative in Social Movements." *Qualitative Sociology* 21, no. 4 (1998): 419–445.

—*It Was Like a Fever: Storytelling in Protest and Politics.* Chicago: University of Chicago Press, 2006a.

—With John Lee. "Is Telling Stories Good for Democracy? Rhetoric in Public Deliberation after 9/11." *American Sociological Review* 71, no. 5 (2006b): 699–723.

Portes, Alejandro, and Ruben G. Rumbaut. *Immigrant America: A Portrait.* Berkeley: University of California Press, 1996.

—*Ethnicities: Children of Immigrants in America.* Berkeley: University of California Press, 2000.

—*Legacies: The Story of Immigrant Second Generation.* Berkeley: University of California Press, 2001.

Portes, Alejandro, and Min Zhou. "The New Second Generation: Segmented Assimilation and Its Variants." *Annals of the American Academy of Political and Social Science* 530 (1993): 74–96.

Prashad, Vijay. *The Karma of Brown Folk.* Minneapolis: University of Minnesota Press, 2000.

—*Everybody Was Kung Fu Fighting: Afro-Asian Connections and the Myth of Cultural Purity.* Boston: Beacon Press, 2001.

Providence Plan. *1990 Census Report.* 1992.

Providence Youth Student Movement. *PRYSM Archival Video footage, November 8, 2002.* Courtesy of Kohei Ishihara, 2005. Film.

—*National Survey on Southeast Asian LGBTQ Youth.* 2008.

—*Testimonies from the Community Safety Act hearings* [video]. September 14, 2016.

—*Private Security Alongside Community Safety.* December 15, 2016.

—Community Defense Project Community Safety Act campaign updates. 2016–2017.

Pulido, Laura. *Black, Brown, Yellow and Left: Radical Activism in Los Angeles.* Berkeley: University of California Press, 2006.

Ramirez, Catherine. "Representing, Politics, and the Politics of Representation in Gang Studies." *American Quarterly* 56, no. 4 (2004): 1135–146.

Ramirez, Horacio N. Roque, and Nan Alamilla Boyd. *Bodies of Evidence: The Practice of Queer Oral History.* New York: Oxford University Press, 2012.

Ramos-Zayas, Ana Y. *National Performances: The Politics of Class, Race, and Space in Puerto Rican Chicago.* Chicago: University of Chicago Press, 2003.

Rampton, Ben. "Youth Culture and Liminality." *Social Semiotics* 9, no. 3 (1999): 355–373.

Reder, Stephen M., and John Finck. *The Hmong Resettlement Study Site Report: Providence, RI.* Washington, D.C.: Office of Refugee Resettlement, July 1984.

Janet V. Reno et al. v. Kim Ho Ma. 2000. No. 00-38.

Returnee Assistance Project. October 22, 2003. Personal Communication.

Rhode Island Historical Society. www.rihs.org.

Rios, Victor M. *Punished: Policing the Lives of Black and Latino Boys.* New York: New York University Press, 2011.

—*Human Targets: Schools, Police, and the Criminalization of Latino Youth.* Chicago: University of Chicago Press, 2017.

Robertson, Geoffrey Q. C. *Crimes Against Humanity: The Struggle for Global Justice.* 4th ed. New York: The New Press, (1999) 2012.

Robinson, W. Courtland. *Terms of Refuge: The Indochinese Exodus and the International Response.* New York: Zed Books, Ltd, 1995.

Rodriguez, Dylan. "The Political Logic of the Non-Profit Industrial Complex." In *The Revolution Will Not Be Funded: Beyond the Non-Profit Industrial Complex*, edited by INCITE! Women of Color Against Violence, 21–40. Cambridge: South End Press, 2007.

Rosaldo, Renato. "Cultural Citizenship, Inequality, and Multiculturalism." In *Latino Cultural Citizenship: Claiming Identity, Space, and Politics*, edited by William V. Flores and Rina Benmayor, 27–38. Boston: Beacon Press, 1997.

Rose, Tricia. *Black Noise: Rap Music and Black Culture in Contemporary America.* Hanover: Wesleyan University Press, 1994.

Roy, Arundhati. "Confronting Empire" speech, January 28, 2003. Porto Alegre, Brazil: World Social Forum.

Rumbaut, Rubén G. "Ties that Bind: Immigration and Immigrant Families." In *Immigration and the Family: Research and Policy on U.S. Immigrants*, edited by Alan Booth, Ann C. Crouter, and Nancy S. Landale, 3–46. Mahwah, NJ: Lawrence Erlbaum Associates, 1997.

Ryan. "Personal interviews," 2003. Phnom Penh, Cambodia.

Rymes, Betsy. *Conversational Borderlands: Language and Identity in an Alternative Urban High School.* New York: Teachers College Press, 2001.

Salaita, Steven. "Ethnic Identity and Imperative Patriotism: Arab Americans before and After 9/11." *College Literature* 32, no. 2 (2005): 146–68.

Sam. "Personal interview," June 2005. Bronx, NY.

Sampson, Robert J., Jeffrey D. Morenoff, and Thomas Gannon-Rowley. "Assessing 'Neighborhood Effects': Social Processes and New Directions in Research." *Annual Review of Sociology* 28 (2002): 443–78.

Santa Ana, Otto. "'Like an animal I was treated': Anti-Immigrant Metaphor in U.S. Public Discourse." *Discourse & Society* 10, no. 2 (1999): 191–224.

Scheufele, Dietram A., Matthew C. Nisbet, Dominique Brossard, and Erik C. Nisbet. "Social Structure and Citizenship: Examining the Impacts of Social Setting, Network Heterogeneity, and Informational Variables on Political Participation." *Political Communication* 21, no. 3 (2004): 315–38.

Schlegal, Ryan. *Pennies for Progress: A Decade of A Boom for Philanthropy, a Bust for Social Justice.* Washington, D.C.: National Committee for Responsive Philanthropy, 2017.

Schlund-Vials, Cathy J. *War, Genocide, Justice: Cambodian American Memory Work.* Minneapolis: University of Minnesota Press, 2012.

Scott, James C. *Domination and the Arts of Resistance: Hidden Transcripts.* New Haven: Yale University Press, 1992.

Scott, Joanna C. *Indochina's Refugees: Oral Histories from Laos, Cambodia and Vietnam.* Jefferson, NC: McFarland & Company, Inc, 1989.

Sentenced Home. David Grabias and Nicole Newnham. The Corporation for Public Broadcasting, 2004. DVD.

Shah, Bindi V. *Laotian Daughters: Working Toward Community, Belonging, and Environmental Justice.* Philadelphia: Temple University Press, 2012.

Sharma, Nitasha, *Hip Hop Desis: South Asian Americans, Blackness, and a Global Race Consciousness.* Durham: Duke University Press, 2010.

Shay, Christopher. "From Teenage Gangster to Exiled Poet: New Documentary Follows Kosal Khiev." *Al Jazeera America*, April 26, 2014. http://america.aljazeera.com /articles/2014/4/26/ cambodian- son-documentaryexile.html.

Sitrin, Marina. *Horizontalism: The Voices of Popular Power in Argentina*. Berkeley: AK Press, 2006.

Smith, Andrea Lee. "Introduction." In *The Revolution Will Not Be Funded: Beyond the Non-profit Industrial Complex*, edited by INCITE! Women of Color Against Violence, 1–20. Cambridge: South End Press, 2007.

Snow, David A., and Robert D. Benford. "Framing Processes and Social Movements: An Overview and Assessment." *Annual Review of Sociology* 26 (2000): 611–39.

Sohoni, Deenesh, and Tracy.W.P. Sohoni. "Perceptions of Immigrant Criminality: Crime and Social Boundaries." *The Sociological Quarterly* 55, no. 1 (2014): 49–71.

Sotheavy. "Personal interviews," 2005. Providence, RI.

Southeast Asian Freedom Network. *Fact sheet for community organizations on deportation compiled from 2000 Census, I.C.E. reports, and personal vignettes*. Washington, D.C.: Southeast Asian Resource Action Center, 2002.

—"Forty Years Later: U.S. Human Rights Violations & The Deportation of Cambodian-American Refugees." March 18, 2015. https://1lovemovement. wordpress.com/ 2015/03/18/40- years-later-us-human-rights-violations-the-deportation-of-cambodian-american-refugees/.

—"SEAFN Campaign Solidarity Letter." October 24, 2015. https://docs. google.com/forms/d/1hof3EhZiU3ofYTYgSzJxkwRUdFriSlJiNPkYGwTkC yo/viewform.

—"SEAFN Video Campaign Series." October 24, 2015. https://www.youtube. com/ watch?v= YYFUn WN -8Ks.

Southeast Asian Resource Action Center (SEARAC). *Southeast Asians at a Glance*. Washington, D.C.: Southeast Asian Resource Action Center, 2011.

Southern Poverty Law Center. *Intelligence Report: Stranger Politics*. Fall 2017. https://www.splcenter.org / fighting-hate/ intelligence-report/2017/ stranger-politics.

Soul Choj Vang. "Letter from the Shore of Dragon River." In *Bamboo Among the Oaks: Contemporary Writing by Hmong Americans,* edited by Mai Neng Moua. Minneapolis: Minnesota Historical Society Press, 2002.

SRI International: Social Sciences Center. *Southeast Asian Refugee Resettlement at the Local Level: The Role of the Ethnic Community and the Nature of Refugee Impact.* Report for the Office of Refugee Resettlement, Social Security Administration, and Department of Health and Human Services, 1983.

Srikanth, Rajini. *Constructing the Enemy: Empathy/Antipathy in U.S. Literature and Law.* Philadelphia: Temple University Press, 2011.

Steven. "Personal interviews," October 2014–July 2017. Providence, RI.

Strauss, Anselm, and Juliet Corbin. *Basics of Qualitative Research: Grounded Theory Procedures and Techniques.* Thousand Oaks, CA: Sage, 1990.

Strom, Dao. *Grass Roof, Tin Roof.* New York: Mariner Books, 2003.

Suong, Sarath. "Personal interviews," 2003–2013. Providence, RI.

Suong, Sovath. "Personal interview," December 2004. Long Beach, CA.

Southeast Asian Freedom Network (SEAFN). #EndDeportation#Right2Return campaign list of demands. 2014.

—Statement on the 40th anniversary of the Khmer Rouge revolution. April 17, 2015.

—#EndDeportation#Right2Return Youtube campaign. 2015–2016.

Southern Poverty Law Center. "Intelligence Report: Stranger Politics: Fall 2017 Issue." August 2017. https://www.splcenter.org/fighting-hate/ intelligence-report/2017/stranger-politics.

Suárez-Orozco, Carola. "Identities Under Siege: Immigration Stress and Social Mirroring Among the Children of Immigrants." In *Cultures Under Siege: Collective Violence and Trauma*, edited by Antonius C.G.M. Robben and Marcelo M. Suárez-Orozco, 194–226. New York: Cambridge University Press, 2000.

Sugano, Masahiro. "Informal conversations," April 24–25, 2014. Boston, MA.

Takahashi, Corey. "American Export." *Vibe Magazine* (December 2003): 194–201.

Takaki, Ronald. *Strangers from A Different Shore: A History of Asian Americans.* New York: Penguin Books, 1989.

Talò, Cosimo, Terri Mannarini, and Alessia Rochira. "Sense of Community and Community Participation: A Meta-Analytic Review." *Social Indicators Research* 117 (2014): 1–28.

Tang, Shirley. "Diasporic Cultural Citizenship: Negotiate and Create Places and Identities in Their Refugee Migration and Deportation Experiences." *Trotter Review: Where is Home? Immigrants of Color in Massachusetts* 19, no. 1, article 4 (2010): 39–58. http://scholarworks.umb.edu /trotter_review/ vol19/iss1/4.

Tarrow, Sidney. *Power in Movement: Social Movements and Contentious Politics.* 2nd ed. Cambridge: Cambridge University Press, 1998.

—*The New Transnational Activism.* Cambridge: Cambridge University Press, 2005.

Taylor, Verta. "Feminist Methodology in Social Movements Research." *Qualitative Sociology* 21, no. 4 (1998): 357–79.

Teranishi, Robert, Libby Lok, and Bich Mai Dolly Nguyen. *iCount: A Data Quality Movement for Asian Americans and Pacific Islanders in Higher Education.* National Commission on Asian American and Pacific Islander Research in Education CARE and Educational Testing Service ETS, 2013.

Thida. "Personal interviews," 2003–2006. Oakland, CA.

Tilly, Charles. *From Mobilization to Revolution.* Chicago: Dorsey Press, 1978.

—*Social Movements: 1768–2004.* Boulder, CO: Paradigm Publishers, 2004.

Tony. "Personal interviews," 2002–2004. New York, NY.

Tran, Tam. "Testimony before the House Judiciary Committee's Subcommittee on Immigration, Citizenship, Refugees, Border Security and International Law." May 18, 2007. http://www.scribd.com/doc/31573121/Tam-Tran-s-Testimony-to-Congress-on-the- DREAM-Act- May-2007#download.

Tran, Tuyen. "Behind the Smoke and Mirrors: The Vietnamese in California, 1975–1994." PhD diss., University of California, Berkeley, 2007.

Troy. "Personal interviews," 2003–2004. Phnom Penh, Cambodia.

Toolan, Michael J. *Narrative: A Critical Linguistic Introduction.* London: Routledge Press, 2001.

Uch, Many. "Unpublished Journal." 2003.

—"Personal interviews," 2005. Seattle, WA.

—"Speech at Hate Free Zone Award Dinner," May 2006.

Um, Khathrya. "Diasporic Nationalism, Citizenship, and Post-war Reconstruct." *Refugee Diasporas and Transnationalism* 23, no. 2 (2006): 8–19.

U.S. Census. "Quick Facts on Rhode Island 2010 Census." http://quickfacts. census.gov/qfd/states/44000lk.html.

U.S. Department of Justice. "Crime Statistics, 2006." www.justice.gov.

U.S. House of Representatives. "Committee on Foreign Affairs Study Mission to Thailand and Laos, July 5–9, 1991." *Refugees and Asylum-Seekers From Laos: Prospects for Resettlement and Repatriation.* Washington, D.C.: U.S. Government Printing Office, September 1991.

U.S. State Department. *Memorandum of Understanding Between the Department of State, United States of America, and the Department of Interior, Cambodia,* June 22, 2002.

U.S. State Department. *Memorandum of Understanding Between the Department of State, United States of America, and Viet Nam,* 2008.

U.S. White House Initiative on Asian Americans and Pacific Islanders. "What's Your Story?" Video Challenge 2012. http://www.whitehouse.gov/blog/2011/08/29/whats- your-story-video-challenge.

Valverde, Kieu-Linh Caroline. *Transnationalizing Viet Nam: Community, Culture, and the Politics in the Diaspora.* Philadelphia: Temple University Press, 2012.

Van Dyke, Nella, and Holly McCammon, eds. *Strategic Alliances: Coalition Building and Social Movements.* Minneapolis: University of Minnesota Press, 2010.

Van Diyke, Teun. *Racism and the Press.* London: Routledge Press, 1991.

Vang, Ma. Summer. "The Refugee Soldier: A Critique of Refugee Recognition and Citizenship in the Hmong Veterans' Refugee Act of 1997." *positions* 20, no. 3 (2012): 685–712.

Vee. "Interview," August 2002. Long Beach, CA.

Vincent, Rickey. *Party Music: The Inside Story of the Black Panthers' Band.* Chicago: Chicago Review Press, 2013.

Vo, Linda Trinh. "Whose School District is This? Vietnamese American and Coalitional Politics in Orange County, California." *AAPI Nexus* 5, no. 2 (2007): 1–32.

—*Mobilizing An Asian American Community.* Philadelphia: Temple University Press, 2003a.

—"Vietnamese American Trajectories: Dimensions of Diaspora." *Amerasia Journal* 29, no. 1 (2003b): ix–xviii.

Vo Dang, Thuy. "The Cultural Work of Anticommunism in the San Diego Vietnamese American Community." *Amerasia Journal* 31, no. 2 (2005): 65–86.

Wang, L. Ling-chi. "The Structure of Dual Domination: Toward a Paradigm for the Study of the Chinese Diaspora in the United States." *Amerasia Journal* 21, no. 1-2 (1995): 149–70, DOI:10.17953/amer.21.1-2. a3tk238521728620c

Ward, Jane. "White Normativity: The Cultural Dimensions of Whiteness in a Racially Diverse LGBT Organization." *Sociological Perspectives* 51, no. 3 (2008): 563–86.

We Shall Not Be Moved. PrYSM, 2002. Self-distribution: www.prysm.org.

Wei, William. *The Asian American Movement.* Philadelphia: Temple University Press, 1993.

Whitten, Marsha. *Narrative, Social Control: Critical Perspectives.* London: Sage, 1993.

Wolf, Eric. "Kinship, Friendship, and Patron-client Relations." In *The Social Anthropology of Complex Societies,* edited by Michael Banton, 1–22. London: Routledge, (1966) 2004.

Wu, Cinthya. "State Violence is Chronic." *Journal of Asian American Studies* 20, no. 2 (June 2017): 295–97.

—"The Mattering of Black Lives for Non-Black People of Color." *Reappropriate,* July 14, 2016.

Yang. "Personal interviews," 2002–2006. New York, NY.

Yang, Kao Kalia. *The Latehomecomer: A Hmong Family Memoir.* Minneapolis: Coffee House Press, 2008.

Zald, Mayer. "Culture, Ideology and Strategic Framing." In *Comparative Perspectives on Social Movements,* edited by Doug McAdam, John McCarthy, and Mayer Zald, 261–74. Cambridge: Cambridge University Press, 1996.

Zhou, Min, and Carl L. Bankston, III. *Growing Up American: How Vietnamese Children Adapt to Life in the United States.* New York: Russell Sage Foundation, 1998.

Zia, Helen. *Asian American Dreams: The Making of an American People.* New York: Farrar, Straus and Giroux, 2001.

Index

Symbols

A

V

Y

APPENDIX A-1: MOU-U.S. & CAMBODIA (2002)

MEMORANDUM BETWEEN THE GOVERNMENT AND THE UNITED
STATES AND THE ROYAL GOVERNMENT OF CAMBODIA FOR
THE ESTABLISHMENT AND OPERATION OF A UNITED STATES -
CAMBODIA JOINT COMMISSION ON REPATRIATION

The government of the United States of America (United States) and the Royal
Government of Cambodia (Cambodia):

Recognizing their mutual international obligations to accept the return of their
nationals in an orderly, prompt, and humane manner;

Desiring to establish and advance the development of normal immigration
relations, in accordance with general recognized principles of international law
and practice;

Desiring to put into effect the principles adopted by both states in the Joint
Statement made in Phnom Penh on April 27, 2000, and subsequently endorsed
by order of the Royal Government of Cambodia on June 21, 2000; and

Desiring to further enhance cooperative and friendly relations between the two
states on the basis of respect for each State's sovereignty, and on the basis of
equality and mutual interest;

Hereby establish the following Principles and Objectives which are intended to
govern the establishment and operation of a joint Commission on Repatriation:

Fundamental Principles

Each repatriation request should be considered and decided individually, on a
case-by case basis, without preconditions.

The United States and Cambodia should act in a spirit of mutual cooperation in
determining the nationality of an individual and in all other matters pertaining
to repatriation.

The United States and Cambodia are committed to the primary objective of
effecting the return of each other's nationals to their home State, taking into

account the humanitarian and compassionate aspects of each case and the principles of internationally recognized human rights.

Nothing in the document imposes, or should be constructed to impose, any legal or financial obligations on either State.

Composition of the Joint Commission and Scheduling of Meetings

The Joint Commission on Repatriation (Commission) should be comprised of four (4) members from the United States and four (4) from Cambodia, representing the ministries of immigration, foreign affairs, and justice, or their equivalent, of such State.

The Commission should meet twice each year, or as mutually agreed, at times and locations to be mutually determined

Procedures/Modalities for Considering Repatriation Requests

Each State should designate a Central Authority for the receipt and initial screening of repatriation requests and related matters.

The Commission should be the primary forum for the discussion and resolution of repatriation policy and individual repatriation requests refused by the Central Authority of the requested State.

Unless otherwise agreed, all repatriation requests shall be initially sent to the Central Authority of the requested State and should include a copy of the final order of removal issued by the competent authority of the requesting State; a copy of the individual's passport, if available, or other documentation evidencing the identity and the biographical history of the individual and his or her status as a national of the receiving State; a copy, if any, of any available record of the individual's criminal violations in the requesting State; two identical photographs of the individual and his or her fingerprints and medical history, if available; any additional information that the Central Authority of the requested State deems necessary.

4. Upon receiving and reviewing a repatriation request, the Central Authority of the requested State may request the assistance and resources of the Central Authority of the requesting State in conducting any additional interview of the individual and verifying any information contained in the request.

5. The Central Authority of the requested State should respond in writing

to the Central Authority of the requesting State not later than 30 days from the date of receipt of the request, unless otherwise agreed. In all cases of refusal, the Central Authority of the requested State should state its reasons in writing and should refer the request to the Commission for consideration. The Commission shall consider all referred requests as its next scheduled meeting.

6. When the Central Authority of the requested State accepts a repatriation request, it should simultaneously issue a travel document, valid for at least 60 days, to permit the individual's return. The requesting State should expeditiously make the appropriate arrangements for the return of the individual to the requested State, and should inform the Central Authority of the requested State at least seven (7) business days in advance of the return itinerary and any special considerations, such as medical, law enforcement, or escort matters.

7. Unless otherwise agreed, all costs of repatriation, including air transportation and escort services, should be borne exclusively by the requesting State.

Signed at Phnom Penh on March 22, 2002, in duplicate, in both the English and Khmer languages with identical value

FOR THE GOVERNMENT OF THE FOR THE ROYAL GOVERNMENT UNITED STATES OF AMERICA OF CAMBODIA

Kent M. Wiedemann
Ambassador of the United States of America

Lt. Gen. Em Sam An Secretary of Ministry of Interior

JOINT STATEMENT

On 26-27 April, 2000, officials of the Royal Government of Cambodia from the Ministries of Foreign Affairs and International Cooperation, Interior, and Justice met with officials of the United States Department of State, U.S. Department of Justice, and the U.S. Immigration and Naturalization Service, and agreed that the following general principles shall govern the repatriation of each other's nationals:

That, in accordance with applicable principles of international law, each state agrees that it shall accept its nationals who have not obtained another nationality;

That there should be an orderly, prompt, and transparent process for considering such returns; That each such case must be considered on its individual merits without preconditions;

That the requesting state shall bear all costs associated with the returns of Cambodian Nationals;

That the final decision whether to accept the repatriation of particular individuals shall rest with the requested state;

That such repatriations shall take into account the humanitarian and compassionate aspects of each case, and that any such repatriation shall be conducted in an orderly, dignified manner, with due respect for human rights and the personal dignity of the individual who is being returned;

That the two Governments commit to cooperate, through appropriate channels, and in a timely fashion, in the determination of the nationality of individuals who the requesting state believes are nationals of the requested state.

That the requesting state shall promptly accept back individuals who have been repatriated to the requested state whenever it is subsequently determined that the repatriated individual is not in fact a national of the requested state.

April 27, 2000 in Phnom Penh

APPENDIX A-2: MOU-U.S. & VIET NAM (2008)

TREATIES AND OTHER INTERNATIONAL ACTS SERIES 08-22

REPATRIATION

Agreement Between

the UNITED STATES OF AMERICA

and VIETNAM

Signed at Hanoi January 22, 2008 with Annexes

NOTE BY THE DEPARTMENT OF STATE

Pursuant to Public Law 89—497, approved July 8, 1966

(80 Stat. 271; 1 U.S.C. 113)—

". . .the Treaties and Other International Acts Series issued under the authority of the Secretary of State shall be competent evidence . . . of the treaties, international agreements other than treaties, and proclamations by the President of such treaties and international agreements other than treaties, as the case may be, therein contained, in all the courts of law and equity and of maritime jurisdiction, and in all the tribunals and public offices of the United States, and of the several States, without any further proof or authentication thereof.

VIETNAM Repatriation Agreement signed at Hanoi January 22, 2008; Entered into force March 22, 2008
With annexes.

AGREEMENT

BETWEEN
THE GOVERNMENT OF THE UNITED STATES OF AMERICA
AND
THE GOVERNMENT OF THE SOCIALIST REPUBLIC OF VIETNAM
ON
THE ACCEPTANCE OF THE RETURN OF VIETNAMESE CITIZENS

The Government of the United States of America
(hereinafter called "the U.S. Government")
and the Government of the Socialist Republic of Vietnam
(hereinafter called "the Vietnamese Government"),

With a wish of developing friendly relations between the two countries, and to establish procedures for cqmpetent authorities of both countries on the prompt and orderly acceptance of Vietnamese citizens who have been ordered removed by the U.S. Government,

In order to establish common procedures for the relevant authorities based on the legal principles of each country and the international responsibility to accept the return of repatriated citizens; and to follow recognized principles of international law, to allow for a case-by-case determination of repatriation, and to recognize the right of the receiving country to determine nationality.

Have agreed to the following:

Article 1
General Provisions

1. The U.S. Government will carry out the repatriation of Vietnamese citizens who violated U.S. law in accordance with U.S. and international law and the provisions of this Agreement. The repatriation should take into account the humanitarian aspect, family unity and circumstances of each person in each individual case.

2. The Vietnamese Government may consider the return of its citizens who violated U.S. law based on the consideration of legal procedures and the status

and circumstances of each individual case. The subject individuals and the acceptance procedure will be based on the terms of this Agreement.

3. Repatriation will be carried out in an orderly and safe way, and with respect for the individual human dignity of the person repatriated. The U.S. Government will allow Vietnamese citizens who have been ordered removed a reasonable time to arrange their personal affairs before returning them to Vietnam.

4. Persons repatriated under this Agreement have the right to transfer their legal money and personal property to Vietnam.

5. The U.S. Government will pay for the cost of returning to Vietnam persons repatriated under this Agreement, as provided in Article 5 and Annex The U.S. Government will also pay for the cost of returning to the United States any person who was mistakenly repatriated, in accordance with Article 3 of this Agreement.

Article 2
Removable Persons and Conditions of Acceptance

1. The Vietnamese Government will accept the return of Vietnamese citizens in accordance with Article 1 and item 2 of Article 2 of this Agreement, if upon investigation the individual meets the following requirements:

(a) The individual is a citizen of Vietnam and is not a citizen of the United States or of any other country;

(b) The individual previously resided in Vietnam and has no current residence in a third country;

(c) The individual has violated U.S. laws and has been ordered by competent authority removed from the United States; and

(d) If the individual has been convicted of a criminal offense (including immigration violation), the person will have completed any imprisonment before removal, and any reduction in sentence will have been ordered by competent authority.

2. Vietnamese citizens are not subject to return to Vietnam under this Agreement if they arrived in the United States before July 12, 1995, the date on which diplomatic relations were re-established between the U.S. Government and the Vietnamese Government. The U.S. Government and the Vietnamese Government maintain their respective legal positions relative to Vietnamese citizens who departed Vietnam for the United States prior to that date.

3 In the case of a citizen of Vietnam who immigrated to the United States from a third country where that person had a permanent residence and who has been ordered removed from the United States, the U.S. Government will seek to return that person to the third country or consider allowing that person to stay in the United States, before requesting removal to Vietnam.

4. In any case where the Vietnamese Government obtains information relevant to the repatriation of an individual that was not previously considered by

the U.S. Government, the Vietnamese Government may request a humanitarian reconsideration based on the specific circumstances of the repatriated person in accordance with United States law.

Article 3
Return of Persons Repatriated in Error

Upon notice by the Vietnamese Government that a person returned to Vietnam by the U.S. Government does not meet all criteria mentioned in Article 2 of this Agreement, the U.S. Government should promptly receive the return of that person to the United States without any special procedure.

Article 4
Acceptance Procedures

1. When the U.S. Government believes that a removable person is a citizen of Vietnam and meets all criteria within Article 2 of this Agreement, the U.S. Department of Homeland Security, on behalf of the U.S. Government, will request appropriate travel documents from the Vietnamese Government and will forward the appropriate files to that Government. Such files will include three sets of documents, the original and two copies. The original and one copy shall be forwarded to the Vietnamese Ministry of Public Security (Immigration Department) by the U.S. Embassy in Vietnam, and the other copy will be sent to the Vietnamese Ministry of Foreign Affairs (Consular Department).

Each file will contain a diplomatic note which requests that the Vietnamese Government accept the returnee, the name of the person the U.S. Government believes should be repatriated to Vietnam, the appropriate forms completed by such· person (an example of which is provided in Annex 2 of this Agreement), a copy of the order of removal, and other documents regarding the person's biography, citizenship, criminal history, sentence imposed, and decision of amnesty or reduction of criminal sentence. The order of removal will be translated into Vietnamese on the standard form, and the criminal history will include a National Crime Information Center (NCIC) record in English accompanied by a code key translated into Vietnamese. All documents and translations will be certified by the competent U.S. authorities.

2. Upon request by the Vietnamese Government, the U.S. Government will arrange and facilitate the interview of persons who fall within Article 2(1) of this Agreement by Vietnamese immigration officials to determine information regarding the Vietnamese citizenship, biographical data, and last place of residence of such persons. The U.S. Department of Homeland Security will arrange a venue for those interviews. The U.S. Government also will facilitate

interviews by U.S.-based consular officers of the Vietnamese Government of deportable persons whom the U.S. believes to be Vietnamese citizens.

3. The Vietnamese Government will provide a prompt response to the U.S. Government on cases referred under this Article after the Vietnamese verification is made. If it is determined that a person whose name and file has been provided to the Vietnamese Government in accordance with this Article meets the requirements of Article 2, the Ministry of Public Security of the Vietnamese Government will issue a travel document authorizing that person's return to Vietnam, and will provide written notification to the U.S. Embassy in Vietnam.

4. When the Vietnamese Government has issued a travel document under this Agreement, the U.S. Government will provide at least fifteen (I 5) days notice of the flight and travel arrangements by which the person will be returned to Vietnam. The U.S. Embassy in Vietnam will inform the Ministry of Public Security (Immigration Department) and the Ministry of Foreign Affairs (Consular Department) of the date and number of the flight, the time of arrival, the port of entry (Noi Bai Airport in Hanoi or Tan Son Nhat Airport in Ho Chi Minh City), and the details regarding any U.S. officers escorting the person to be returned (such as names, dates of birth, passport numbers, estimated times of stay in Vietnam, etc.), and allow the Vietnamese side to confirm receipt of the returnees.

When a person under medical treatment is returned to Vietnam under this Agreement, the escorting U.S. officers will provide a copy of the person's health record to the receiving Vietnamese officials at the port of entry. The escorting and receiving officers will sign a joint report verifying the person's repatriation.

Article 5 Expenses

1. The U.S. Government will pay for the cost of transporting Vietnamese citizens to Vietnam under this Agreement.

2. The U.S. Government will pay for the costs of receiving repatriated

persons including; verifying fee, the receipt at the airport and transportation of the persons from airport to the place of residences in accordance with the enclosed Annex 1.

3. The U.S. Government will pay for the cost of arranging interviews by relevant Vietnamese officials of persons whom the U.S. Government believes to be Vietnamese citizens and subject to repatriation under this Agreement.

4. The U.S. Government will pay for the cost of returning to the United States persons who were repatriated in error, as provided in Article 3 of this Agreement.

Article 6
Entry into Force and Duration

1. This Agreement will enter into force sixty (60) days from the date of signature by both Governments.

2. Upon entry into force, this Agreement will be valid for five years. The Agreement will be extended automatically for terms of three years thereafter unless written notice not to extend is given by one Government to the other at least six months prior to the expiration date of the Agreement.

Article 7
Amendment and Supplementation

This Agreement may be amended or supplemented by written agreement of the Vietnamese Government and the U.S. Government through appropriate diplomatic channel.

Article 8
Resolution of Disputes

Any disputes regarding the interpretation and implementation of this Agreement will be resolved through appropriate diplomatic channels.

Article 9
Suspension or Termination

This Agreement may be suspended or terminated by either Government. Such suspension or termination of this Agreement will come into effect after thirty days (30) from the date one Government receives the written notification from the other Government of its intention to suspend or terminate.

Done at Hanoi, on 22 January 2008 in duplicate in the English and Vietnamese languages, both texts being equally authentic.

FOR THE GOVERNMENT OF THE UNITED STATES OF AMERICA

FOR THE GOVERNMENT OF THE SOCIALIST REPUBLIC OF VIETNAM

EXPENSES FOR REPATRIATION *(Annex I)*

Content	Expenses for Repatriation
1. Expenses for verification (including verification through the Vietnamese Embassy in the U.S.,) and receipt at airports in Vietnam.	$140/person
2. Transportation fee for the repatriated person from airport to the place of residence.	$10/person
Total:	$150/person

Appendix A-2: MOU-US & Vietnam, 2008

APPENDIX B: AAPA STATEMENT ON VIET NAM (1969)

AAPA October 1969 Volume No.1, Issue No. 6
AAPA Position on Vietnam

"The history of mankind is one of continuous development from the realm of necessity to the realm of freedom." (Mao Tse-Tung)

The Asian American Political Alliance supports all oppressed peoples and their struggles for liberation. A simple glance at the Viet Nam situation clearly defines our stand. The Vietnamese people have been oppressed for thousands of years--first by the Chinese, then the French, the Japanese, and finally by the United States. This oppression has progressed from merely paying tribute to being bombed daily. The entire Vietnamese people are determined to mobilize all their physical and mental strength, to sacrifice their lives and property in order to safeguard their independence and liberty.

In 1945, the Vietminh forces, many who had given their lives working with the Allies through the Office of Special Services, made the mistake of believing U.S. rhetoric. As in 1919, when the U.S. promised China territorial integrity and preached self-determination for all peoples, so it was in Viet Nam in 1945. Viet Nam was officially split in the Geneva Agreement of 1954 to be unified before July 20, 1956. At that time, Ngo Dinh Diem, U.S. puppet and head of the South Vietnamese government, refused to hold the 1956 referendum on reunification. The Vietnamese and Chinese people have now learned to watch the man's hands and not his mouth.

The Vietnamese people not only watch but feel the "peace moves" of the U.S. Even though U.S. troops are slowly being withdrawn from Viet Nam proper, the tempo of the war is increasing. The Paris Peace talks are just a maneuver by the U.S. government to give the proper facade for its senseless war. Monthly U.S. bombings in Viet Nam have increased since Nixon took office. Nixon wants to "win" his war, even if through annihilation of the Vietnamese. Without people there can be no liberation struggle. One-third of the rural population of South Viet Nam has been driven to the cities and six percent of the land has been defoliated. The killing, bombing, starvation, and disease exceed that caused by the Germans in World War II.

The war is a struggle of survival for the Vietnamese. It is a necessity. America is conducting a war of technological genocide in Viet Nam. Any human being, who agrees to participate in this senseless, inhuman war to defend the "free world" (domino theory), deserves to bear the suffering of the Vietnamese people.

America must prove her superiority over Viet Nam; prove that a nuclear power can mobilize the kind of force required to contain guerilla warfare; prove her position as the protector of "certain inalienable rights," such as life, Liberty and the pursuit of Happiness.

The Vietnamese people, struggling for independence; democracy, peace, and neutrality, are resolved to drive out any imperialist forces from Viet Nam. Theirs is a war of human bonds and enduring spirit. They see their comrades, men, women, and children of all ages, die; they see a senseless destruction of the land. In their struggle for survival, ideology and organization has become almost meaningless; human relationships deepen and become the source of strength for the people.

The Asian American Political Alliance supports the ten demands of the National Liberation Front and recognizes the Vietnamese as people.

APPENDIX C: LY HUONG NGUYEN SPEECH FOR NATIONAL DAY OF ACTION (2002)

National Day of Action Speech - API ForCE
Ly Huong Nguyen

The history of how SEAs came to this country as refugees, our struggle to survive and achieve freedom, justice and future for families, our journey to America is well-known. Yet there is another side to our story that is not being portrayed, our stories of the continuing struggle to survive and our present-day struggle to achieve freedom, justice and future for our families in this, our new country. We are here today to tell this story.

Southeast Asian communities are relatively new to this country. Like many third world communities in the US--Native Americans, Blacks, Latinos, Middle Eastern--our experience is one marked by extreme violence, the violence of war and the violence of poverty. SEA came here as refugees as a direct result of US military and political incursions during the VN war. The US government bears a direct responsibility for the social, economic and environmental devastation created by decades of secret military operations, weapons of mass destruction, counterinsurgency campaigns, war crimes, economic sanctions, the legacy of dioxin and land mines, and the plight of SEA refugees. We are here, because America was there. US involvement in Southeast Asia was not just a "mistake", it was immoral and criminal.

Our families came to this country, the beacon of democracy and freedom, to seek safety, freedom from violence and persecution. As with most immigrants, we were not welcomed. The US refused to take SEA refugees until forced to do so by international pressure. Families languished for years in inhumane conditions in refugee camps in the meanwhile. When our families finally were able to come to this country, our communities were randomly divided up. The immediate result was to continue the US's long-standing practice of breaking down community networks, separating families, placing immigrants and non-whites into urban poverty, poor neighborhoods and substandard housing without jobs or provision for negotiating the legal system, obtaining social services or resources for the many who lacked education & skills or had suffered severe trauma. 80% of Southeast Asians live in linguistic isolation and our community has the highest poverty rates of any race or ethnicity in the US. The US again refuses to take responsibility for our communities' welfare and created the conditions for our communities to be plunged into poverty.

Criminalization of Immigrant Youth

Beginning in the 80s, the US mounted a campaign criminalizing Southeast Asian youth as the latest segment in its racist and xenophobic history of criminalizing non-whites and immigrants. Paranoid media depictions of gang violence led to public support for increased police harassment of and brutality against Southeast Asian youth. The spending on Prisons has increased exponentially at the same time that education and social services are being drastically reduced. Especially in this post-9/11 era, public opinion and the government willingly endorse the criminalization, policing and incarceration of all immigrants and non-white youth.

Most of the Cambodian refugees now being targeted for deportation came here as children. The US has been the only home that they know. Most do not have living relatives or material connection to Cambodia. They have already served their time and have the right to be reunited with their families. Deportation constitutes double jeopardy, denies due process, and violates human rights. Many of those slated for deportation are primary income earners in their families. Deportation will force thousands of families into poverty. Deportation punishes our families and hurts our communities.

The paranoid and xenophobic logic behind deportation assumes that by deporting criminals the US would be rid of internal threats and dangers. However, this is based on several arbitrary assumptions about crime and criminality. The concept of crime in the US is framed to directly punish and incarcerate immigrants and non-white youth. "Crime" serves as a tool to exert power, control and physical force over targeted populations especially poor communities. This fails to recognize state crimes and "white collar crimes."

Criminality is not imported by or inherent in refugees and immigrants; crime is brought about by the inhumane conditions in the US -- lack of resources, lack of family networks, the lack of basic human rights like food, water, shelter, education, and health care. As longs as these wretched conditions exist, citizens and non-citizens, all people, will do what they have to survive. The condition in which poor people in the US live is itself criminal and violates our human rights.

From the historical perspective, citizenship itself is an arbitrary, exclusivist and racialized category that the US has historically used as a tool to deny rights to non-whites, Native Americans, freed slaves, African, Asian, Pacific Islander and Latino immigrants whose labor built this country. Restrictive shifts in immigration, naturalization and citizenship policy and laws are deeply linked to racism and xenophobia but in particular to white supremacist ideology and scapegoating of immigrants. Deportation is the most recent form of this historical white supremacism and xenophobia. The central logic is that if you are not a citizen, if you are not white, you do not deserve basic human rights.

As with other immigrants and non-whites, Southeast Asian communities in the US are being targeted simultaneously for poverty, criminalization, incarceration and deportation. The US never wanted Southeast Asians here and will do everything it can to get rid of us.

Like other communities in this country and peoples of the world, Southeast Asians are and have always been the collateral damage of US wars, the Vietnam war, the War on Drugs, the War on Poverty, and today the War on Terrorism.

What is happening to the SEA community is part of a longer history of anti-immigrant laws, racism and human rights abuses since the foundation of this country on slavery and the genocide of indigenous peoples. When slavery was finally brought to an end in this country, the US wanted to deport freed slaves to Africa. Those freed slaves had grown up in the US, had established families, lives, connections and roots. The black community struggled against this injustice and to obtain rights denied to them as human beings. Deportation was not a just solution then, and it is not a just solution now.

History teaches us that injustice can only be transformed by people coming together to struggle against it. Today third world communities across this country have come together to demand justice and human rights for our communities. Justice for all people!

APPENDIX D: SEAFN STATEMENT ON DEPORTATION (2002)

Political Analysis: Cambodian Deportation Committee against Southeast Asian Deportation (SEA Dep) By Ly Huong Nguyen and Loan Dao

Introduction

API Force believes that we are all living in an unbalanced power structure in this society with an unequal distribution of wealth where the minority of wealthy elite oppress the majority of people. This power structure supports white supremacy and protects the wealthy. The involuntary detention and deportation of Southeast Asians is a part of that agenda. The forcible deportation of Cambodian refugees is the intersection of the continuing attacks against immigrant communities and families, the criminalization of poor and immigrant youth, and US violations of our human and legal rights which created the refugee situation in the first place and continues with the "war on terrorism."[1]

The current Memorandum of Understanding (MOU) between the Cambodian government and the United States government violates the legal and human rights of immigrant and refugee people, most of whom came to the U.S. as infants and children. This initiative sets the precedent for further anti-immigrant legislation, for similar negotiations with Viet Nam and Laos, and more power concentrated in the Department of Justice (DOJ) and the INS. Its impact on our communities will be devastating as families are torn apart, youth are disproportionately targeted, and deportees face cruel and unusual punishment.

API ForCE believes that the involuntary deportation of immigrants and refugees is an unjust violation of human rights! Deportation is a continuation of existing attacks on our communities, both here and in our homelands. Already Southeast Asia is being targeted as the "second front" of US terrorism in the world. People in Singapore, Malaysia and the Philippines are being rounded up by the US; US death squads terrorize people in the Philippines.[2] Asian and Pacific Islander communities are all too familiar with the horrors of war and militarism and the devastating impact on our families and countries, where it is the innocent people who suffer most. Our communities are suffering because of US domestic and international policies and actions.

---

1   For API ForCE's political analysis of the "War on Terror" see <www.apiforce. org/features/war.html>

2   AP "Powell: Southeast Asia is 'second front'", 7/28/2002

We oppose the deportation of immigrants and refugees, DOJ imposition of virtual martial law, INS police raids and indefinite detention; we oppose the criminalization of youth and the attacks against immigrants. We challenge the flawed logic behind involuntary deportation, the lack of due process and the violation of human rights for refugee and immigrants. We demand a moratorium on all deportations and that all deportees be granted the right to defend themselves.

There is a growing movement of community members and activists to stop US human rights violations and to demand social justice. We must continue to challenge the dominant view that deportation protects the US from internal threats and bad elements and challenge the state manipulation and traumatization of Cambodian refugees. We must also make connections to what is happening in our SEA community and what is happening to all immigrants and to all third world peoples and communities.

Overview of Cambodian Deportation

Since the passage of the reactionary Immigration & Welfare Reform Act of 1996 (IRWA), all non-citizen immigrants in the US have been subject to mandatory deportation if ever convicted of an "aggravated felony" as loosely defined by the DOJ regardless if it was a non-violent crime or if they had already served time for the crime. This legislation is unconstitutionally retroactive in scope.[3] Because of the Cold War political climate, the US did not have diplomatic relations with the Southeast Asian countries of Viet Nam, Cambodia and Laos for the last 25 years. With no "repatriation" agreements between the US and those nations, Southeast Asian refugees being affected by this legislation were being indefinitely detained by the INS in federal penitentiaries far from family and community. Many of those being deported now were falsely promised by the INS that they would never be deported if they signed voluntary deportation agreements in exchange for release from indefinite detention and return to their families. This coercion denies them due process.

Catalyzed by successful civil liberties lawsuits against indefinite detention and renewed patriotic backlash against immigrants, the US conducted secret negotiations and finally obtained an MOU with Cambodia in March 2002 allowing Cambodian refugees to be forcibly deported to Cambodia. There are reportedly at least 1400 Cambodians who have received notices of deportation; virtually all of them came to the US as small children.[4] The MOU has not been

---

3   IRA text <http://www.networkusa.org/fingerprint/page2/fp-104-208-immigration.html>

4   http://www.searac.org/cambrepbak6_02.html

finalized, however six Cambodian men who have lived in the US approximately 20 years have already been deported as of June, 2002.

The US is probably already engaged in the process of secret negotiations with Viet Nam and Laos to deport Viet and Lao refugees. There are 9,000 deportable Laotian and Viet in the US. It is only a matter of time before deportation will affect Hmong, Mien, Lao and Viet communities.

Historical context: Southeast Asians in the US

Southeast Asian refugees came to the US as a direct result of US military and political incursions in our homelands and the subsequent social, economic and environmental devastation wrought by decades of US secret military operations, counterinsurgency/anti-people campaigns, bombings, warfare and economic sanctions in Cambodia, Laos and Viet Nam. An estimated three million Southeast Asians died during the Viet Nam war; many more continue to suffer from its after effects (such as death and dismemberment from land mines and birth defects as a result of Agent Orange). US secret bombings of Cambodia and military funding set up the conditions for the Khmer Rouge's rise to power and for massive displacement and famine directly leading to three million Khmer deaths. Thus, US involvement/interference in Southeast Asia created the conditions for total social disruption, destruction of families, mass displacement, economic instability, famine and refugee exodus. The US did *not* succeed in winning the "hearts and minds" of Southeast Asians, but it *did* succeed in destroying the countries' economies, destabilizing society and setting up the conditions for social breakdown after its withdrawal. US involvement in Southeast Asia was itself criminal.

The US initially refused to acknowledge any responsibility for the impact of its war on Southeast Asian people, ignored the subsequent dire humanitarian situation of what is called the "Killing Fields of Cambodia" and refused to accept Cambodian refugees in the late 70s early 80s. Because of its role as a primary instigator, the US was finally forced to take responsibility and accept Southeast Asian refugees by mounting international pressure.[5] The US still refuses to take any responsibility for abandoned American land mines throughout Southeast Asia and continues to deny the serious medical impact of Agent Orange. We would not be here as refugees if the US did not wage war in our homelands.

---

5 W. Courtland Robinson. Terms of Refuge: The Indochinese Exodus & the International Response. Zed Books 1998. J. Hein. From Vietnam, Laos, and Cambodia: a refugee experience in the United States. Twayne Publishers 1995. Ngoan Le. "Policy for a community 'at-risk,'" The state of Asian Pacific America: a public policy report. LEAP Asian Pacific American Public Policy Institute and UCLA Asian American Studies Center 1993.

Most of the Cambodian refugees who came to the US were agrarian women, infants and children who survived the trauma of US bombings and landmines, famine, the "Killing Fields," the dangerous escape, and the refugee camps. US resettlement policies haphazardly divided up the Cambodian (and other Southeast Asian) refugees all over the nation – primarily to small cities and towns – to facilitate the assimilation of refugees. The immediate result was to continue the US's long-standing practice of splintering community networks and separating families and placed Southeast Asian refugees into urban poverty, impoverished neighborhoods and substandard housing without the guarantee of living wage jobs. Refugees were minimal government assistance for an ever decreasing amount time and there was no provision for concrete and long term assistance in acculturating to US society and language, negotiating the legal system or for other social services and resources for the many who lacked education & skills or had suffered trauma.[6] 80% of Southeast Asians live in linguistic isolation and have the highest poverty rates of any race or ethnicity in the US.[7] Once again, the US refuses to take any further responsibility for the welfare of Southeast Asian refugees and inserted our refugee communities into poverty.[8]

Criminalization of Immigrant Youth

Beginning in the 1980s, the US media mounted a campaign criminalizing Southeast Asian youth as the latest its history of criminalizing people of color. Paranoid media depictions of alleged Vietnamese and Cambodian gang violence -- in addition to long-standing anti-immigrant and criminalization of "minority" youth backlash -- led to public support for increased police harassment of and brutality against Southeast Asian youth and other third world peoples. Just to take one example, the San Jose and Orange County PD are notorious for racial profiling, police harassment and brutality, and the outright framings of Southeast Asian youth. There have been a few successful legal challenges, but with the passage of Prop 21, Prop 187, Prop 209 in the last decade and especially in this post-9/11 era, public opinion and the government willingly endorse the

---

6 Ibid.
7 see SEARAC <http://www.searac.org/statstab.html>; Asian-Nation http://www. asian-nation.org/issues8.html; also, E. Tang. "Refugee reality: Clinton's Vietnam Fiction," Colorlines. 29 Nov 2000. <http://www.arc.org/C_Lines/CLArchive/ story_web00_06.html>
8 see also, the documentary "Eating Welfare" by CAAAV—Organizing Asian Communities. Bronx, NY 2001. <www.caaav.org>

criminalization, policing and incarceration of our youth.[9] Not surprisingly, Southeast Asians have the highest rising rates of incarceration in the nation.[10]

Most of the Cambodian refugees now being targeted for deportation came here before the age of 10. The US has been the only home that they know. Most do not have living relatives or material connection to Cambodia. Cambodian refugees are being excessively penalized: the injustice of US devastation of the homeland, the devastating living conditions in the US, is compounded by the injustice of incarceration and deportation from their home and their family in the US. Many of those slated for deportation are the primary income earners in their families. Deportation will force thousands of families into poverty. Deportation punishes our families and hurts our communities.

Deportation based on flawed logic

The paranoid and xenophobic logic behind deportation assumes that by deporting criminals the US would be rid of internal threats and dangers. However, this is based on several incorrect and backwards assumptions about crime and criminality. The concept of crime in the US is framed to directly punish and incarcerate young people of color. "Crime" serves as a tool to exert power, control and physical force over targeted populations. Criminal is a code for young people of color from economically impoverished communities. This fails to recognize state crime and "white collar crime." Criminality is not imported by or inherent in refugees and immigrants; crime is brought about by the inhumane conditions in the US -- lack of resources, lack of family networks, the lack of basic human rights like food, water, shelter, education, and health care. Furthermore, the conditions of refugees and poor people in the US are criminal and violates our human rights. Deportation is a further injustice that the US is perpetrating on third world peoples.

Southeast Asian communities in the US are being targeted simultaneously for impoverization, criminalization, incarceration and deportation. The US never wanted Southeast Asians here and will do anything in its power to get rid of us.

Attack on Immigrants and Refugees

The INS has steadily been increasing its power since its inception in the early

---

9   These California propositions increased the criminalization of third world peoples by respectively trying youth as adults, denying immigrants basic human rights such as health care and education, and re-instituting white supremacist hiring & admissions policies. These reactionary and xenophobic propositions were a watershed for other states and for national policies.

10   Southeast Asian Student Coalition, UC Berkeley 2002.

1900s, adding substantial military powers to its range in the last few decades (e.g. the US-México border). [11] The IRA substantially increased the INS' ability to create and enforce punitive actions on immigrants. Following 9/11 the US public and legislative branches have given increasing international powers and autonomy to the INS.[12] The INS has its own military force, its own domestic and overseas intelligence agents, its own armed criminal enforcement (i.e. the policing of immigrants), incarceration system and ability to render indefinite/ lifetime sentences, and the selective use of its legal powers ("prosecutorial discretion").[13] The centralization of powers in the INS sets a dangerous precedent for the erosion of immigrant rights and human rights and marks an era of intense political repression and a right-wing agenda.

INS is a despot

As a federal agency with jurisdiction over immigration matters, the INS currently has discretion in determining involuntary detention and deportation without judicial review or any form of checks and balances in the enforcement, persecution and prosecution of immigrants and refugees. This autonomous power in conjunction with anti-immigrant backlash has led to a loose and arbitrary definition "aggravated felony" to include non-violent crimes – such as check fraud, marijuana possession shoplifting and other non-violent crimes – as grounds for mandatory deportation regardless if the person have served their sentence and are rehabilitated and productive members of society. This constitutes at the very least "double jeopardy" – that is, being punished twice for committing a single crime, serving one's sentence and then being deported – and violates international human rights as a cruel and unusual punishment.

Because the INS has such broad powers – discretionary and enforcement – no one caught in the INS snare is guaranteed Miranda Rights.[14] Not only is the INS enabled to detain and deport immigrants and refugees virtually at will, but indigent deportees do not have the right to a court appointed lawyer. For poor Southeast Asian refugees, this de facto denies them adequate legal counsel. Furthermore, deportees who are detained or are undergoing "removal proceedings" are jailed with the general prison population regardless of the nature

---

11 INS powers < http://www.ins.usdoj.gov/graphics/lawenfor/index.htm> For more on INS militarization, National Border Patrol Strategy <http://www.ins.usdoj.gov/graphics/lawenfor/bpatrol/strategy.htm>

12 Operation Global Reach http://www.ins.usdoj.gov/graphics/publicaffairs/factsheets/globalreach.htm; http://www.ins.usdoj.gov/ graphics/lawsregs/whatsnew.htm

13 http://www.ins.usdoj.gov/graphics/lawenfor/index.htm

14 Miranda Rights <http://www.dui.com/duieducation/Miranda.html>

of their past conviction. Since the INS does not have as yet its own detention facilities, it ships potential deportees to prisons all over the nation regardless of their place of residence. The INS deliberately isolates the deportee from their families and their community support networks and makes it more difficult for action to be taken against the deportation proceedings. The deportation issues has been one cloaked in legal abuses and human rights abuses.

International dimension

The economic success of the US depends on the displacement and marginalization of the majority of the world and of the US population. Cheap or slave labor and cheap resources fuel US economic success. There has historically been an ever-growing struggle to concentrate more capital, resources, and power in the hands of a few countries, of the "First World", of a few corporations, and in the ruling class.

This effort has always been opposed by collective action of the people directly affected in the US and internationally. The power structure has tried to suppress this dissent through many forms, such as anti-immigrant legislation and policies and through deportation. The more wealth and power is concentrated into the hands of the few, the more people will oppose and join the disenfranchised majority in the movement for social justice. And thus the more force will be used throughout the world, and the more our constitutional rights and liberties and human rights as citizens and non-citizens living in the US will diminish.

Historically the US "opens" its borders for immigration of cheap labor to bolster its economic growth. The US pushes its surplus labor into the prison system and uses deportation as a "safety-valve".[15] The unemployment rate is rising while social services for the people are being cut. With the economic situation weakening, there is much potential for growing instability and discontent of people all over the world, including here in the US. The US ruling elite needs more than ever, ways to maintain its profit level for the rich while squashing dissent worldwide. The fear and paranoia of 9.11 allowed them to strengthen forces internationally as well as remove constitutional rights and civil liberties domestically. Over the last four decades, the prisons have expanded at an exponential rate into an industry to control poor and immigrant communities. Deportation is a false solution to perpetuate this agenda.

We believe that the US is once again trying to get away with human rights violations under the guise of national security. We oppose the deportation of immigrants and refugees, INS police raids and indefinite detention; we oppose

---

15 See for example the Bracero program.

the criminalization of youth and the attacks against immigrants. We challenge the flawed logic behind involuntary deportation and the violation of human rights for refugee and immigrants. We demand that all deportees be granted a deferred action status and the right to defend themselves.

APPENDIX E: SEAFN DEMANDS TO U.N. HUMAN RIGHTS COUNCIL (2015)

REFUGEES
MARCH 18, 2015/ 1LOVEMOVEMENT
The Universal Periodic Review of the United States of America
Second Cycle | Twenty-Second Session of the UPR | Human Rights Council
Southeast Asian Freedom Network

2015 marks 40 years since Southeast Asian refugee communities were displaced by militarism and war, and began being resettled in the US. In recognition of our community's deep resilience and power in the face of struggle, we continue our fight for justice and declare the following systemic US human rights violations against the Cambodian community over the course of the last five decades:

Universal Declaration of Human Rights, Article 3. Right to Life, Liberty and Security

Between 1965-1973 the US dropped 2,756,941 tons of bombs, in a secret and illegal military campaign, across the countryside of Cambodia, which was an internationally declared neutral country. The destruction of 8 years of bombing led Cambodia into the hands of the rising, and genocidal leadership of the Khmer Rouge.

April 17, 2015 will mark 40 years since the Khmer Rouge marched on Phnom Penh and vacated the city, forcibly leading families and children into the Killing Fields for the next 3 years, 8 months, and 20 days. During this time nearly 2 million people, approximately 21% of our population, lost their lives to genocide.

Universal Declaration of Human Rights, Article 25. Right to Food, Shelter and Health

Beginning in the 1970s, there was a mass influx of Southeast Asians to the US due to war and political upheavals in their countries. A total of 1,146,650 Southeast Asians were resettled in the US from 1975-2002. Upon our arrival, the structures of support needed for our community to heal, survive, and grow, were not in place. Families were exploited for cheap labor, apartments and houses were falling apart, and as refugees we experienced deep trauma and mental health issues. A 2004 survey revealed that 70% of Cambodian-Americans exhibit signs of post-traumatic stress disorder (PTSD) due to the loss of family members, experience of labor camps, and war.

Universal Declaration of Human Rights, Article 26. Right to Education, & Article 7. Right to Equality Before the Law

Most Southeast Asian refugees were resettled into inhumane conditions in impoverished neighborhoods, making us vulnerable to poverty, crime, violence, structural disadvantage, racism, discrimination and profiling. Many young people fell through the cracks in an under-resourced education system unfit to meet their needs, leaving only 65% of Cambodian-American youth graduating from high school. Many enter into a highly functional and highly funded School-to-Prison Pipeline. Law enforcement agencies in cities across the country began coding Cambodian communities as "gang infested" and we were surveilled and profiled for arrest and incarceration. Over-policing of our community led to racial profiling, police brutality, and high incarceration rates, higher than any other Asian ethnic group in relation to the size of our population.

Universal Declaration of Human Rights, Article 10. Right to Due Process, Article 16. Right to Family Unity, & Article 9. Right to Freedom from Arbitrary Arrest, Detention, Exile

In 1996, the US passed the Illegal Immigration Reform and Immigrant Responsibility Act (IIRIRA) and Anti-terrorism and Effective Death Penalty Act

(AEDPA). These laws expanded "aggravated felony" to include offenses that are neither aggravated nor felonious under criminal justice law, but lead to deportation under immigration law. Judicial discretion and individualized deportation hearings were eliminated for those being deported for such "aggravated felonies," leaving individuals stripped of their right to due process. Deportation for "aggravated felonies" also became permanent with no right to return, and was applied retroactively, leading to international human rights violations regarding proportionality of punishment, double jeopardy, and fairness under the law.

Universal Declaration of Human Rights, Article 21. Right to Democracy

On March 22, 2002 the US signed a Repatriation Agreement with Cambodia and began deporting Cambodian-Americans. This agreement was signed without transparency, insight, or accountability to the community impacted. It was signed swiftly and secretly.

Repatriation Agreements must be seen as human rights contracts, because they impact the livelihood and survival of individuals and families. These agreements need to reflect the unique conditions and experiences of the diaspora they apply to, and participating countries must be accountable to the impact of deportation on the diaspora, as well as the history and conditions of their displacement. As such, the creation of such agreements must be done through transparent, open, and democratic processes that prioritize the will of the people and insight of directly impacted communities.

As a Cambodian-American refugee community, we have been rooted in an intergenerational struggle over the last five decades to keep our families together against unjust forces of US militarism, war, systemic poverty, education inequity, imprisonment, institutionalized racism, discrimination, and deportation. With over 500 Cambodian- American families broken apart since 2002, and over 4000 more awaiting the same fate, our human rights fight today, is deportation.

REQUESTED ACTION

We call for immediate recourse to begin to rectify over five decades of US human rights violations that have torn Cambodian families apart from Cambodia to the US, and back again:

1. We call for an immediate suspension of US deportations to Cambodia.

2. We call for an open review process of the US-Cambodia Repatriation Agreement, which includes and prioritizes democratic oversight and input of impacted communities in the US and Cambodia.

3. We call for amendments to the Repatriation Agreement that tailor its impacts to consider the individual and community experience of US human rights violations, and will protect those with these experiences from deportation.

4. We call for amendments to the Repatriation Agreement that ensure humane, just, and fair structures of support for impacted families and individuals in the US and Cambodia, including economic stability, human and social services, employment infrastructure, visitation rights, and the right to return.

QUESTIONS TO THE US GOVERNMENT

1. Will the United States commit to suspending US deportations to Cambodia until human rights issues can be rectified through amendments to the US-Cambodia Repatriation Agreement?

2. Will the United States commit to undergoing an open review process of the current Repatriation Agreement with Cambodia which includes and prioritizes democratic oversight and input of impacted communities in the US and Cambodia?

############

The Southeast Asian Freedom Network (SEAFN) is a national collective of Southeast Asian grassroots organizing groups that works towards radical & transformational change led by those most impacted by systemic injustice.

SEAFN Member Groups: 1Love Movement, Freedom Inc., ManForward, Mekong NYC, Providence Youth Student Movement, SOY-Shades of Yellow, and VAYLA New Orleans.

APPENDIX F: SEAFN 40TH ANNIVERSARY STATEMENT (2015)

SEAFN STATEMENT: April 17, 2015

TODAY, marks 40 years since our country was taken over by the Khmer Rouge revolution. It was revolution that was rooted in political theory, but not liberatory action. Revolution built on communist ideology, but practiced through dictatorship and mass murder. Revolution that promised life, but led to the genocide of our people. Revolution that cherished our homeland, but led us to displacement.

TODAY, as SEAFN reflects on the deep resistance and resilience of our community, we also commit to recognizing the historic root causes of our experience. We know that French colonialism, and US imperialism and militarism bear responsibility for creating the conditions that led our country into the Killing Fields. We experience this oppression through continuous cycles of violence from one side of the world to the other, from war to displacement to poverty to incarceration to deportation. We are the collateral damage and human cost of colonialism, imperialism, and militarism. And we know that we will continue to carry the weight of all of this systemic violence for generations to come, and that we must heal through determined resistance and resilience.

TODAY, we are called to reclaim the meaning of revolution for our communities. We must continue to break the cycle of isolated trauma, and ground ourselves in collective healing, and actions rooted in our historic experience and our current conditions. And we have already begun. Our revolution has been our survival and our determination to re-build and re-center our lives, our families, and our people. Our revolution has been our resilient creation of new pathways for us to experience family, love, healing, and community. As we continue to struggle with the impact of intergenerational systemic oppression, we are building a new foundation that honors our humanity and dignity.

TODAY, our revolution honors our ancestors, our history, and our struggle. Our revolution is about action rooted in love. It is about building vision through support for each other and our experiences. It is about taking back our dignity by reclaiming and redefining our art, our culture, our music, and our expression. It is about challenging the ways that we have internalized systemic imbalance and oppression, and taking accountability for the ways this has caused us to enact violence on each other. It is about doing the work of continuously acknowledging our systemic privileges, and deepening our solidarity with other oppressed communities in a country founded on white supremacy, anti-blackness and indigenous genocide. It is about identifying our movement purpose through analysis of root causes and systemic responsibility. It is about fighting back against the separation of families from generation to generation.

TODAY, 40 years later, we are called to be revolutionary, and move together in the fight of our generation...the fight for our families, the fight for our communities. Today, that means ending deportation.

Notes

Chapter One Notes

1   Frantz Fanon, *The Wretched of the Earth*, trans. Richard Philcox (New York: Grove, 1963/1990), 206.

2   Loan Dao, "We Will Not Be Moved: The Mobilization Against Southeast Asian Detention and Deportation" (Ph.D. diss., University of California, Berkeley, 2009).

3   For M.O.U.s, see Appendix A.

4   Loan Dao, "Refugee Representations: Youth, Hip Hop, and Southeast Asian Deportation," *Amerasia Journal* 40, no. 2 (2014): 88–110.

5   The Southeast Asian Youth Leadership Project (YLP) was a social justice youth program created by Communities Against Asian American Violence (CAAAV) in the northwest Bronx, New York, that organized Southeast Asian American youth and their families. YLP became independent from CAAAV in 2011 and is referred to as Mekong in later chapters.

6   Espiritu, *Body Counts*; Nguyen, "Refugee Memories and Asian American Critique"; Thu-Huong Nguyen-Vo, "Forking Paths: How Shall We Mourn the Dead?" *Amerasia Journal* 31, no. 2 (2005): 157–75; Kieu-Linh Caroline Valverde, *Transnationalizing Viet Nam: Community, Culture, and the Politics in the Diaspora* (Philadelphia: Temple University Press, 2012).

7   Loan Dao, "What's Going On with the Oakland Museum's 'California & the Vietnam Era' Exhibit," *AmerAsia Journal: 30 Years AfterWARd: Vietnamese Americans & U.S. Empire* 30, no. 2 (2005): 88–108.

8   Aihwa Ong, *Buddha Is Hiding: Refugees, Citizenship, and the New America* (Berkeley: University of California Press, 2003); Alejandro Portes and Ruben G. Rumbaut, *Legacies: The Story of Immigrant Second Generation* (Berkeley: University of California Press, 2001); Min Zhou and Carl L. Bankston, III, *Growing Up American: How Vietnamese Children Adjust to Life in the United States* (New York: Russell Sage Foundation, 1998).

9   For more on AAM origins and history, see Diane C. Fujino, "Who Studies the Asian American Movement? A Historiographical Analysis," *Journal of Asian American Studies* 11, no. 2 (2008): 127–69; Kim Geron, "Serve the People: An Exploration of the Asian American Movement," in *Asian American Politics: Law, Participation, and Policy*, ed. Don Nakanishi and James Lai (Lanham, MD: Rowman & Littlefield, 2003), 163–79; Michael Liu, Kim Geron, and Tracy Lai, *The Snake Dance of Asian American Activism* (London: Lexington Books, 2008); Daryl Maeda, *Chains of Babylon: The Rise of Asian America* (Minneapolis: University of Minnesota Press, 2009); Glenn Omatsu, "The Four Prisons and the Movements for Liberation," in *Asian American Politics: Law, Participation, and Policy*, ed. Don Nakanishi and James Lai (Lanham, MD: Rowman & Littlefield, 2002), 135–62.

10   I am using Pew Research Center's generational categorization (April 11, 2018), in which Millennials are those who were born between 1981 and 1996, and post-Millennials were born from 1997. http://www. pewresearch.org/facttank/2018/04/11/generationsdefined2017/.

11   MAAs are organizations that began in the 1970s and 1980s by co-ethnic refugees to assist newer cohorts of arrivals with resettlement in the United States. They operated mainly through funding from the U.S. Office of Refugee Resettlement (ORR), private foundations, and donors. MAAs developed in response to the crisis of refugee resettlement when the U.S. government agencies and resettlement agencies, largely religious and formed out of the refugee influx from Europe post-WWII, were ill-equipped to support the unique needs of Southeast Asian refugees. These large, Euro-American agencies frequently received funding from the ORR and subcontracted a portion to MAAs, which subsisted on shoestring budgets. Many MAA leaders became the representational voices and gatekeepers of the refugee communities, and later played instrumental roles in forming national, ethnic-specific advocacy organizations. For more on the development of MAAs, see Chan, *Not Just Victims*; Jeremy Hein, *From Vietnam, Laos, and Cambodia: A Refugee Experience in The United States* (New York: Twayne Publications, 1995); and Tuyen Tran, "Behind the Smoke and Mirrors: The Vietnamese in California, 1975–1994" (PhD diss., University of California, Berkeley, 2007).

12   Eric Tang uses Wacquant's concept of the hyperghetto to describe the socio-economic conditions of the northwest Bronx in New York City, where Cambodian and Vietnamese refugees were resettled in the 1980s and suffered severe isolation, neglect, exploitation, and criminalization.

See Eric Tang, *Unsettled: Cambodian Refugees in the New York City Hyperghetto* (Philadelphia: Temple University Press, 2015).

13   My emphasis that the refugee is "no longer a refugee" harkens to ongoing debates about the concept of the perpetual refugee (Fung 2010) in both refugee studies and Southeast Asian American studies whereby one is forever burdened and haunted by the label and the assumed responsibilities attached to it, literally and figuratively. In regard to MAAs, the retreat from funding by the state, particularly the Office of Refugee Resettlement, and private funders from Southeast Asian refugee organizations from the American War in Southeast Asia toward newer refugee populations, forces a reckoning with the material evidence of the end of an era for refugee resettlement from Laos, Cambodia, and Viet Nam.

14   Erica Kohl-Arenas, "Governing Poverty Amidst Plenty: Participatory Development and Private Philanthropy," *Geography Compass* 5, no. 11 (2011): 10. For more on the "non-profit industrial complex," see INCITE! Women of Color Against Violence, *The Revolution Will Not Be Funded: Beyond the Non-profit Industrial Complex* (Cambridge: South End Press, 2007); Tim Bartley, "How Foundations Shape Social Movements: The Construction of an Organizational Field and the Rise of Forest Certification," *Social Problems* 54, no. 3 (2007): 229–55; Susan Ostrander, "Legacy and Promise for Social Justice Funding: Charitable Foundations and Progressive Social Movements, Past and Present," in *Foundations for Social Change: Critical Perspectives on Philanthropy and Popular Movements*, ed. D. Faber and D. McCarthy (Lanham, MD: Rowman & Littlefield, 2005), 33–59.

15   INCITE! Women of Color Against Violence, *The Revolution Will Not Be Funded*; Andrea Del Moral, "The Revolution Will Not Be Funded," *LiP Magazine*, April 4, 2005, accessed September 11, 2020, http://www.lipmagazine.org/articles/featdelmoral_nonprofit_p.html.

16   Craig Jenkins and Abigail Halci, "Grassrooting the System?: The Development and Impact of Social Movement Philanthropy, 1953–1960," in *Philanthropic Foundations: New Scholarship, New Possibilities*, ed. E. C. Lagemann (Bloomington: Indiana University Press, 1999).

17   Dylan Rodriguez, "The Political Logic of the Non-Profit Industrial Complex," in *The Revolution Will Not Be Funded: Beyond the Non-Profit Industrial Complex*, ed. INCITE! Women of Color Against Violence (Cambridge: South End Press, 2007), 21–40.

18   Cristina M. Balboa, "How Successful NGOs Set Themselves Up for Failure on the Ground," *World Development* 54 (2014): 273–87; Nicola Banks, David Hulmes, and Michael Edwards, "NGOs, States, and Donors Revisited: Still Too Close for Comfort?" *World Development* 66 (2015): 707–18; Alnoor Ebrahim, "Making Sense of Accountability: Conceptual Perspectives for Northern and Southern Nonprofits," *Nonprofit Management & Leadership* 14, no. 2 (2003): 191–212; Geoffrey Q. C. Robertson, *Crimes Against Humanity: The Struggle for Global Justice*, 4th ed. (New York: The New Press, 2012); Adil Najam, "NGO Accountability: A Conceptual Framework," *Development Policy Review* 14, no. 4 (1996): 339–54; Stein (1984); Eric Wolf, "Kinship, Friendship, and Patron-client Relations," in *The Social Anthropology of Complex Societies*, ed. Michael Banton (London: Routledge, 2004), 1–22.

19   Conversation with Doua Thor of SEARAC (May 2013).

20   501(c)3 status is a federal Internal Revenue Service (IRS) designation for tax-exempt, charitable organizations, that operate for the public good and not for profit. This identification restricts political activity and legislative activities outlined by the IRS at https://www.irs.gov/charities-non-profits/charitable-organizations/the-restriction-of-political-campaign-intervention-by-section-501-c-3-tax-exempt-organizationss.

21   Soo Ah Kwon, *Uncivil Youth: Race, Activism, and Affirmative Governmentality* (Durham: Duke University Press, 2013), 58.

22   Paul Kivel, "Social Service or Social Change?" in *The* Revolution *Will Not Be Funded: Beyond the Non-Profit Industrial Complex* (Boston: South End Press, 2007), 129–50.

23   Mimi Thi Nguyen, *The Gift of Freedom: War, Debt, and Other Refugee Passages* (Durham: Duke University Press, 2012), 183.

24   1.5-generation refers to refugees and immigrants who immigrated as minors (before the age of 18). I also interchangeably refer to this population with the legal term "childhood arrivals." 1.8-generation are childhood arrivals who migrated before they were of school age and spent their entire K-12 educational experience in the United States. Second-generation refers to children of immigrants and refugees who were born in the country of resettlement, but retain similar characters of 1.5-generation due to their family migration history. For more, see Portes and Rumbaut, *Legacies*.

25   Cathy J. Schlund-Vials, *War, Genocide, Justice: Cambodian American Memory Work* (Minneapolis: University of Minnesota Press, 2012), 184.

26   Harvey C. Dong, "The Origins and Trajectory of Asian American Political Activism in the San Francisco Bay Area, 1968–1978" (PhD diss., University of California, Berkeley, 2003); Fujino, "Who Studies the Asian American Movement?"; Maeda, *Chains of Babylon*.

27   Benedict R. Anderson, *Imagined Communities: Reflections on the Origin and Spread of Nationalism* (London: Verso Books, 2006).

28   Maeda, *Chains of Babylon*, 98–99.

29   For more on AAM's stance against the Viet Nam War, see Grace Lee Boggs, "Interview," *Democracy Now*, July 13, 2007; Grace Lee Boggs with Scott Kurashige, *The Next American Revolution: Sustainable Activism for the Twenty-first Century* (Berkeley: University of California Press, 2011); Dong, "The Origins and Trajectory of Asian American Political Activism in the San Francisco Bay Area, 1968–1978," "AAPA Position on Vietnam [from October 1969. *AAPA Newspaper* 14]" in *Stand Up! An Archive Collection of the Bay Area Asian-American Movement 1968–1974*, ed. Harvey Dong (Berkeley: Asian Community Center Archive Group, 2009), 32–33; Fred Ho, *Legacy to Liberation: Politics and Culture of Revolutionary Asian Pacific America* (San Francisco: AK Press and Big Red Media, 2000); Yuri Nakahara Kochiyama, *Passing It On—A Memoir*, ed. Marjorie Lee, Akemi Kochiyama-Sardinha, and Audee Kochiyama-Holman (Los Angeles: UCLA Asian American Studies Center Press, 2004); Steve Louie and Glen Omatsu, eds., *Asian Americans: The Movement and the Moment* (Los Angeles: UCLA Asian American Studies Center Press, 2001); Maeda, *Chains of Babylon*; Laura Pulido, *Black, Brown, Yellow and Left: Radical Activism in Los Angeles* (Berkeley: University of California Press, 2006).

30   Ruth Wilson Gilmore, "In the Shadow of the Shadow State," in *The Revolution Will Not Be Funded: Beyond the Non-profit Industrial Complex*, ed. INCITE!: Women of Color Against Violence (Cambridge: South End Press, 2007), 41–52; Kohl-Arenas, "Governing Poverty Amidst Plenty"; Omatsu, "The Four Prisons and the Movements for Liberation"; William Wei, *The Asian American Movement* (Philadelphia: Temple University Press, 1993).

31   Fujino, "Who Studies the Asian American Movement?"; Omatsu, "The Four Prisons and the Movements for Liberation."

32   Jeff Chang, *Can't Stop Won't Stop: A History of the Hip-Hop Generation* (New York: St. Martin's Press, 2005); Omatsu, "The Four Prisons and the Movements for Liberation."

33   Yen Li Espiritu, *Body Counts: The Viet Nam War and Militarized Refugees* (Berkeley: University of California Press, 2014), 101.

34   Viet Thanh Nguyen, "Refugee Memories and Asian American Critique," *Positions* 20, no. 3 (2012): 924.

35   Yen Le Espiritu called for scholars to engage in a "[Critical Refugee Studies) that is refashioned in the fields of Vietnamese Studies, Asian American Studies and American Studies, not around the benign narratives of American exceptionalism, immigration, or even transnationalism, but around the crucial issues of war, race, and violence." See Yen Le Espiritu, "Toward a Critical Refugee Study: The Vietnamese Refugee Subject in U.S. Scholarship," *Journal of Vietnamese Studies* 11, no. 2 (2006): 426.

36   Throughout the book, I reference four different generations in relation to activism. In this context, generation means when a critical mass reach a stage at which they have the political awareness and organizing skills to lead campaigns, be the spokespeople, or even be gatekeepers for the community. The first generation is the originators of the Asian American Movement, ethnic studies, and the anti-war movement during the 1960s and 1970s. The second generation is predominately the professionalized class that formed the non-profit organizations in the 1980s and 1990s. The Millennial generation, including the founders of PrYSM, emerged as youth leaders just around September 11, 2001. The post-Millennial leaders are youth who came of age to lead around 2016, the majority of whom have gone through political development as youth members in the SEAA youth organizations and were born and raised in the post-9/11 environment.

37   For more on Southeast Asian refugee migration and resettlement to the U.S., see Nancy D. Donnelly, *The Changing Lives of Refugee Hmong Women* (Seattle: University of Washington Press, 1994); James Freeman, *Hearts of Sorrow: Vietnamese American Lives* (Stanford: Stanford University Press, 1989); David W. Haines, ed. *Refugees in America in the 1990s: A Reference Handbook* (Westport, CT: Greenwood Press, 1996); Hein, *From Vietnam, Laos, and Cambodia*; W. Courtland Robinson, *Terms of Refuge: The Indochinese Exodus and the International Response* (New York: Zed Books, Ltd., 1995).

38   Robin D. G. Kelley, *Freedom Dreams: The Black Radical* Imagination (Boston: Beacon Press, 2002), 196.

39   Charles Tilly, *Social Movements: 1768–2004* (Boulder, CO: Paradigm Publishers, 2004). See also Jeff Goodwin and James M. Jasper, eds., *Rethinking Social Movements: Structure, Meaning and Emotion* (New York: Roman & Littlefield, 2004); Francesca Polletta, *It Was Like a Fever: Storytelling in Protest and Politics* (Chicago: University of Chicago Press, 2006a); Francesca Polletta with John Lee, "Is Telling Stories Good for Democracy? Rhetoric in Public Deliberation after 9/11," *American Sociological Review* 71, no. 5 (2006b): 699–723; Sidney Tarrow, *The New Transnational Activism* (Cambridge: Cambridge University Press, 2005); Charles Tilly, *From Mobilization to Revolution* (Chicago: Dorsey Press, 1978).

40   Lisa Marie Cacho, *Social Death: Racialized Rightlessness and the Criminalization of the Unprotected* (New York: New York University Press, 2012); Dao, "We Will Not Be Moved," "Refugee Representations"; Bill Hing, *Defining America through Immigration Policy: An Interpretive History* (Philadelphia: Temple University Press, 2004), *Deporting Our Souls: Values, Morality, and Immigration Policy* (New York: Cambridge University Press, 2006); Kwon, *Uncivil Youth*.

41   Carolyn Ellis, Tony E. Adams, and Arthur P. Bochner, "Autoethnography: An Overview," *Historical Social Research* 36, no. 4 (2011): 273.

42   James C. Scott, *Domination and the Arts of Resistance: Hidden Transcripts* (New Haven: Yale University Press, 1992).

43   I attended the 2002 Freedom Training organized by the Youth Leadership Project of the Committee against Anti-Asian American Violence (CAAAV) in the Bronx in New York City that formed SEAFN and sat on the SEAFN steering committee until 2004. As the lead in the campaign against detention and deportation in Oakland, California, I assisted families with their legal cases and social needs, serving as a liaison with pro bono lawyers, mobilizing people to fill the courtrooms for hearings, and identifying social services for other issues, such as depression. I organized campaign events and protests, spoke to media and at events and rallies, and created a method of gathering and tracking individual experiences to find patterns that would be the basis of future campaigns.

44   Tony E. Adams, Stacy Holman Jones, and Carolyn Ellis, *Autoethnography: Understanding Qualitative Research* (New York: Oxford University Press, 2014); Verta Taylor, "Feminist Methodology in Social Movements Research," *Qualitative Sociology* 21, no. 4 (1998): 357–79.

45   Christina Chavez, "Conceptualizing from the Inside: Advantages, Complications, and Demands on Insider Positionality," *The Qualitative Report* 13, no. 3 (2008): 474–94.

46   Linda Trinh Vo, "Whose School District is This? Vietnamese American and Coalitional Politics in Orange County, California," *AAPI Nexus* 5, no. 2 (2007): 1–32.

47   Milan Kang, "Researching One's Own: Negotiating Co-Ethnicity in the Field,» in *Cultural Compass: Ethnographic Explorations of Asian America*, ed. Martin Manalansan (Philadelphia: Temple University Press, 2000).

48   Kelley, *Freedom Dreams*.

49   Kathy Charmaz, *Constructing Grounded Theory: A Practical Guide Through Qualitative Analysis* (London: Sage, 2006).

50   Merideth Minkler, *Community Organizing and Community Building for Health and Welfare*, 3rd ed. (New Brunswick: Rutgers University Press, 2012).

51   Charmaz, *Constructing Grounded Theory*, 60–63.

52   Charmaz, *Constructing Grounded Theory*; B. G. Glasser and A. L. Strauss, *The Discovery of Grounded Theory* (Chicago: Aldine Press, 1967); Anselm Strauss and Juliet Corbin, *Basics of Qualitative Research: Grounded Theory Procedures and Techniques* (Thousand Oaks, CA: Sage, 1990).

53   I followed Blee and Taylor's guide in conducting qualitative interviews in a social movement context. See Kathleen M. Blee and Verta Taylor, "Semi-Structured Interviewing in Social Movement Research," in *Methods of Social Movement Research*, vol. 16 (Minneapolis: University of Minnesota Press, 2002), 92–117.

54   Alexander L. George and Andrew Bennett, *Case Studies and Theory Development in the Social Sciences* (Cambridge: MIT Press, 2005).

Chapter Two Notes

55 Yuri Kochiyama, *Passing It On: A Memoir*, 170.

56 Nguyen, "Refugee Memories and Asian American Critique."

57 Tang, *Unsettled*, 13.

58 Tang, *Unsettled*, 54.

59 Stephen M. Reder and John Finck, *The Hmong Resettlement Study Site Report: Providence, RI* (Washington, D.C.: Office of Refugee Resettlement, July 1984), 2.

60 United States Census, "Quick Facts on Rhode Island 2010 Census," http://quickfacts.census.gov/qfd/states/44000lk.html; U.S. Census (2000).

61 Southeast Asian Resource Action Center (SEARAC), *Southeast Asians at a Glance* (Washington, D.C.: Southeast Asian Resource Action Center, 2011).

62 PrYSM and CSEA, National Survey on Southeast Asian LGBTQ Youth, 2008.

63 SEARAC, Southeast Asians at a Glance.

64 Diana Bui, *Cambodian Resettlement in Rhode Island* (Washington, D.C.: Office of Refugee Resettlement, 1981); North and Sok, *Profiles of Some Good Places for Cambodians to Live in the United States* (Washington, D.C.: Family Support Administration, March 1989); Reder and Finck, *The Hmong Resettlement Study Site Report*.

65 Reder and Finck, *The Hmong Resettlement Study Site Report*, 9.

66 Reder and Finck, *The Hmong Resettlement Study Site Report*, 11.

67 Center for SouthEast Asians of Rhode Island, www.CESARI.org.

68 Tuyen Tran, "Behind the Smoke and Mirrors: The Vietnamese in California, 1975–1994" (PhD diss., University of California, Berkeley, 2007).

69 North and Sok, *Profiles of Some Good Places for Cambodians to Live in the United States.*

Chapter Three Notes

70 Rhode Island Historical Society, www.rihs.org.

71 Reder and Finck, *The Hmong Resettlement Study Site Report*, 4.

72 Gilmore, "In the Shadow of the Shadow State."

73 Victor Rios, *Human Targets: Schools, Police, and the Criminalization of Latino Youth* (Chicago: University of Chicago Press, 2017).

74 Hanhardt, *Safe Space*, 5.

75 Ong, *Buddha Is Hiding.*

76 Rios, *Punished*, 40.

77 Rios, *Punished*, 41.

78 Edmund F. McGarrell, Natalie Kroovand Hipple, Nicholas Corsaro, Timothy S. Bynum, Heather Perez, Carol A. Zimmermann, and Melissa Garmo, *Project Safe Neighborhoods –A National Program to Reuce Gun Crime: Final Project Report* (Washington, D.C.: Department of Justice, April 2009), iii.

79 McGarrell et al., *Project Safe Neighborhoods*, vii.

80 U.S. Department of Justice, "Crime Statistics, 2006," www.justice. gov, 97–98.

81 U.S. Department of Justice, "Crime Statistics, 2006," 100.

82 U.S. Department of Justice, "Crime Statistics, 2006," 100.

83 U.S. Department of Justice, "Crime Statistics, 2006," 98–100.

84 Patricia Hill Collins and Sirma Bilge, *Intersectionality: Key Concepts* (Cambridge: Polity Press, 2016), 2.

85   Kimberlé Crenshaw, "Mapping the Margins: Intersectionality, Identity Politics, and Violence Against Women of Color," *Stanford Law Review* 43, no. 6 (July 1991): 1282.

86   Carlos Muñoz, Jr., *Youth, Identity, Power: The Chicano Movement* (London: Verso Books, 1989), 6.

87   Collins and Bilge, *Intersectionality*, 2.

88   David L. Eng, "Out Here and Over There: Queerness and Diaspora in Asian American Studies," *Social Text* 52/53 (1997): 31–52; Michael Hames-Garcia and Ernesto Javier Martinez, eds., *Gay Latino Studies: A Critical Reader* (Durham: Duke University Press, 2011).

89   Crenshaw, "Mapping the Margins," 1252.

90   I use "queer" interchangeably with LGBTQ+ as it is the term of choice by PrYSM and SEAFN members.

91   Monisha Das Gupta, *Unruly Immigrants: Rights, Activism and Transnational South Asian Politics in the U.S.* (Durham: Duke University Press, 2006); Sunaina Marr Maira, *Missing: Youth, Citizenship and Empire after 9/11* (Durham: Duke University Press, 2009); Rajini Srikanth, *Constructing the Enemy: Empathy/Antipathy in U.S. Literature and Law* (Philadelphia: Temple University Press, 2011).

92   Victor Rios defines hypercriminalization to describe the conditions of Latino youth in East Oakland, California: "The process by which an individual's everyday behaviors and styles become ubiquitously treated as deviant, risky, threatening, or criminal, across social contexts" (xiv). He uses sociologist Loïc Wacquant's concept of the hyperghetto, in which the culture of the prison and the ghetto are indistinguishable. See Victor M. Rios, *Punished: Policing the Lives of Black and Latino Boys* (New York: New York University Press, 2011).

93   Hing, *Deporting Our Souls*.

94   Dao, "We Will Not Be Moved"; Tanya Maria Golash-Boza, *Deported: Immigrant Policing, Disposable Labor, and Global Capitalism* (New York: New York University Press, 2015); Maira, *Missing*; Srikanth, *Constructing the Enemy*.

95   PrYSM, "About," www.prysm.us.

96   Valerie Lehr, *Queer Family Values: Debunking the Myth of the Nuclear Family* (Philadelphia: Temple University Press, 1999); Russell Leong, ed., *Asian American Sexualities: Dimensions of the Gay and Lesbian Experience* (New York: Routledge, 1995); Catherine Ramirez, "Representing, Politics, and the Politics of Representation in Gang Studies," *American Quarterly* 56, no. 4 (2004): 1135–146.

97   Ong, *Buddha Is Hiding*, 235.

98   Ong, *Buddha Is Hiding*, 240.

99   Portes and Rumbast, *Legacies*.

100   Lehr, *Queer Family Values*.

101   Collins and Bilge, *Intersectionality*, 68.

102   Combahee River Collective, "First Official Statement on CRC Formation," (1973/ 1995).

103   Collins and Bilge, *Intersectionality*, 69.

104   Pulido, *Black, Brown, Yellow and Left*, 238.

105   bell hooks, *Teaching to Transgress: Education as a Practice of Freedom* (New York: Routledge, 1994), 244–245.

106   Elizabeth Armstrong, *Forging Gay Identities: Organizing Sexuality in San Francisco, 1950–1994* (Chicago: University of Chicago Press, 2002), 3.

107   hooks, *Teaching to Transgress*, 243.

108   Armstrong, *Forging Gay Identities*, 34.

109   Armstrong, *Forging Gay Identities*, 61–62.

110   Christine B. Hanhardt, *Safe Space: Gay* Neighborhood *History and the Politics of Violence* (Durham: Duke University Press, 2013), 31.

111   Portes and Rumbaut, *Legacies*.

112 hooks, *Teaching to Transgress*, 246.

Chapter Three Notes

113 Robin D. G. Kelley, *Race Rebels: Culture, Politics, and the Black Working Class* (New York: The Free Press, 1994).

114 Doug McAdam and W. Richard Scott, "Organizations and Movements," in *The Nature of the Nonprofit Sector*, ed. J. S. Ott and L. Dicke (Boulder, CO: Westview Press, 2012), 257–72.

115 Horacio N. Roque Ramirez and Nan Alamilla Boyd, *Bodies of Evidence: The Practice of Queer Oral History* (New York: Oxford University Press, 2012); Chong-suk Han, "Geisha of a Different Kind: Gay Asian Men and the Gendering of Sexual Identity," *Sexuality & Culture* 10, no. 3 (Summer 2006): 3–28; Ana Y. Ramos-Zayas, *National Performances: The Politics of Class, Race, and Space in Puerto Rican Chicago* (Chicago: University of Chicago Press, 2003).

116 Kochiyama, *Passing It On—A Memoir*; Boggs, *The Next American Revolution*.

117 Sucheng Chan, ed., with Audrey Kim, *Not Just Victims; Conversations with Cambodian Community Leaders in the United States* (Urbana and Chicago: University of Illinois Press, 2003); Shinhee Han, "Asian American Gay Men's (Dis)claim on Masculinity," in *Gay Masculinities*, ed. Peter M. Nardi (Thousand Oaks, CA: Sage, 2000), 206–21; Han, "Geisha of a Different Kind"; Pulido, *Black, Brown, Yellow and Left*.

118 Aldon Morris and Naomi Braine, "Social Movements and Oppositional Consciousness," in *Oppositional Consciousness: The Subjective Roots of Social Protest*, ed. Jane J. Mansbridge and Aldon Morris (Chicago: University of Chicago Press, 2001), 20–37; Ramos-Zayas, *National Performances*; Cosimo Talò, Terri Mannarini, and Alessia Rochira, "Sense of Community and Community Participation: A Meta-Analytic Review," *Social Indicators Research* 117 (2014): 1–28; Linda Trinh Vo, *Mobilizing An Asian American Community* (Philadelphia: Temple University Press, 2003a); Helen Zia, *Asian American Dreams: The Making of an American People* (New York: Farrar, Straus and Giroux, 2001).

119 ProvPlan 1990 Census Report (1992).

120   In accordance with generally accepted norms for discussing transgender oral histories, I refer to Heng's childhood with his preferred pronouns, "he/his/him." For more information on writing about transgender individuals, please refer to http://www.glaad.org/reference/transgender.

121   Tang, *Unsettled*, 73.

122   Nikki Jones, *Between the Good and the Ghetto: African American Girls and Inner City Violence* (New Brunswick: Rutgers University Press, 2010).

123   Maeda, *Chains of Babylon*, 134–135.

124   Manuel Castells, *Networks of Outrage and Hope: Social Movements in the Internet Age*, 2nd ed. (Cambridge: Polity Press, 2015).

125   Muñoz, *Youth, Identity, Power*, 78.

126   Hames-Garcia and Martinez, *Gay Latino Studies*.

127   Heng never explicitly stated what kind of activities would generate more profits for his boss, but he implied that they were of a sexual nature.

128   Donnelly, *The Changing Lives of Refugee Hmong Women*.

129   Frances Fox Piven, *Challenging Authority: How Ordinary People Change America* (New York: Rowman & Littlefield Publishers, 2006).

130   Marshall Ganz and Emily S. Lin, "Learning to Lead: Pedagogy of Practice," in *Handbook for Teaching Leadership: Knowing, Doing, and Being*, ed. Scott Snook, Nitin Nohria, and Rakesh Khurana (Thousand Oaks, CA: Sage, 2011), 359.

131   Ganz and Lin, "Learning to Lead," 361.

132   Kelley, *Race Rebels*.

133   Bindi V. Shah, *Laotian Daughters: Working Toward Community, Belonging, and Environmental Justice* (Philadelphia: Temple University Press, 2012).

134   Shah, *Laotian Daughters*, 131.

135   Shah, *Laotian Daughters*, 128.

136   Karen L. Ishizuka, *Serve the People: Making Asian American in the Long Sixties* (New York: Verso Books, 2016); Louie and Omatsu, *Asian Americans*; Zia, Asian American Dreams.

137   Han, "Asian American Gay Men's (Dis)claim on Masculinity"; Jane Ward, "White Normativity: The Cultural Dimensions of Whiteness in a Racially Diverse LGBT Organization," *Sociological Perspectives* 51, no. 3 (2008): 563–86.

138   Karin Aguilar-San Juan, *Little Saigon: Staying Vietnamese in America* (Minneapolis: University of Minnesota Press, 2009); Armstrong, *Forging Gay Identities*; Chavez, "Conceptualizing from the Inside."

139   Shah, *Laotian Daughters*, 114.

140   Shah, *Laotian Daughters*, 119.

141   Kohl-Arenas, "Governing Poverty Amidst Plenty."

142   Rodriguez, "The Political Logic of the Non-Profit Industrial Complex."

143   Ishizuka, *Serve the People*, 202.

144   Gray Brakke, "Linda Heng interview," *Brown* Political *Review*, November 4, 2015.

145   Polletta, *It Was Like a Fever*, 176.

146   Cacho, *Social Death*, 27–28.

147   Cinthya Wu, "The Mattering of Black Lives for Non-Black People of Color," *Reappropriate*, July 14, 2016.

148   Cinthya Wu, "State Violence is Chronic," *Journal of Asian American Studies* 20, no. 2 (June 2017): 296.

149   Clayborne Carson, In *Struggle: SNCC and the Black Awakening of the 1960s* (Cambridge: Harvard University Press, 1995); Estella Habel, *The San Francisco International Hotel: Mobilizing the Filipino American Community in the Anti-Eviction Movement* (Philadelphia: Temple

University Press, 2007); Ishizuka, *Serve the People*; Peter Medoff and Holly Sklar, *The Streets of Hope: The Fall and Rise of an Urban Neighborhood* (Boston: South End Press, 1994).

150   Medoff and Sklar, *The Streets of Hope*, 259.

151   Okihiro, *The Third World Studies*, 119.

152   Shah, *Laotian Daughters*, 160.

153   Marshall Ganz, "Leading Change: Leadership, Organization, and Social Movements," in *Handbook of Leadership Theory and Practice*, ed. Nitin Nohria and Rakesh Khurana (Boston: Harvard Business Press, 2010a), 509–50.

154   Freire, *Pedagogy of the Oppressed*.

155   Habel, *The San Francisco International Hotel*; Ho, *Legacy to Liberation*; Liu, Geron, and Lai, *The Snake Dance of Asian American Activism*; Maeda, *Chains of Babylon*; Pulido, *Black, Brown, Yellow and Left*.

156   Frances Fox Piven and Richard Cloward, *Poor People's Movements: How They Succeed, and Why They Fail* (New York: Vintage Books, 1979).

157   Barkan, "Plutocrats at Work"; Kohl-Arenas, "Governing Poverty Amidst Plenty."

Chapter Four Notes

158   Kelley, *Freedom Dreams*, 198.

159   Fujino, "Who Studies the Asian American Movement?"

160   Joseph Kahne, Ellen Middaugh, Nam-Jin Lee, and Jessica Feezell, "Youth Online Activity and Exposure to Diverse Perspectives," *New Media & Society* 14, no. 3 (2011): 492–512.

161   Marshall Ganz, "The Power of Story in Social Movements," in the Proceedings of the Annual Meeting of the American Sociological Association, Anaheim, California (August 18–21, 2001), 19.

162   Francesca Polletta, "Contending Stories: Narrative in Social Movements," *Qualitative Sociology* 21, no. 4 (1998): 425.

163   I refer here to Kohl-Arenas's summary of the post-9/11 philanthropic focus on civic participation, which emphasizes positive engagement and participation within the system for historically marginalized groups, thus placing the burden of change on the individual rather than on funding grassroots organizing that directly challenges systems of oppression through direct action and other forms of political organizing. See Kohl-Arenas, "Governing Poverty Amidst Plenty," 78–79.

164   Ishizuka, *Serve the People*, 6.

165   I use *first-generation* to mean someone who immigrated to the country of resettlement as an adult; *1.5-generation* to mean someone who immigrated as an adolescent; *1.8-generation* to mean someone who immigrated pre-adolescence; and *second-generation* to mean someone who was born in the country of resettlement to immigrant parents. For more information, see Rubén G. Rumbaut, "Ties that Bind: Immigration and Immigrant Families," in *Immigration and the Family: Research and Policy on U.S. Immigrants*, ed. Alan Booth, Ann C. Crouter, and Nancy S. Landale (Mahwah, NJ: Lawrence Erlbaum Associates, 1997), 3–46; and Khatharya Um, "Diasporic Nationalism, Citizenship, and Post-war Reconstruct."

166   Medoff and Sklar , *The Streets of Hope.*

167   Elizabeth Armstrong and Mary Bernstein, "Culture, Power, and Institutions: A Multi-institutional Politics Approach to Social Movements," *Sociological Theory* 26, no. 1 (2008): 74–99; Bartley, "How Foundations Shape Social Movements"; Lauren Langman, "Virtual Public Spheres and Global Justice: A Critical Theory of Inter-networked Social Movements," *Social Theory* 23, no. 1 (March 2005): 42–74; Marina Sitrin, *Horizontalism: The Voices of Popular Power in Argentina* (Berkeley: AK Press, 2006).

168   Freire, *Pedagogy of the Oppressed.*

169   Ishizuka, Medoff and Holly Sklar, *The Streets of Hope: The Fall and Rise of an Urban Neighborhood* (Boston: South End Press, 1994), .

170   Ben Kiernan, *The Pol Pot Regime: Race, Power, and Genocide in Cambodia under Khmer Rouge*, 3rd ed. (New Haven: Yale University

Press, 2008); David Marr, *Viet Nam 1945: The Quest for Power* (Berkeley: University of California Press, 1997).

171   Nguyen, "Refugee Memories and Asian American Critique."

172   Cacho, *Social Death*; Tang, *Unsettled*.

173   Marshall Ganz, "Public Narrative, Collective Action, and Power," in *Accountability Through Public Opinion: From Inertia to Public Action*, ed. Sina Odugbemi and Taeku Lee (Washington, D.C: The World Bank, 2011), 273–89; Homero Gil de Zúñiga, Nakwon Jung, and Sebastian Valenzuela, "Social Media Use for News and Individuals' Social Capital, Civic Engagement and Political Participation," *Journal of Computer-Mediated Communication* 17, no. 3 (2012): 319–36.

174   Castells, *Networks of Outrage and Hope*; Kahne et al., "Youth Online Activity and Exposure to Diverse Perspectives."

175   Tony, "Personal interviews," 2002–2004. New York, NY.

176   Yang, "Personal interviews," 2002–2006. New York, NY.

177   Anderson, *Imagined Communities*.

178   Debra Joy Perez, "Existing is a Natural Part of Philanthropy: Learning from it? Not So Much," *The Foundation Review: Exit Strategies* 9, no. 1 (2017): 103–6.

179   McAdam and Scott, "Organizations and Movements"; Dietram A. Scheufele, Matthew C. Nisbet, Dominique Brossard, and Erik C. Nisbet, "Social Structure and Citizenship: Examining the Impacts of Social Setting, Network Heterogeneity, and Informational Variables on Political Participation," *Political Communication* 21, no. 3 (2004): 315–38.

180   Kohl-Arenas, "Governing Poverty Amidst Plenty," 69.

181   Ostrander, "Legacy and Promise for Social Justice Funding"; Doug McAdam, John D. McCarthy, and Mayar N. Zald, *The Trend of Social Movements in America: Professionalism and Resource Mobilization* (Newark: General Learning Press, 1973).

182   Kelley, *Freedom Dreams*.

183   Marshall Ganz, *Why David Sometimes Wins: Leadership, Organization, and Strategy in California Farm Worker Movement* (New York: Oxford University Press, 2010b).

184   Polletta, *It Was Like a Fever.*

185   Ganz, "Public Narrative, Collective Action, and Power," 273–74.

186   Espiritu, *Body Counts*; Nguyen, "Refugee Memories and Asian American Critique."

187   PrYSM archives (2002–2006).

188   Habel, *The San Francisco International Hotel*, 25.

189   Four Freedoms Fund, www.carnegie.org/four-freedoms-fund/.

190   Habel, *The San Francisco International Hotel*, 176–177.

191   Ellen O'Connor, "Minding the Workers: The Meaning of 'Human' and 'Human Relations' in Elton Mayo," *Organization* 6, no. 2 (1999): 223–48.

192   Carson, *In Struggle.*

193   The Development, Relief, and Education for Alien Minors Act, or "DREAM Act," S. 729 and H.R. 1751, was introduced in 2009 to provide relief to undocumented childhood arrivals. It narrowly failed to pass in Congress in 2010 but would have provided a pathway to legal status for undocumented students who had arrived as children. The piecemeal legislation was a strategy used to bypass the more contentious debates on comprehensive immigration reform. It attracted a great deal of support because of the news media's and major policy groups' narrative framing of these DREAMers as model contributors and potential citizens who came to the United States through no fault of their own.

Chapter Five Notes

194   Interview with Kimho Ma, deportee, S-21 prison tour, June 2002.

195   For more on transnational and diasporic anti-Communist movements to overthrow Communist regimes in Laos, Cambodia, and Viet Nam, see Aguilar-San Juan, *Little Saigon*; Hein, *From Vietnam,*

Laos, and Cambodia; Tran, "Behind the Smoke and Mirrors"; Valverde, *Transnationalizing Viet Nam.*

196 Elora Halim Chowdhury, *Transnationalism Reversed: Women Organizing against Gendered Violence in Bangladesh* (Albany: State University of New York Press, 2011).

197 Tarrow, *The New Transnational Activism.*

198 Herbert J. Gans, "Second Generation Decline: Scenarios for the Economic and Ethnic Futures of the Post-1965 American Immigrants," *Ethnic and* Racial *Studies* 15, no. 2 (1992): 173–92; Marjorie Orellana, Barrie Thorne, Anna Chee, and Wan Shun Eva Lam, "Transnational Childhoods: The Participation of Children in Processes of Family Migration," *Social Problems* 48, no. 4 (2001): 572–91; Ramos-Zayas, *National Performances.*

199 Civil Rights Congress petition (1951).

200 Donnelly, *The Changing Lives of Refugee Hmong Women.*

201 Piven, *Challenging Authority.*

202 Ganz and Lin, "Learning to Lead," 359.

203 Ganz and Lin, "Learning to Lead," 361.

204 Kelley, *Race Rebels.*

205 Shah, *Laotian Daughters.*

206 Shah *Laotian Daughters*, 131.

207 Shah, *Laotian Daughters*, 128.

208 SEAFN public list of demands for the Right2Return campaign 2014.

209 SEAFN statement on the fortieth anniversary of the Khmer Rouge revolution, April 17, 2015.

210 Tang, *Unsettled.*

211　Michelle Alexander, *The New Jim Crow: Mass Incarceration in the Age of Colorblindness* (New York: The New Press, 2010); Susan Koshy, "From Cold War to Trade War: Neocolonialism and Human Rights," *Social Text* 58 (1999): 1–32; Mae Ngai, *Impossible Subjects: Illegal Aliens and the Making of America* (Princeton: Princeton University Press, 2004); Robertson, *Crimes Against Humanity.*

212　Samera Esmeir, *Juridical Humanity: A Colonial History* (Stanford: Stanford University Press, 2012), 9.

213　Esmeir, *Juridical Humanity*, 12.

214　Kwon, *Uncivil Youth*, 129.

215　Nguyen, "Refugee Memories and Asian American Critique."

216　SEARAC memos (2017–18).

217　Boggs, *The Next American Revolution*, 175.

218　Golash-Boza, *Deported*, 210.

219　The Immigration Detention Transparency & Human Rights Project (2015).

220　Cecelia Menjivar and Leisy J. Abrego, "Legal Violence: Immigration Law and the Lives of Central American Immigrants," *American Journal of Sociology* 117, no. 5 (2012): 1000.

221　Loan Dao, "Out and Asian: How Undocu/DACAmented Asian Americans and Pacific Islander Youth Navigate Dual Liminality in the Immigrant Rights Movement," *Societies* 7, no. 3 (2017): 3. DOI:10.3390/soc7030017.

222　Roberto G. Gonzales, "Left Out but Not Shut Down: Political Activism and the Undocumented Student Movement," *Northwestern Journal of Law and Social Policy* 3, no. 2, article 4 (2009): 223.

223　Dao, "We Will Not Be Moved."

224　Gilmore, "In the Shadow of the Shadow State," 11–12.

Chapter Six Notes

225 PrYSM-Providence Community Safety Act coalition updates (2016–17).

226 Simone Browne, *Dark Matters: On the Surveillance of Blackness* (Durham: Duke University Press, 2015); Cacho, *Social Death*.

227 Maeda, *Chains of Babylon*, 79.

228 Kwon, *Uncivil Youth*, 80.

229 L. Ling-chi Wang, "The Structure of Dual Domination: Toward a Paradigm for the Study of the Chinese Diaspora in the United States," *Amerasia Journal* 21, no. 1-2 (1995): 149–70, DOI:10.17953/amer.21.1-2.a3tk238521728620.

230 Hames-Garcia and Martinez, *Gay* Latino *Studies*; Han, "Geisha of a Different Kind."

231 Hanhardt, *Safe Space*, 74–75.

232 Dao, "We Will Not Be Moved."

233 Joey L. Mogul, Andrea J. Ritchie, and Kay Whitlock, *Queer InJustice: The Criminalization of LGBT People in the United States* (Boston: Beacon Press, 2011), 121.

234 PrYSM Statement (December 15, 2016).

235 Mogul et al., *Queer InJustice*, 157–58.

236 Browne, *Dark Matters*.

237 Ryan Schlegal, *Pennies for Progress: A Decade of A Boom for Philanthropy, a Bust for Social Justice* (Washington, D.C.: National Committee for Responsive Philanthropy, 2017), 8.

238 Del Moral, "The Revolution Will Not Be Funded."

239 Tilly, *Social Movements*.

240   Funders Collaborative on Youth Organizing (2013).

241   Southern Poverty Law Center (Fall 2017).

242   Sitrin, *Horizontalism*.

243   Andrea Lee Smith, "Introduction," in *The Revolution Will Not Be Funded: Beyond the Non-profit Industrial Complex*, ed. INCITE! Women of Color Against Violence (Cambridge: South End Press, 2007), 98.

244   Funders Collaborative on Youth Organizing (2013).

245   Kwon, *Uncivil Youth*.

246   Jenkins and Halci, "Grassrooting the System?"

247   Robert J. Sampson, Jeffrey D. Morenoff, and Thomas Gannon-Rowley, "Assessing 'Neighborhood Effects': Social Processes and New Directions in Research," *Annual Review of Sociology* 28 (2002): 443–78.

248   www.whcf.org.

249   Bartley, "How Foundations Shape Social Movements."

250   Lisa Duggan, *The Twilight of Equality: Neoliberalism, Cultural Politics, and the Attack on Democracy* (Boston: Beacon Press, 2003); Robert L. Goldstone and Todd M. Gureckis, "Collective Behavior," *Topics in Cognitive Science* 1, no. 3 (2009): 412–38, DOI:10.1111/j.1756-8765.2009.01038.x.

251   Perez, "Existing is a Natural Part of Philanthropy."

252   Rodriguez, "The Political Logic of the Non-Profit Industrial Complex."

Chapter Seven Notes

253   Kenneth T. Andrews and Bob Edwards, "Advocacy Organizations in the U.S. Political Process," *Annual Review of Sociology* 30 (2004): 479–506.

254   Hing, *Deporting Our Souls*.

255   Nguyen, "Refugee Memories and Asian American Critique."

256 Armstrong and Bernstein, "Culture, Power, and Institutions"; Browne, *Dark Matters*; Mark Hager, Patrick Rooney, and Thomas Pollak, "How Fundraising is Carried Out in US Nonprofit Organisations," *International Journal of Nonprofit and Voluntary Sector Marketing* 7, no. 4 (2002): 311–24. DOI:10.1002/nvsm.188.

257 Kelley, *Freedom Dreams*, 196.

About the Author

 Loan Thi Dao, Ph.D. (she/her/hers) is an Associate Professor and Director of Ethnic Studies at St. Mary's College of California. She specializes in Southeast Asian refugee migration and community development, immigrant and refugee youth, social movements, and Community-Based Participatory Research (CBPR). Dao has published on topics related to memory and war in cultural productions, Vietnamese American female leadership, undocumented AAPI activists, transnational activism, and Southeast Asian American deportation. She teaches interdisciplinary ethnic studies courses, and her service has included leadership positions in student groups, cultural productions, diversity and inclusion initiatives and training, immigrant rights and policy advocacy, and on boards of Southeast Asian American community organizations. She previously served on the Commonwealth of Massachusetts Asian American Commission and as a Governor-appointed advisor to the Massachusetts Office of Refugees and Immigrants.